To Peter + Br...
With Be...
October 2013
Chris Maddocks

For Eleanor...

Read this, and you won't be forced
to watch any of my old racing videos!

www. chrismaddocks . co. uk

Printed in Great Britain by Short Run Press, Ltd

INDEX

MONEY WALKS

An autobiography by five-time Olympian Chris Maddocks

FOREWORD

The story of a remarkable Devonian whose athletic career personified the true Olympic Corinthian spirit, written in his own words and pulling no punches regarding the obstacles he overcame. Read on to be informed, amazed and often amused by Chris "Mad Max" Maddocks' long and winding road to five Olympiads.

Edmund "Edbanger" Shillabeer

INTRODUCTION

'Hey, you're Chris Maddocks, aren't you?'

I looked across and caught my questioner's gaze. His accent was undoubtedly Devonian, face vaguely familiar, name definitely unknown. Before I could think, he spoke again.

'My mate here doesn't believe me that you've been to the Olympics.'

My heart sank. I should have been flattered that someone recognised me. However, I was in the process of leaning my Royal Mail bicycle against a wall and extracting the next bundle of letters from my pannier bag. I nodded an insincere smile. I was doing a job that did not nourish my soul. Eleven years had passed since I had experienced halcyon days that included my last competitive race in Sydney, Australia. At that moment I would rather have stayed an anonymous postman.

My inquisitor, who would remain nameless, downed tools and spoke to me like a long lost friend. In fact he was several school years below me and even back then in the 1970's I had no recollection of our paths ever crossing. Undeterred, he saw the vicarious bond that we apparently had and gestured knowingly towards his friend standing non-plussed with shovel in hand that the man before them clutching a banded bundle tight to his chest was indeed an Olympic medallist. My heart sank further.

'Huh, no,' I said. My smile had become more an uncomfortable grimace as I walked slowly on towards the next flight of concrete steps leading up to the next letter box. 'I didn't win a medal. I won a lot of races,' I added in a slightly more upbeat tone, before mumbling, 'but not an Olympic medal.'

In the time that it took me to post the letters, surreptitiously stride across a stretch of grass, hop over a wall and post more letters before descending neighbouring steps, allowed for a brief exchange of dialogue the manner of which I had *endured* any number of times before. Whether at a party, in a pub, or simply by the roadside and reluctantly chatting to council workers going about their business, the conversational route invariably scaled giddy heights prior to an inevitable plummet back down to earth. This one at least had the advantage of missing out the rise of my athletic status and quite quickly cutting to the chase. No need here for answers to the slightly inebriated pub-style questions of:

'So, you do a bit of sport?'

'Yes.'

'What?'

'Athletics.'

'What event?'

A sharp intake of breath is usually required at this point. 'Race walking.'

An ever widening smirk often preceded the next question: 'What...that thing where they wiggle their bum? You any good?'

'I'm okay.'

'Have you won anything?'

'A few races.' At this point I would be glancing around for my so-called friends to rescue me from this mortifying debacle.

'What kind of races? What level are we talking about here?'

My tolerance level for the company would dictate how this particular line of questions was dealt with. If *she* was pretty, I might have started at county level working my way up to national and international level winning performances. If *he* was ugly and spat beer in my face, I was straight to the upper echelons of my sporting achievements. No matter what, I nearly always regretted it. As was the case when my long lost buddy from school queried my recollection of whether or not I had actually won an Olympic medal.

'So, you didn't win a medal.'

'No.'

'Oh! You did go to the Olympics. More than once, wasn't it?'

With this latest question, and for fear that more might follow, I did not feel compelled to dignify it with the more accurate answer that I had been to the Olympics five times. More times in fact than any other man in British athletics history. Though I didn't really care that this well meaning chap was contributing to the delay of the Royal Mail getting through, more importantly he was beginning to slow me up from finishing work as soon as possible. Re-mounting my bike, I merely offered an affirmative, 'Yes.'

'What was your best result?'

With a sharp intake of breath I readied myself to cycle on. 'Sorry, I gotta go...hmm.' For the life of me, I still could not remember his name. 'Good seeing you again. Bye.' With that, I put pressure to the pedal and moved away.

'Yeah, and you mate. Hey...'

From behind I heard his broad West Country accent one last time as he called out, '...At least you gave it a go.'

At least I gave it a go. Oh, God, he did say that. Damned by faint praise, I was not going to allow it to spoil my day. The sun was shining. I had my health, and beyond a bag of letters, a few parcels and too much junk mail, I also have good memories with so much more to look forward to.

At 55 years old, some would say that I still looked young for my age; a few bits of grey maybe around my temples but, other than that, my short brown hair was the same as it was when I *officially* retired in 2002. I say officially because I took my last competitive step during the 2000 Sydney Olympic Games, but could only bring myself to officially announce my retirement almost a year and a half later. By then any realistic hopes I may have had of competing for England in Manchester later that year at what would have been a fifth consecutive Commonwealth Games, were diminishing as quickly as my weight was rising.

Interviewed in Plymouth by Hamish Marshall from BBC TV Spotlight, I said then that although my racing days were finally over, I was returning to university in order to qualify as a journalist. I seriously doubt the mischievous nod and wink I gave suggesting that I might be back after his job resulted in him losing any sleep on my account.

In fact, the move north to Leeds to embark on a one year post-graduate course did conclude with a two month work experience first back in Plymouth with the Spotlight team and then at the BBC in London. Working as part of the Simon Mayo 5-live radio team, and on TV sport was hard but great fun. As much as I loved it, that was as far as it went. There was no paid job on offer at the end. Under increasing pressure to earn some money, I applied for two advertised positions at the BBC without success. Three months later I was a policeman in the Avon & Somerset force; two totally unrelated career paths that can only be explained as 'Plan A' and 'Plan B'. Plan B temporarily won out.

It was not long before I realised that I was not cut out for a new career in the police service. This feeling was confirmed when I was out one evening on solo foot patrol on the streets of Taunton. Catching sight of my reflection in a shop window I thought I looked like someone in fancy dress. Job satisfaction was low on my radar. Beyond duties that included the tugging of a few criminal collars, laborious amounts of repetitive form filling and dealing routinely with drunken *dickheads* at the weekend, tendering my resignation was ultimately disappointing but definitely the right thing to do.

Within a couple of weeks I was back in uniform of a different kind. Delivering letters was supposed to have been the proverbial six month stopgap job whilst I sorted myself out. Eight years on, I'm still sorting myself out.

During much of this time I wrote my life story, first, as a semi-autobiographical novel. I thought it was quite good, I still do! Whilst I sought to get it published, others who knew me well suggested that I was making a mistake. Tell it as it really was, they said...*from the beginning to the end, it's pretty unbelievable anyway*. So, very begrudgingly, I started again, and here it is: All the highs and lows, all the wrong turns, a long mad athletics career that began when I was 10 years old running a marathon before drawing to a close 33 years later during a tumultuous final racing year that ended in epic circumstances. A true story...

PART ONE

The formative years: Little fat Buddha to International athlete

Born in Tiverton, Devon in1957, weighing 8lb 3ozs, I was the heaviest of Tina and John Maddocks' five children. By all accounts, I was also the laziest – not attempting to walk until I was19 months old. If I was plonked in the middle of the living room with at least one toy to amuse myself I was, according to Mum, quite content to sit there indefinitely like *a little fat Buddha*. There was no shortage of her friends willing to take me out in a pram, safe in the knowledge that I could be returned as spotless as I was when we left. This all changed when the baby became a little boy.

Together with my mates on the housing estate where I grew up, we played games, climbed trees, made camps, and, much to the exasperation of our respective mothers, invariably arrived back home either with a scraped knee, sporting a tasty new bruise, shielding something ripped, or at the very least, grass stained and mud-splattered mucky. The joy derived from playing competitive sport came early too. We played football almost every day, often in the street, two against two, one in goal. Liverpool was my team, Roger Hunt my favourite player. As much as I wanted to score goals like him, he probably wasn't my first *real* hero. That accolade instead went to a fictional character whose exploits I loved reading about every week in a comic. Alf Tupper *was, The Tough of the Track.*

Reading comics, lots of them, was a weekly ritual amongst me and my friends. Initially I was more interested in sharing stories about the adventures of Dennis the Menace, the Bash Street Kids, and the likes of Roger the Dodger, The Banana Bunch, and Desperate Dan. The more discerning reader like my eldest brother Patrick read the *Victor*. Unlike the comic characters found in the likes of the Beano, the Dandy and the Topper, where mischievous children and general naughtiness was the general theme, the Victor appeared to be dominated by war heroes and sports characters. Pat was very protective of his comic so it was quite difficult for me to lay my hands on it without being found out and getting in trouble with our Mum or having my arm twisted by him.

Undeterred, I got my sneaky reads. Flying ace Matt Braddock VC was good, as was reading football stories surrounding super-rich aristocrat club owner Gorgeous Gus and his ever loyal butler, Jenkins. Best of all I was inextricably drawn by the adventures of Alf, the eternal underdog, who had a talent for running far beyond most of his contemporaries and yet always seemed to be continually battling against officialdom. Not least because of his working class roots he was regarded as a *guttersnipe* by the so-called posh blokes from the AAA's. His often dishevelled appearance at races were typically as a result of late shifts at work, a restless night sleeping on his mattress at Aunt Meg's home under the railway arches, rescuing someone in distress on the way to a race, falling asleep on the bus or train and arriving late, some form of skulduggery by rival runners from the universities, any such scenario he may have fallen foul of before winning with a final desperate lunge for the line.

A welder by trade, Alf's staple diet appeared to be eating fish 'n' chips bought from a shop and wrapped in old newspapers. Abrasive sometimes, helpful to those in need at other times, he was a local star who did not always win, but through grit and determination did eventually become a world class miler. I was captivated by it all. In due course, parallels may be drawn to my own life, leading to suspicions that I unwittingly became his alter-ego.

Certainly growing up, I think it would be fair to say that I was instinctively competitive. As unattractive as it may have been, I was one of those insufferable kids only really happy if he was winning everything. Neither of my parents was particularly sporty; my three brothers did little sport beyond school days, and the only running I recall my attractive sister doing was away from the boys!

Joining the cub scouts when I was 10 offered up numerous other opportunities to burn excessive energy. Mum's professional sewing skills were soon utilised. Before long my cub uniform was covered in cloth activity badges. Half-term school holidays were sacrificed come bob-a-job week. I just had to raise the most money. I quickly headed for Post Hill, a notoriously affluent area one mile out of town where I deduced prospective clientele might only be too willing to pay well for my hard labour. It wasn't always so, but cars were cleaned, paths swept, potatoes peeled, gardens weeded. So long as I totted up more money than the other cubs by the end of the week and there was another badge up for grabs, no job was too big or too small.

Alf Tupper may have sown the seeds of interest, but it was not until I was a cub that my skinny legs first tasted serious running action. Well that is how I saw it. Day long picnic refreshment was provided during the sponsored marathon walk. Parents and adults alike were there taking part, some accompanying the less than enthusiastic participants. Of course now, any person encouraging children as young as 10 years old to walk or run the full marathon distance might expect a visit from social services. Back then it never bothered me. It might have taken most of the day, but crossing the finish line first was more important to me than drinking copious amounts of lemonade and how many free sandwiches I could eat.

I should perhaps mention that throughout my adolescence and adult life, the attraction of an eating competition would periodically play some small part in my life, whether at a village fete, at college, at work, or indeed any kind of social gathering. Before I list just a few of the culinary delights to pass my lips on various competitive occasions over the years, I suggest that readers of a delicate disposition might consider skipping the next bit.

Cold baked beans, eaten with a spoon, straight from the tin – seven and a half tins in all.

Thirty-three buffet sausages scoffed in two minutes.

Seventeen custard cream pies (all consumed after eating a full roast dinner, and done so as a result of a dare by 16 colleagues in a works canteen who were prepared to forego their individual tart in order to see if I could eat the entire dessert menu).

If I didn't win, I seemed to have a habit of being a close second as happened the time a big bloke ate half a tin of beans more than me during a jamboree in town up near the canal, when I was 13 years old. I was gutted. It took me ages to push my bike home afterwards. Mum was concerned for a while when I said that I didn't feel like my tea that night. At college I had to settle for second position again, although to this day I would argue that I was robbed by dubious refereeing. When the whistle blew, that other student's cheeks were positively bulging with sausages. My interpretation of sausage *eating* contest is that said sausages should be swallowed. To have lost on an important technicality still grieves me to this day!

Returning again to 1967, I was vaguely aware of the American led flower power movement. During the summer school holidays my mates and I from the Cottylands council housing estate messed around outside, playing games. For a brief period we probably looked ridiculous wearing flowers in our hair without having the faintest clue as to what it symbolised. It seemed cool at the time, as we pranced around. In truth, around that period we were more interested in building camps, riding our bikes and talking about the latest great film at the cinema.

One Saturday, the merits of the *Jungle Book* were dissected as we lounged about on the school playing fields eating crisps and chocolate, laughing as we slurped back Coca-Cola in the late afternoon sun. Trespassing on school property? It didn't worry us. If anything it added to the fun of it all.

This was a wonderful carefree time where even the simplest silly little things could make you snigger, to the point that bubbles from fizzy drinks were inextricably sucked up the nose causing eyes to bulge with water. The sight of Mark, the more rotund one amongst us reappearing after a furtive pee behind the nearest tree was one such time. Brothers Kelvin and Gary could not resist mimicking Baloo the Bear singing the bare necessities of life as he ambled back towards us obviously struggling to zip up his oversized khaki shorts. The more he cursed the more we laughed. Unimpressed, he collapsed in a heap next to us blissfully unaware of the running track chalk marks staining his clean shirt. We were not going to tell him, but sure as hell his mum would later. In the meantime, we had an idea.

Whether the challenge of last *man* running wins was a *bright idea* could be disputed. And, I say *we* reservedly because I would still deny it was actually me who originally suggested that all of us line up and run the six lanes of 80 metre sprint track back and forth until all but one dropped out, literally. But start, we did.

One by one, bodies fell to the grass each writhing in various states of distress. Unsurprisingly, given the pre-challenge nourishment, the stitch was the most common complaint, followed by aching legs, sheer breathlessness and an unquenched thirst. Mark was a revelation as he hung on for bronze, Gary taking silver. I continued on ignoring the less than enthusiastic words of encouragement ringing in my ears.

'What's he doing?'

'Ah, flipping heck, he's not stopping.'

'Hey, Maddocks you've won, you don't have to do anymore.'

I was in my own selfish groove and with thick skinned tenacity carried on, determined to notch up at least 100 lengths. Yes, it was more than 20 necessary to claim victory but once that milestone was reached I sorely tested the patience of my friends. I had resolved to run on until I counted 111. It was too much for some.

'Boring...'

Finally, I got there. Folding like a pack of cards I rolled onto my back smiling deliriously up towards a bruising sky. It felt great. My disgruntled friends had already begun to peel away, more mindful of our respective parents' suppertime curfew. Meanwhile, I deduced that 111 had a pleasing look to it, a perfect symmetry. This kind of unconscious rationale would, over the coming years, crop up with surprising frequency.

Watching the 1968 Mexico Olympics on a small grainy black and white television screen did not detract at all from its huge spectacle. It certainly gave me the extra inspiration to sign up at the local athletics club. Being part of like-minded runners in the Tiverton Harriers team was great fun. Particularly exciting at that time, was winning a cross-country medal a few days later in my first race over muddy fields near Exeter. Boarding the coach returning home I vividly recall Gary, who joined the club at the same time as me, saying the medal I had won would be the first of many leading to a medal at the Olympics one day. My chest felt like it would burst with youthful optimism.

Tuesday and Thursday evenings was club night training, where it was usual afterwards to go on to Dominos' and buy the biggest bag of fish 'n' chips we could afford. For a while I *was* Alf Tupper.

Not doing sport every day during schools days was unimaginable. Football, rugby, swimming, gym, I was happy to fit any of it around my desire to run. As most of us learn to appreciate, if you are lucky enough to be the *best* at something in your year at school, it carries a certain amount of gravitas that may go some way to diverting attention away from any limitations elsewhere, like good homework marks and success with the gentler sex. By virtue of winning most PE cross-country runs I had arguably proven to be the best runner.

I was 12 years old. It was during my second year at secondary modern school that I first noticed Jackie Cousins. Up until then, I hadn't been too bothered about girls. She was in my class and for some reason, I suddenly fancied her rotten. I was sure that she was throwing me the odd flirty glance across the classroom floor. Clueless, it was enough to fan the flames of puppy love and keep the fires burning until I worked out what to do about it.

My mates would nudge me in the ribs and ask, 'Have you kissed her yet?'

'Yeah,' I would say, lying through my teeth.

'Tongues?'

A dismissive shrug of the shoulders, a scoff and a hearty smirk usually was enough to divert the baying hounds off the scent until I came up with a strategy.

I hatched a plan for the next cross-country run. The plan was not infallible. I hadn't bargained on our Games teacher, Mr Grundy saying that the leading finishers in the run would get a gold star on their next report. Love, I considered, could wait another week.

It would not have been the first time that a *woman* might have been partly responsible for the premature end of a budding career. By loafing around at the back, it felt really weird running through the woods watching all my mates disappear away into the distance; I was even behind the fat kids. Fortunately, Jackie had picked up my overt signals and similarly hung back. If she hadn't, I guess there would have been a mad chase to try and catch up and salvage something from the day. Alas, plan B was not necessary.

I now cringe at the thought of it. What we must have looked like, trotting through the woods and across the fields, smiling winsomely our fingers entwined as we held hands. *Aagh*! Just thinking about it; it really is too horrible for words.

My reputation as the best cross-country runner in our year was temporarily in tatters. I didn't care. I was a stud. I was a Casanova. I'm not even sure we did tongues.

When I heard that our local youth centre staged an annual 50 mile sponsored walk, I just had to do it. I was 13 years old. I cried when the organisers refused my entry on the day.

'You're too young son,' they said. 'Come back next year. You can have a go then.'

So I did. I finished fourth and made the front page of the Gazette. I was disappointed. Leading for the first 35 miles I ran, until I got caught firstly by 29 year old Alan Luke and then by two other men. Whilst they steamed on ahead, I alternated between walking and running till eventually coming home in eight hours 35 minutes. Five more efforts in consecutive years resulted in two 4ths, two 2nds, two wins, and one course record. Six hours 30 minutes it took me to run over the hills and on through the towns and villages of Cullompton, Willand, Wiveliscombe, and Bampton before finishing back where we started at the Tiverton Youth Centre.

One of my proudest memories from those 50 mile runs was the time that Mum had a go one year. She managed 17 miles before stopping. It was a novelty that the local press was quick to pick up on. We were pictured together under the headline *And Mother Came Too* – an amusing homage to the TV hit comedy of the

11

day *And Mother Makes Three* starring Wendy Craig.

More conventional running ambitions continued during my early teens with track and road events. For three years up until the age of 15, I also belonged to the local sea cadet unit. It was during this time when I was 14 that I had my first competitive walk, when taking part in a regional multi-sport event held at RAF Chivenor in North Devon. Pitted against other sea, army and air cadets, around 100 competed in a competition that included cycling, an assault course, running, a pool swim, and a one mile walk. It was no big surprise that I won the three mile run. As for walking fast, I did not have a clue. Eight minutes later... *Natural ability* they called it after I won that event as well. Two winners medals from one weekend. The newspaper photograph of me in my sea cadet uniform flanked by my cadet teammates found its way into what became the first of a dozen volumes of scrapbooks.

The first time I appeared on TV was not for running or for my race walking exploits, but rather it was whilst playing rugby for school. Our rugby XV was chosen as the first opponents to a team of 10 and 11 year olds from a nearby junior school. Until then no children of that age had played competitive rugby in the county of Devon. Mr Grundy was a big proud man who loved his rugby. On the coach journey to Crediton he stood up and said that anyone who scores a try will get a gold star on his report. Mr Grundy liked to dangle those particular carrots. The feisty light bulb in my head pinged on again.

By halftime we were 30-0 up. We were slaughtering the poor little mites. It probably did not look too good on camera and for that reason it came as no surprise that Mr Grundy instructed us to ease up, and whisper that we might even let the boys score.

I can only imagine that the spirited acting by our bigger boys looked less than convincing as they seemingly struggled in a defensive scrum, grunting and straining to hold back the force of those juniors as they pushed over the score line for their one and only try of the game. We ran out 43-3 winners.

As we did not get the HTV channel in our house, I had to go around to a mate's house at teatime to watch the two minutes they showed on the telly with his mum and dad. I felt distinctly uncomfortable at the sight of me dashing down the wing, the wind in my hair, ball tucked under my arm, and my teammates, their head and arms flaying desperately trying to keep up, screaming at me to pass the ball. Unlike them, I looked quite happy as I went over for my fourth try. To my eternal shame, the word, *greedy* was mentioned more than once afterwards.

A few weeks later I was scheduled to run the junior track 1500m at Yeovil in Somerset. Driven there by my coach Jack Snow, we turned up too late and so looked for an alternative option. I entered the only walking race on the programme that day – the men's 5000m where I beat all but three. Suddenly, people I had never met before were excited for me. I was told that I was quite a good prospect. Buoyed by this, the next few years I mixed the two different disciplines of running and walking until it was decided in my late teens that I should concentrate on one. Jack helped me most with my formative race walking career and I said as much when I read a eulogy at his funeral a number of years later.

Jack was so much to so many at the club. At different times, other than being club chairman, secretary, treasurer, I remember him best as our club coach. Bald headed from the first day I saw him, I always thought he must have been quite old. In fact he was a fit man in his late fifties. He competed himself, and in those early days when I showed a desire to develop my walking speeds, he learned what he could from other specialists and guided me as best he knew how. At first he would run shoulder to shoulder with me, cajoling me to faster times as we meandered through mile upon mile of country lanes. As I got faster and my ambitions grew, so Jack switched to cycling alongside and barking instruction at his fast improving young charge.

'C'mon, lengthen your stride,' he'd shout. 'Swing those hips, pump those arms, keep your head still.'

It was a lot for me take in, but over time, I improved.

Ageing limbs meant Jack eventually resorted to using his car, a development that in turn helped give my ears a bit of a rest. To this day, if I see a vintage Morris Minor I recall memories of him in his black car out there in all weathers showing me the way.

Throughout the 1970's I was just about into everything, except perhaps school. It would not be true to say that I disliked school. In fact I was quite capable, but lacked any real application. At the risk of shirking the responsibility, my educational cause was not helped by our Mum's attitude to school homework.

'It can wait until after you've done your jobs,' she'd say.

In other words, until after we had done all the chores relating to our pets. Of all the five siblings, I think it fair to say that my sister Jane and I came off worst in this area. Michael, our youngest brother by 11 years or more, might reasonably argue otherwise. It was after all, a comical sight to see the poor mite in his school uniform trying to lead a stubborn goat on a leash away from home towards the country lanes, whilst cursing its penchant for eating anything within its greedy range. Mum insisted that *Snowy* needed both the exercise and daily change of scenery! Thank God that was later, long after I'd left school.

For me, it was no hardship to walk the family dogs, I quite liked doing that. Caring for our rabbits and guinea pigs was another matter. We would have been happy with two of each. Of course, in no time at all, *two* equalled loads of the damn creatures. Deemed our fault, we were told by Mum that we had to keep all of them.

Row upon row of wooden hutches there were at the end of our garden. Every day we had to clean out the hutches and feed them all with freshly picked wild food, fondly remembered by us as, *rabbit's food*, or more precisely, dandelions, dandelion leaves, clover, and sweet, tender grass. Finding this in plentiful supply was not difficult near where we lived, though memories of gathering it up in polythene bags still makes me recoil with cringing embarrassment.

As far as I was concerned, Higher Cottylands was a great place to live. It was a large post-war red-brick council estate on the edge of town where I think it true to say, most residents took some pride in their homes. Our house was one of four in an elevated position overlooking acres of green fields. Lower Cottylands on the other hand seemed less desirable, partly I think because it was built near the old *pre-fabs* – prefabricated homes also built post-war but as cheap and supposedly temporary accommodation, yet decades on still in use, tired and in some cases dilapidated with overgrown gardens, gardens that contained rich pickings for those out hunting for rabbit's food!

It may sound pitiful, but I believe residents got used to us knocking on their doors and asking, 'Please can we pick some rabbit's food?'

Few said, *no*. Why would they? We were offering to weed their garden, for free; not all at once I grant you, but, dependant on size of garden, and quantity of goods, perhaps over the course of a few days. Anything other than freshly picked, and we risked the wrath of our mother.

Jane and I found other supply sources in the grounds of a few old Victorian houses a quarter mile beyond our estate where one or two had big elevated gardens, so unkempt that our weeding services were invariably met with a smile. It was not without its drawbacks. It was commonplace to be in the process of picking a bag of the green stuff when the school bus would trundle by with all the out-of-town kids on board. It was imperative for reasons of self respect that I was not spotted by anyone staring out of the window. The familiar sound of the bus's engine usually allowed enough time to dash behind the nearest tree or around the side of the house. Occasionally, I was caught daydreaming at the crucial drive past moment. Wet or dry, it was necessary to dive face down spread-eagled in the grass and hope that no one saw this demeaning act. I worried I might not have always pulled off my escape. Sure enough one day my worst fears were realised when I was standing near a smart-arse grammar school boy who thought he'd share his thoughts with two friends.

'Hey, I hear the Maddocks' are so poor that they eat grass.'

When I ploughed headlong into the comedian little consideration was given to the fact that I was seriously outnumbered. It was lucky for my sake that we were soon pulled apart.

I had a low boredom threshold when it came to reading books. I can thank Richard Jarman for one of my less celebrated educational moments. We routinely sat together in class, usually in the corner at the back. Those of you reading this who adopted the same tactic will recognise strategic seat positioning best suited to avoidance at being asked too many questions by teacher. This too was not an infallible plan.

English exams were less than a year away. One by one, Mr Saunders randomly selected pupils to stand and tell the class what books they had read. This was definitely a time to keep my head down. By the time four or five had spoken, I thought I'd got away with it. I also couldn't believe just how many books some of the *creeps* had supposedly read. Then, it happened. Eye contact had been made.

Old man Saunders had craned his neck everyway which way and caught my inadvertent gaze. It was a school boy error. Rooted to my chair, the sweat pores opened up.

'Yes...you at the back...Maddocks. I can see you,' he said.

I was in denial for a few long painful seconds. If I was left in any doubt, the nudge in the ribs from Richard was confirmation that I had to stand. I could have done without the sniggering that accompanied my slow rise. My mouth felt dry when asked again, *how many books have I read*. As I totted them up in my head, the silence was rudely interrupted by chairs scraping on the floor as more heads turned towards me.

Richard obviously thought he could help me out. 'Huh, I think it's one, Sir. Chris has read one book.'

I looked down at him.

He looked up at me, smiled and said, 'Black Beauty, about three years ago, wasn't it?' The smirk was damning.

My God, I thought. Was he still sore about those sweets that I'd nicked out of his desk? Whatever, I had just been betrayed by one of my so-called mates. Richard of course glorified in spinning his version of the same story years later at my wedding during a comedy double act with brother Peter and their joint best man's speech.

The fact that I left with seven good graded CSE's was probably more to do with last minute revision during the final few months than any serious academic prowess. It would be a while before I appreciated that CSE's were practically useless in relation to job prospects unless of course you had grade 1's. I had one...in geography. Grade 2's nah, forget it!

Away from school I think I was instinctively more prepared for the long haul. I seemed drawn by challenges that by their very nature would take a long time to complete. Doing those 50 mile sponsored walks was one thing, but I knew that I would not be happy until I had won the event; and even then, I had to win it a second time for good measure.

Around the same period, I had a similar attitude to the *Ten Tors* expeditions. This two-day annual hiking challenge on the rugged terrain of Dartmoor in Devon still goes on today and is for young people between the ages of 14 and 20. Three alternative distances are tackled in teams of six depending on age and level of training. Not satisfied with doing it once, I ticked off each of the respective 35, 45 and 55 mile routes within four years. First, I was a nominated captain of a well drilled school team; two years later the principal navigator as part of a police cadet team; and one year on after resignation from the police force, I was back on the moors helping to complete the numbers of a motley team of college hippies. Far from the identikit navy blue serge team of a year earlier, our undertrained ramshackle argumentative lot were a mishmash of tied-dyed jeans, cheesecloth shirts and long hair. Against the odds, we triumphantly descended down from the peak of the final tor to base camp at Oakhampton, finishing the 55 miles with barely 20 minutes to spare.

Then there was *The Duke of Edinburgh Award scheme:* Bronze, silver *and* Gold – what else? I collected my Gold lapel badge at Buckingham Palace from the Duke himself. All those years of getting my D of E book ticked off for community work, police service assistance, first aiding, athletics coaching all seemed particularly worthwhile when I was escorted to London by a proud Mum and Jack. Mum's lasting memory of the event – the brass taps in the super-clean toilets!

Munich in 1972 was the first Olympic Games where I had any real understanding of its significance. Swimmer, Mark Spitz, gymnast, Olga Korbet, and runner, David Bedford were a few of my early sporting inspirations. The Israeli Arab atrocities were beyond my comprehension at that time. Sport and politics were already undesirable bedfellows, a fact of which I would all too soon become an indirect victim.

By the time of the mid-seventies I had fanciful dreams of competing at the Montreal Olympic Games. In truth, I was nowhere near ready. Traditionally, the two Olympic walk distances for men were 50 kilometres or 31.1 miles and 20 kilometres, 12.2 miles. In 1976, Montreal, and for one Olympiad only, the shorter of the two events was contested and the best men were covering that in less than 90 minutes. I simply could not walk that fast. When you are young it is difficult sometimes to appreciate the huge difference between being an aspiring club athlete who trains hard and an international competitor with experience who knows how to develop sufficiently in order to step up to Olympic level.

Aside of all the crazy long runs that I had done, the furthest I had race walked by this time was 10 miles on the road. If Montreal was too soon, then the Moscow Olympics in 1980 had the potential to be just right.

The sensible thing to have done would have been a gradual increase of race distances in reasonable increments over the next four years. After all, there were many intermediate road and track walking events up to and even beyond 50 kilometres. So, the right way to go would be to try a number of 20km races and see how fast I could go. Beyond that, a 30km or 35km race, and maybe, just maybe, a 50km race when I felt ready. What did I do? Walk 42 miles from Plymouth to Dawlish, of course. That's 67kms in new money. Hindsight is a wonderful thing. At least the race got me noticed.

It was springtime 1977 and I was in the green vest of my new club, Dawlish & South Devon. From the start, wearing my trademark union jack shorts, I was followed out of the Citadel, home base of 29 Commando Regiment of the

Royal Artillery, by walkers who soon formed a long snake-like line on the road that wound its way out of Plymouth. It was 30 miles up the dual carriageway until veering off onto undulating winding country roads that descended down into Dawlish. My impetuosity once again saw me lead the way for three-quarters of the race, until I slipped back to third position at the finish, beaten once again by more experienced men than me. There was no prize money at stake, only the promise of a fresh Devon cream tea for all finishers.

Our club president Eric Shillabeer, a retired gent sporting a pencil-thin moustache, always impeccably attired in collar and tie, was convinced that this special inducement would attract the finest walkers to our annual event. This ploy was never really proven. True, a smattering of lithe super-fit men with highly tuned smooth walking actions did indeed travel from afar to grace the event. There was however a fair share of enthusiasts, men and women alike, all adding to the numbers. Amongst those who brought up the rear, the Grunters and the Twitchers, armed with less talent but with bucketfuls of admirable determination.

The strawberry jam and delicious cream was barely wiped from my chops, before I heard that my third position result had caught the attention of the British international selectors. Later that year I was joining other junior walkers at Aldershot army training barracks and rubbing shoulders with senior athletes in a combined national squad. It was interesting to briefly be part of a group of men who were better than me and to see them train. The notion of doing specific speed work and alternating track and road work with hard hill training would however remain an alien concept to me. With the benefit of hindsight, I think I just needed more time for it all to sink in. Back home in Devon, I continued training in my own unorthodox way.

I returned to the Citadel the following spring, this time winning the 42 miler in a record time of six hours 40 minutes. Following me along the busy dual carriageway where passing cars came within inches of the competing walkers, was my Mum with drinks in hand hollering encouragement. When she wasn't telling me what to do, she was speaking to the local television crew. They were there filming the event for airing the next evening on regional TSW. By the time I reached the finish line in amongst the leafy trees on Dawlish Green just yards from the seafront, the cameras were poised, ready to film *Devon's next great hope at the Moscow Olympics.*

I was booked for a studio interview in Plymouth the next evening with sports presenter Chris Fear. It was exciting. As things transpired, *interview* would hardly best describe what evolved that night.

Chris Fear introduced me, and then, over a short clip of the race, he asked his opening question. Approximately six minutes elapsed before I drew breath and stopped talking. Off air the studio crew fell about laughing. Bemused, I wondered if it was something I had said. A cameraman spoke up and asked if Mr Fear would have the audacity to pick up his wages that week? If I learned anything that day, it was that a rhetorical question generally requires no answer. I also learned that in future I might try more concise answers to certain questions.

1978 was a memorable year for so many other reasons. A few weeks after the Dawlish win, I was in Stratford-upon-Avon. Winning the British 50km trial race in 4 hours 23 minutes was good but not good enough to qualify for the European athletic championships. I had fallen short of the qualifying time by a mere three minutes – about the same amount of time that I had stopped, sat in a chair, tended to my sore blood-blistered feet, and made a futile change of shoes and socks. This injury affected result was all the more disappointing given that I had routinely followed the advice of the day; that the best way to avoid blisters was by applying regular dabs of vinegar to the soles of your feet in order to harden the skin. It smelt horrible and it did not work.

It was supposedly the same principle as when we used to toughen horse chestnuts by soaking them in vinegar before conker fights. Unfortunately, it would be years before I was made to realise that conkers hardened this way, still cracked, and when they did, the extra dryness meant that they quickly split to the point of disintegration resulting in game over. Memories of the skin cracks in my heels are enough to make me wince even now.

In September I did answer the call from the selectors to make my senior international debut. Cordoned off roads in Sheffield city centre for multi-lap road walking hardly seems glamorous now, but at the time I was thrilled. Great Britain v West Germany in a full sided senior and junior, male and female international match was good enough for me. It also captured the imagination of the local press.

Photographed outside our council house, I stood proudly in my pristine red, white and blue GB tracksuit, my long hair held in place with my usual racing stripy cotton headband cobbled together by Mum. The newspaper editor presumably had seen the images noting an apparent similarity to a certain Swedish tennis legend and ran the headline, *the Bjorn Borg of walking.* At 21 I was described as one of the youngest athletes ever to compete in the walk. The full page spread went on to say how like all amateurs I had to hold down a full time job. My day started at 4am at the bakery where I worked six days a week. Work ended around 1pm. I said in the article that when I returned home *I couldn't sit down and put my feet up – if I did, I was finished.* I would change straight away into my training gear and start with a few exercises – up to 200 press ups and 60 odd sit ups. My Dad had well defined muscles and, before he left home for the final time, an abiding memory I have was him always doing loads of press ups.

After the exercises, it was out onto the roads and covering between five and fourteen miles. Late afternoon, after a relaxing bath it was outside again for a therapeutic recovery stroll with Rascal, our family border-collie cross. I explained that I would make time in the evening to see my girlfriend Kim, although there was seldom any late nights because I was up again around 3am to start all over again. I risked Kim's displeasure by telling the newspaper that in answer to the question about my success that there was indeed, like many great men, a great woman behind him: *My Mum helps me more than a coach,* I said. *She supports me at*

18

races, and I get an incredible lift from her being there. She washes my stuff and feeds me – she even cooks me a steak when she can afford it.

I saw no reason to mention that for a time, seven of us lived in our three bedroom council house. It was only five by then anyway. My eldest brother Patrick had left home several years earlier to join the Police cadets, and our Dad was long gone.

Mum and Dad divorced around the time I was 15. Exactly when, I'm not sure because dad told me about it in a pub several months after it had happened. I should add that we were not in the habit of going to the pub together. Indeed, when he suggested that we might drive out to the Rose & Crown for a drink and a chat, I was too excited to have had any suspicions.

'When are you coming home dad?'

'I'm not, son.'

Stunned by the manner and finality of those cold, matter-of-fact words, the pain could not have felt worse had a knife been thrust into my heart and twisted every which way. In spite of all the fights, arguments and separations, I had until then, rather naively hoped that they would still get back together again. They never did.

Although I never thought about it at the time, my Mum was an attractive lady. Freed from an unhappy marriage, she was vivacious in her forties. Peroxide blonde, good humoured and in spite of having five kids she appeared to have what I believe would be considered the perfect slim figure. I hated it when the men came calling. One did seem to make her happier than any other. I probably hated Brian most of all. A large moustachioed man, who's greased thinning black hair and heavy wafts of aftershave, marked his ever presence. He had all the trappings of wealth – a good job, fine clothes, a flash car, and jewellery. I always remember the oversized rings and gold chains hanging around his neck. I think he took Mum to interesting places and bought her nice clothes. My sister and younger brothers received presents, while I stubbornly refused anything that he offered. It was difficult to know just how long that particular relationship lasted, but when it came to an end it was bitter and traumatic.

Walking towards our home I saw suitcases strewn outside. I ran in when I heard the sound of raised angry voices. Stepping into the lobby I saw Mum with tears running down her face, screaming at Brian to get out whilst shoving him towards the door. I could hear crying in the other rooms. I shouted at him to leave. He looked at me with utter contempt. Mum pleaded with me to help. I shouted again. He laughed.

Filled with rage, I leapt at him and locked my arm around his neck and wrestled what felt like an almost immovable beast to the floor. More out of fear than any bravery, I pinned him to the floor and squeezed my arm lock as tight as I could muster and demanded that he leave once I released my grip. He was choking so much that he could barely respond. I could smell cigars and stale coffee on his breath as he spat out his submission. If necessary I think I would have broken his neck but instead made him repeat his promise to get up and go if I agreed to release my stranglehold. Mum was crying. She said to let him go.

I hesitated at first, then slowly pulled my arm and body away and stood up. He rubbed his neck, stood up, dusted himself down, looked me in the eye and punched me full on in the face. Clutching my face in my hands I sunk to my knees. Brian walked out of the door. I never saw him again, although I believe he and Mum stayed in touch for a while.

I cleaned myself up in the bathroom and got changed into my training kit. I was angry, so angry and humiliated that I ignored Mum's pleas for me to calm down and stay indoors. The eight mile run that afternoon was probably the fastest I had done till then. I pushed myself so hard that no amount of physical discomfort could feel worse than the aching pain of total disillusionment.

My Mum was a kind person who deserved better. I wanted her to be happy, and if anything I did in my life might help her towards that end, then I vowed to do my utmost. I could only hope that I might make her proud.

So, it was only right that I should mention her in the newspaper article and of course she was there to share the joy when I first wore that British International vest.

As it turned out, fifth place over 50kms in a new personal best time of four hours 21 minutes meant I should have been able to hold my head high at the civic hall evening prize presentation function. Alas, the opportunity was largely missed. I was so disappointed by Mum not being allowed to accompany me into the function room and share the experience that I spent much of the time arguing outside with officials. Only with some determined persuasion by her, did I eventually join the smoke filled, brandy swilling after dinner presentations and speeches, while my best supporter retreated to her B&B down the road.

Come October, my first excursion training overseas with the national junior squad should have been happier. For a short time it was, until...*BANG*!

It was the second day of our time in rural France. Led by head coach, Julian Hopkins in a support vehicle, about a dozen of us were out together fast walking our way through tree-lined quiet country roads. An hour into the session and exchanging words of breathless banter, walking two, maybe three abreast I was suddenly sent hurtling six feet into the air.

In a surreal moment, time almost stood still. I recall feeling little pain as I hung mid-air staring at a powder-blue sky. The next moment I'm plummeting and feel a sickening thud as I hit the ground. Lying flat on my back in the middle of the road I remember being confronted by faces assuring me that everything's going to be alright. My head hurt all the more at the sound of an irate Frenchman gesturing with flailing arms that it was my fault! With the front nearside wing of his car dented, he was far from happy.

I may have only tipped the scales around 10 stone in weight, but wisely it was four or five men who took the precautionary measure to carefully lift me into the transit van that was used to take me to the nearest hospital.

A few hours later, Julian and I returned to the training hostel where the squad were in the last throes of a late lunch. My head, both arms, right leg were all swathed in bandages. The cacophony of barbed comments and applause that accompanied me and the two men chair-lifting me to a spare seat in the dining hall did little for my thumping headache.

'Hey guys, look whose back.'

'Wow, bet that hurts.'

'Make him walk. We got training tomorrow morning.'

'I've eaten your dinner, you don't mind, do ya?'

I returned a weak wry smile. I knew that I had been lucky. Somehow I had come away from the accident with no more than cuts and bruises. How that was possible still baffles me. My recovery was swift.

PART TWO

Bombshells, salad days, and rock 'n' roll: 1979 – 1984

The start of a new year was a watershed marker for me. Four years working as a lowly paid baker with no meaningful future prospects. I had had enough. Early morning starts, afternoon training totalling up to 70 or 80 miles a week, I was constantly knackered. Occasionally I would saunter into the local job centre. Anything that caught my eye invariably demanded more academic qualifications than I had to offer. Handing my notice into my boss was a shock to him.

'What are you going to do,' he asked.

'I'm going back to college,' I replied. 'I'm going to try and get some more 'O' levels; get a better job.' He shook my hand, wished me luck. I walked out of the shop. I don't think we ever saw each other again.

A month or two before my impromptu walk out, I had started a home study correspondence course. I knew that I needed extra help if I was going to get the three extra 'O' levels to go with the two equivalent ones I already had. All indications at the job centre pointed to the magic five, so long as they included maths and English.

When I first spoke to the lady in reception at the East Devon College of Further Education, or *Tech* as we all knew it, I felt small, meek and thick. It was January and I had less than six months before exams started. She could not have been more helpful. I was introduced to staff, all of whom listened and allowed me to join their classes respectively in English, sociology and my pet-hate, maths. When I needed it, they even gave me some private tuition, sensing my determination to get at least the three C-grade passes that I needed.

When I was not training, I was studying. Apart from winning a South West Championship 10 miler at Salisbury at the end of February, I did not race again until our club 42 mile event on Mayday bank holiday weekend. After improving my course record from the previous year by 14 minutes to six hours 26 minutes, I put all my thoughts and energy to getting ready for those impending exams. For a short time I had the house to myself – great for revision. Together with my two youngest brothers Peter and Michael, Mum moved home from our council house to a three bedroom bungalow in the small hamlet of Cove five miles away. It was a fresh start for all the family. For me, it also meant that the road hills that I trained on became routinely mountainous; good for strength, less so for speed.

Come August, I deliberately avoided the rush of students all wanting to see their results pinned up on the college walls. If there was going to be moments of self loathing and humiliation on my part, I wanted it to be a private affair. Arriving at the college towards the end of the day, it was as quiet as I had hoped. I could feel myself trembling like nothing I had felt before, not even before an important race. So the aim was to go in and get out without being seen nor heard. My worst fears were realised when I heard by name called.

'Chris.'

I looked up and around. Leaning heavily on a wide opened second floor window was the college Principal. He called again.

'Chris,' he let out a heavy sigh and tutted. 'Come up to my office. I want to speak to you.'

My head dropped. Like a man walking to the gallows I stepped forward.

When I walked away from the college sometime later, I was still trying to hold back the tears welling up in my eyes. I felt 10 feet tall. I wanted to punch the air. I did. Anything was possible from that moment on. Two A's and a glorious C in maths; on entering his office, Mr Dixon had failed to retain his stern, rather disappointed look for little more than a few seconds. I could still feel the firmness of his handshake as I walked on.

In September I lined up with the best of the British at Hove Park in West Sussex. Against us were some of the best walkers in Europe. It was the semi-finals of the Lugano World Cup. Three teams could advance to the finals in Germany four weeks hence. The 20km event had already taken place earlier that day. The scores from that team performance would be added to those achieved by the four man team in the 50km event. I started as I so often did in those days, fast...usually too fast for my own good. The British squad did eventually qualify third, two points behind winners West Germany, and just one point behind Sweden. For my part, I was the second placed Briton in an overall ninth position. It had taken me four hours 23 minutes. The grotesque blood blisters on my feet meant that I could not walk properly for days after. I assured the team selectors that I would be fine if they picked me for the finals team.

The truth was that I struggled to train at all well. The sore feet restricted my training regime and splitting up with Kim, my girlfriend of four years was tough, especially given the emotional turmoil that comes with that kind of disappointment. I defy anyone who utters those immortal words *let's just be friends*, to mean it. That would have been bad enough but I also managed to be late to the airport and missed my flight to Eschborn in Germany.

The extra hours kicking my heels around Heathrow felt like an eternity. I spent much of this unwanted free time trying to persuade anyone who would listen to get me on a plane. Eight hours later I was airborne and on the way to Cologne. It may have been hundreds of miles from where I needed to be, but I had at least in the meantime got word to British team management that I was in Germany and would need a lift to Eschborn. The taxi ride in the dead of night down the autobahn often at speeds in excess of 100mph was exhilarating. Less exciting was the feeling I got from team management at the breakfast table when I rather sheepishly slipped in. They were not impressed with me. Unprofessional they called it. Disrespectful was another description. I thought I had done well to be there at all, but I kept those thoughts to myself. With the benefit of hindsight, something else that I should perhaps have kept to myself was a potential problem with my choice of racing socks. I needed advice. Seeking it roadside just before the commencement of the first race was undoubtedly bad timing. There was bad news and good news.

The bad news was my socks had holes in them. The good news was that I had the luxury of two pairs. If I chose to wear both, the holes would roughly overlap and almost be covered. My question to team management was should I wear the usual one pair or experiment with two? After much grinding of teeth, opinion seemed to be divided. I sensed that more than one person would have preferred to have seen me go before a firing squad. Two pairs won the day. My old worn out pair of racing shoes stayed out of sight until the last minute.

All three senior races were staged on the same 2.5km town circuit. The first race was the woman's road 5kms where Britain scored a one-two finish with Carol Tyson winning. A great start that was impossible for the British men to emulate. Woman's race walking around the world was in its infancy. By contrast men's walking was long established. We as a nation may have provided Olympic champions in the shape of men like Harold Whitlock, 1936 Champion, Don Thompson, 1960 and Ken Mathews in 1964. Paul Nihill in 1968 was our last Olympic medallist when he won silver and one year on became a European 20km champion. But, times and performance levels had moved on, and they were about to be blown further away by some extraordinarily fast walking over the next two days. First the 20kms: The Mexican team led the way with a revolutionary style that saw a move from strong power walking as exemplified by the likes of the East Europeans to a super-fast cadence and super fast times closer to 80 minutes rather than 90. It was awesome to watch. And watch I did, along with 25,000 others lining the streets. I had never seen anything like it before. The claxon horns were sounding, bells ringing, crowds cheering.

Surely the 50km walk the next day could not match it as a spectacle. Well it probably did, though I saw it from within the iron railing boundaries and at a painful distance. Before this day, the best 50km walkers were recording times around the four hour mark. Now the leaders were up to ten minutes quicker all led by the Mexicans. They were the new superstars of world walking. There had been prior warnings when Daniel Bautista won Olympic gold in Montreal. Now his countrymen were there in his slipstream.

After a fast start that saw me go through halfway in around two hours I slipped back to a lowly 43rd position, eventually struggling home in four hours 27 minutes. Everything hurt, particularly my feet. I thought I might have made some progress by hardening them with methylated spirits rather than vinegar. No. My feet were in shreds again. I was distraught, although few had sympathy for me.

It would be several more years before it was clearly explained to me that hardened feet was an old fashioned concept. I would have many more races compromised by painful blisters until I learned that smooth well conditioned feet minimised the prospect of problems caused by excessive friction.

Although I did not know it at the time, when I did seek the help of a chiropodist it was just my luck that I found a useless one amongst the profession. He may have been new to the job, I don't know. I noticed that he appeared nervous each time I visited. I thought it might have been because he said that he had never had an international athlete step through his door before. I was flattered. I was also stupid. By the third or fourth visit I was more nervous than flattered and surprised that any of his patients ever returned. Sat in the patient's chair I would watch his hands begin to tremble whilst I let him hack away at my feet with his scalpel sometimes until they bled, though to be fair if a cut went too deep it was met with an instant apology. Undeterred, while beads of sweat formed on his bloated face, he would then set about patching up my tender plates with tiny cuts of cloth, a procedure that he once likened to the building of an aircraft. I never returned after that. More than a decade would pass before I trusted a chiropodist to touch my feet again.

Back home from Germany, I was encouraged to enrol full time at the Tech'. Combining two 'A' levels in law and sociology together with a secretarial course including typing and shorthand would keep me busy at the college for the next two years.

I was determined that that my experience in Eschborn should not be the end of my racing season. A few weeks later, I managed to blag my way on to a small British party of walkers travelling to Lassing in Austria. It may well have been my third 31 mile race in two months but I was determined that this would produce a better result. Bob Dobson was our British record holder. His best had been done 12 months earlier at the same venue. As was his pre-race aim, he improved his record again, taking another minute off his best by winning in 4:07.23. For my part, I walked a boringly controlled race where I did not charge off at speed and slowly fall apart in the latter stages. Instead I walked an even-paced four hours 16 minutes. It removed five minutes from my previous best time done at Sheffield. I was ready to get drunk.

Carol Tyson predictably won the woman's race. She was slim, red headed with attractive elfin-like features and a world champion to boot. With her more professional sober head on, she left the evening celebrations early and headed the mile back to the log cabin accommodation. On a straight road surrounded by mountains lit beautifully by a full moon, she hardly needed any act of chivalry from me in escorting her safely home. She got it anyway.

It must have been her idea to take a shortcut up the steep dewy-grassed embankment towards the cabin. It was more than my race-weak, alcohol-sodden legs could manage. To her eternal credit, my face was partially saved by her perseverance in lending me a hand and helping me to the top. The delicate peck on my cheek prior to wishing me goodnight before shutting the door in my face is still a treasured moment. I trudged slowly back to the evening celebrations with a resigned yet reasonably satisfied smile on my face.

The musical sound of *Another brick in the wall* by Pink Floyd helped all of us see out the 1970's and welcome in the 1980's. Overseas, as more soviet tanks rolled into Afghanistan, increasing political unrest was filling the front pages of our national newspapers. This and more were discussed by me and other invited guests in a TV studio debate in Plymouth. Eminent Exeter University academic Dr Peter Travers, teenage swimmer Sharron Davies and decathlete Brad McStravic were among the panel of contributors that helped fan the flames of a lively exchange of views. The depth of my understanding at the time meant that as far as I was concerned, a British team should go to the Moscow Olympic Games regardless of political troubles elsewhere.

Around my study time, Jack Snow continued to meet with me several times a week for training. Dependant on how he felt would determine whether he cycled alongside me, or if he used his car. All looked good until my first race of the year in February at Basingstoke. Ten miles around the Hampshire countryside should have been a good opener for the year; however, disqualified after only three miles by roadside race judges meant that my walking technique was not holding up under scrutiny. As trained race walkers we all know the two clear rules that distinguish us from runners. Here is the technical bit; I shall try to be brief:

1. Walkers should maintain contact with the ground at all times by placing the heel of the lead foot to the ground before the toes of the trailing foot leave the ground, or *heel and toe* as some still like to call it.

2. The supporting knee of a walker on each stride also needs to be straight. This is as opposed to the supporting knee of a runner which is invariably bent on each stride. The fastest walkers will also straighten their knee on each stride as the forward heel strikes the ground...something that is commonly done at a rate of three to four strides per second.

I am not proud of this but, in my early years of racing, if I was disqualified it was not uncommon for me to have a stand up argument with any judge who had the *audacity* to call my name and number. Now, with a little more maturity, I tried to take such disappointments on the chin and learn from it. On this occasion in Basingstoke, the judge took my race numbers from me explaining that I was probably overstretching on each stride and as a consequence lifting both feet off the ground. I begrudgingly listened and decided to vent my frustration by continuing on and completing the 10 miles for training purposes. Out of respect to Carl Lawton who won in a few seconds over 74 minutes, I stayed a few paces in arrears allowing him to cross the finish line ahead of me.

The following Saturday I won the 10 mile South West Championship at Salisbury in 74.54 – a time that was more than two minutes ahead of Edmund Shillabeer, a club teammate 17 years my senior, and a man whose friendship would in the future become vitally important. Two weeks later the hand of friendship was probably extended too far. My next 50km race was on a Sunday morning in the heart of London. The day before, I travelled with the Dawlish team in a transit van to Bournemouth for an afternoon six mile race on the seafront promenade. I had promised Ed that I would help pace him to a good time. Despite the high winds blowing sand from the beach into our faces, Ed finished 6th and pleased with his 46 minutes. It was almost midnight when I got to my hotel room in Kensington.

When I toed the line at 9.30am with around 30 others I could not believe how tired I felt. As we all stood there waiting for the starter's pistol, matters were not helped by the warmth of the sun already being trapped between the high granite facades of London Walls.

A little over two hours and 25kms later I was still contesting the lead. Like those walkers around me, I was saturated by sweat and by sponges handed to us by volunteer helpers. My race was soon about to unravel as I became overwhelmed with fatigue and the pain of a blistered heel. After two hours 48 minutes and 34kms I was sitting on the kerbside with my head in my hands, exhausted.

With the sweat barely out of my eyes, I was approached by someone who said that a small group of British walkers were going to Poland in six weeks time. 'It's another 50km race. One of the team has dropped out. Are you interested?'

'Sure,' I said. 'I'll do it.'

I allowed myself a week to recover from the disappointment of the London retirement. After that, I trained like a demon, averaging 90 miles a week.

Julian Hopkins welcomed me at Heathrow. Julian was one of the most studious men I knew in walking. A physics teacher at Liverpool Polytechnic, there was nothing he didn't know about the event; his only flaw – he was a rubbish walker. No, he did not walk quite as badly as the strutting Professor Wallofski, the comic creation of old time music hall entertainer Max Wall, but it would not be too wide of the mark to say that they looked alike and shared a similar balding pate. As hard as Julian tried, his technique was awful. Coaching was his forte. Bob Dobson as usual looked fit, as did Ian Richards who by reputation was known to be a prolific trainer often covering more than 120 miles a week in training. New Zealand international walker Mike Parker together with his coach John Cook made up the party. I felt fit and privileged to be in such inspirational company.

Flying via Warsaw, our destination was the shipyard town of Gdansk. Walking into the airport lobby was jaw dropping. I had never seen armed guards before, particularly ones that looked like they might use their guns if necessary. Out on the snowbound streets, I lost count of the number of stationary tanks I saw. All the people were going about their business, sombre looks on their faces; everything looked grey and drab, yet there was still an undercurrent of energy in the air, an indefinable sense of imminent change. Perhaps if I had taken more notice of national news I would have been emotionally prepared. We had after all entered an area of the world that had become the focal point of attention. The Polish Solidarity movement led by union activist Lech Walesa was affecting the political landscape of not only that country but that of Eastern Europe.

In our hotel room that night we rested. Any reference to what we had seen outside was limited. Selfish or not, we were there to race and that is what we all needed to concentrate on.

Sunday morning: Race day. If I had been on holiday, a first ever ride on a rickety old tram probably would have been a more enjoyable experience. As it was, the bitterly cold half hour ride from our hotel to Gdynia seemed to take ages.

Finally, on our arrival at the race venue, we discovered that the scheduled 10 o'clock start time had been delayed. Barely a degree or two above freezing, the parkland race circuit was submerged beneath inches of snow and patches of icy water. The local army were already out busy with ploughs and brushes sweeping the course. We had to just wait and see. Over an hour passed before we were all told to prepare to race.

1130 we were off – 35 men, many of whom on paper were so much faster than me. I felt strong throughout, covering any of the breakaway surges. Incredibly, one by one the extreme weather conditions seemed to get the better of those around me. Well beyond halfway I was up to second position and tracking Poland's Felix Selwinski, a man with a pre-race best time of 3:58. To my surprise he was obviously concerned, taking regular opportunities to glance over his shoulder to see if his British pursuer was still there. I finally caught and overtook him on the penultimate lap. Julian was jubilant and there to see me cross the finish line in a new British record time of 4:06.43. More significantly, it was well inside the 4:10 qualifying time that had been set for the Moscow Olympics. The Pole crossed the line 17 seconds behind. Ian Richards came through the carnage of those failing to finish by recording 4:07.57 in third. Bob Dobson had a disappointing walk and was way back, Mike Parker was amongst those who had dropped out.

I sat with Julian on a wooden bench in the changing rooms trading thoughts on what had just gone before. The magnitude of what I had achieved was only just beginning to sink in. Across the way, a foreign athlete, looking cold and bedraggled raised a half smile and gestured that I might care to swop my union jack shorts for the polythene bag of goodies he was holding up in his hand. Initially, I thought why not...I can always get another pair of shorts back home. Before I could ease myself up off the bench, Julian tugged my arm and shook his head. It was his belief that I was being offered some drugs. Drugs, what drugs? I didn't have a headache! Julian pursed his lips, stared at me with a look that could easily have been interpreted as either *you are so naive* or *you're an idiot, Maddocks.* The penny eventually dropped. My union jack shorts were going nowhere.

Sat on the flight home, Bob Dobson bought me a celebration drink; a brilliant gesture from a noble man. Not wishing to appear unappreciative, my best efforts to disguise the distaste of whisky meant that in all probability I may well have looked as if I had swallowed a wasp as I supped away. If Bob knew, he never let on. His playful smile might have been a clue.

The following Saturday I was setting a new personal best of 12 minutes 43 seconds for 3000m on the track at Exeter in a Phillips Trophy league match. That short race was one thing, but I did not really feel up to racing another 50kms eight days later. There seemed little choice. It was the first of two Olympic trial events at Moorgate Polytechnic for the British 20km and 50km teams. All athletes were told that it was necessary for them to contest at least one of the trial events if they wanted to be considered for Olympic selection.

On a cold, windy day, weather conditions were not conducive to fast times. In the space of two weeks, Ian had turned the tables on me.

50kms. Top three race result:
1st	Ian Richards, Coventry	4:10.53
2nd	Chris Maddocks, Dawlish	4:15.42
3rd	Adrian James, Enfield	4:15.47

The general consensus was that as Ian and I already had qualifying times from Poland, and together with our top two finishes in the official trial, our tickets for Moscow were virtually assured. Well, no!

The second of the two trials was a mere five weeks later. I did not want to do it, and said so. Apart from anything else, I had law exams just two days before. You *must* do the race, they said. Well, Ian won in a time of 4:08.28. Ten years my senior, over three tough races he had shown incredible consistency; his place on the team seemed secure. For my part, I dropped out at the 35km point whilst lying second. I was exhausted. My place on the team now apparently hung in the balance. I protested. I am not sure if anyone who mattered was listening.

Eric Shillabeer, in his capacity as honorary secretary of our walking club decided to write to Peter Marlow imploring him and other members of the walks selection committee to recommend to the board of Olympic selectors that I should be in the team. A copy of that letter is now in my scrapbook, from which this extract is taken:

Chris is young and to be made to do a third 50k in seven weeks is grossly unfair. At one time it was decided that you could choose one of the two trials and Chris decided on the first as he would be in the middle of exams for the second trial. If he had been older and with more experience he would probably have done what Bernie Ford did in the marathon i.e., refused to do the trial and risk that no one beat his time, they did not, and Bernie Ford was selected. Chris not only has the best time this year, but also broke the UK record. We know the West Country would be very disappointed if Chris is not selected as he is the first ever race walker to attain such heights from this area. Eric added a postscript: *if any walkers are selected for Moscow we wish them the very best.*

When the British Olympic team was announced, my name was not amongst those on the lists. No one rang me. No one saw fit to tell me the devastating news personally. It just popped up on the early evening local TV news while I sat at the table eating a meal with my brothers Peter and Michael.

Film clips of several selected West Country sportspersons were shown, including one of Sharron Davies. The final piece of film in the news item featured an archive clip of me walking.

The narrator said, 'Meanwhile, excluded from the British team, Chris Maddocks...' In the moments that followed, if anyone around the table spoke, I did not hear them. In my head a voice grew ever louder as it repeatedly said, *you're not in the team; you are not in the team; Maddocks you are not in the team...* Surreal or not, I felt as if the TV announcer was standing by my side leaning into my ear and screaming, *did you not hear me Maddocks, I said, you are NOT in the team!* My chest tightened. I could hardly breathe.

I downed my knife and fork, grabbed my car keys and rushed for the door. Mum made a desperate attempt to stop me.

'Please Chris, don't,' I heard her cry.

I walked to my car, got in and drove off at speed. I had no idea where I was going. Minutes later I was turning a corner and nearly collided with an oncoming lorry. Its horn sounded a loud disapproving noise as it roared on past. Frightened back into the present, I rammed my foot to the pedal causing a screech of brakes that brought me to a body shuddering stop outside the grounds of a deserted school in the village of Bolham. I slumped forward at the wheel and cried.

Government politics and the Soviet invasion of Afghanistan ensured that there were only funds to send a smaller British team than anticipated to Moscow. Three qualified athletes per athletic event could have been selected. Ian Richards proved his worth by ultimately finishing a commendable 11th in the Russian capital. Roger Mills in the 20km race also walked well for a fine 10th placing.

Margaret Thatcher's Conservatives ignored the old maxim that politics and sport should not mix by arguing that while the Afghans were under attack by the same country hosting the Olympics, British athletes on moral grounds should not go to Moscow. A boycott of the games by the athletes was called for from the politicians. Not wishing to be seen in conflict with the Government, many businesses who had planned on providing funds for the British Olympic

Association withdrew their promised financial support. Political intervention was one thing, and some may call it paranoia, but I was angry, very angry.

I felt sure that officials from the British walking hierarchy had not done enough to present my case to the selectors for inclusion in the team. These suspicions were confirmed in August when I was in the changing rooms shortly after competing in a seven mile road race at Gloucester. I overheard walkers saying that my name had not even been put forward to the Olympic selectors by walking officialdom. The months of sweating on selection or not was in fact all in vain. If the hearsay was to be believed, I was never going to be selected for the Moscow Olympic Games. I also heard on more definite authority that there was to be a four sided International walks competition in Paris between GB, France, Switzerland and Spain in September. As I had not heard anything about this I deduced that I no longer figured in the selectors minds, not even in a four man team.

On the return journey home, my Dawlish team mates understood my grievance and agreed to pull over and allow me to make a telephone call to one unsuspecting selector.

We did not think you would be interested in another 50km race, he argued. Fuming, I demanded the right to have at least be asked and said, rather arrogantly, that I would not only do the race but break the British record again.

Columbus – a province of Paris. With the formalities of the civic reception and the national anthems over, the 50km road race got underway at 4pm. Weather conditions were ideal, warm with a slight breeze. From the starter's gun Ian Richards burst into the lead, leaving me trailing in an isolated second position with four men a short distance back contesting third. Ian had built up a two minute lead by 13kms before stomach troubles reduced his speed allowing me to catch and overtake him within the next two kilometers.

The 5.3km course was undulating with some parts of the route going through the *busy* town centre. In typical continental style, as the lead athlete I was headed by the official escort vehicle with flashing lights, music, and commentary of the race for the benefit of the watching crowds.

At one point, my rhythm was briefly affected by the sounds of church wedding bells and a gloriously happy bride and groom outside being showered in confetti by jubilant guests. They looked set to cross the road just as I was approaching. In the nick of time the honking escort car alerted the party. Some turned to cheer as I passed on by relentlessly.

The sun had set when I was finally directed off the road circuit towards the track in the local athletics stadium; my lead over Spain's Manuel Alcalde had lengthened to over 16 minutes. Breaking the tape in a barrage of flash photography I was immediately pursued by a posse of people wanting a post-race interview. I had already eyeballed the large spongy high jump mat as a suitable resting place. Stepping off the track I flopped on to my back breathing heavily, grinning deliriously up at a darkening sky. Within seconds I was confronted by faces and an array of microphones and tape recorders.

I was happy in spite of my increasingly sore stomach muscles that had developed over the final 10kms and almost certainly prevented me from staying on schedule for an historic sub four hour walk. Removing another one minute and 14 seconds from my British record was some compensation.

Contentious or not, by the year end I had been voted UK walker of the year, ahead of Ian Richards and Roger Mills. I had already informed Julian Hopkins that I would decline the opportunity for my name to be added to the national walks squad for winter training. For a few days our phone at home was hot from enquiring journalists who wanted to know more about my apparent *controversial* withdrawal from the national squad. Whether it was naivety, stupidity or sheer arrogance, I merely wanted to make a stand against those who I felt had let me down. I said that I did not need their help and that from now on, I would do it my way.

It would be two and a half years before I would race again in an international vest. It mattered less to me as my heart was not in it anymore. During that time I passed my college A-level exams, and whilst learning how to type and take shorthand I dated the prettiest girl in the secretarial pool. It should be said that as the only man in a class of 17 girls, I probably did have the distinct advantage of some novelty value. Once I fell out of favour with Heather, so my popularity in class plummeted. Though not totally ostracized by my classmates, it did mean that I could at least refocus on the repetitive practice necessary to reach ultimate typing speeds of 30 words per minute and 70 words per minute shorthand. At the time I was quite proud of these new skills, skills that would unfortunately become almost completely redundant for the best part of the next 20 years, by which time my competence levels would in the interim decline to pathetic.

One area of training in which I never lost interest was gym work, in particular lifting weights. So much of athletics training is a solitary experience, whereas the camaraderie and challenges found in most gyms is quite intoxicating. I first discovered this as a teenager at our local youth club – the same one from where the annual 50 mile walks was organised, the same one where on a Friday night my mates and I would go and chat up the girls at the disco. The gym around the back of the youth centre was open to all those over 18. I think we were 17 when we first started. Some would describe it as a spit & sawdust gym, nothing fancy, just free standing weights, a bit tawdry, and lots of sweat and grunting. It was a man's world, figuratively and literally. I don't think I ever recall seeing a female during the five years or so that I was there.

Snow in the early days of 1982 meant travelling into town was slippery and unsafe. Not wishing to miss out on weight training saw me and my brother Peter walk the short distance up to the farm, where our cousins Gary and Graham lived. Such was the size of the Victorian farmhouse, they could afford to dedicate one room for a group workout with weights that we had bought together some months earlier. Bravado is a dangerous thing when unsupervised young men get-together. Connoisseurs of weight lifting will know that the dead lift is a particularly useful exercise if done properly and with care. For the uninitiated it means bending over and grabbing a steel bar, usually loaded with heavy weights, and whilst remaining angled over the bar lifting it off the floor towards the chest keeping the back firm and straight. It is an exercise primarily aimed at strengthening back muscles. I can only surmise that in the chattering company I was not concentrating properly. One minute we were joking and cajoling, the next I was in excruciating pain. Part way through my turn at the dead lift I let the bar fall to the floor, with me dropping to my knees.

For days I could barely put one foot in front of the other. The doctor said that I had almost certainly pulled muscles to my lower vertebrae. Six weeks of regular physiotherapy saw minimal improvement. It would take nine months more of endless specialists' visits before I felt comparatively free of pain. X-rays had revealed that in addition to the damage done, I also had spondylolisthesis – a congenital condition that can cause nerve pain. From all my various physiotherapy treatment sessions, I gleaned what I considered the best of the mobility and back strengthening exercises and meticulously did them on a daily basis – a best practice that I would carry through for the rest of my racing career; a career that at one stage, according to my own GP was probably over. Determined to prove him and other doubters wrong I set about getting fit again.

Averaging around 40 – 50 miles a week I continued to train at a level that allowed me to start winning regional races again. Winning and enjoying it went hand in hand. However, by the summer of 1982 I received a rude awakening. I thought there was little to fear before the start of the 10km walk at the South Western Counties athletic track championships at Yeovil in Somerset. That was until I saw the bearded figure of Roger Mills warming up.

Down from his home in Essex, he was on holiday with his wife and thought he would make a guest appearance in the walk. Here was a man who in addition to being a Moscow Olympian had on numerous occasions, competed under the bright lights at Crystal Palace setting various records in sprint walks the latest of which had been 6 minutes 9 seconds for a new one mile world record. This walk was likely to be no more than a hard training session for him. And so it proved.

Twenty or so walkers were called to the start line. Roger turned to me and casually asked, 'What sort of time are you hoping for?'

'Huh, maybe a personal best,' I replied. 'I'd quite like to go sub 45,' I said. Needless to say there was a huge amount of bravado in stating that I wanted to achieve a sub 45 minute personal best time. I wasn't really fit enough to do it. The die had been cast.

'Okay,' he said with an air of supreme confidence. 'I'll pace you. Stay close to me and I will help you do it.'

Suddenly I felt nervous. It was too late. The starter's gun fired. Roger shot straight to the front with me in his slipstream. The other walkers immediately tailed off. For 24 laps I watched the back of his muscular frame mindful, not to clip his heels. Occasionally he would grunt words of encouragement particularly if I slipped back.

The tone of his voice sometimes bordered on the abusive. 'C'mon, stay close. Don't wimp out on me now.'

For a few brief moments on the 25th and final lap I thought that I might make the audacious move and overtake him. Pulling out wide into the second lane with 100m to go I moved up alongside. I flicked a look across at him. His wry smile could easily be confused with wicked. He pushed ahead to cross the line two seconds in front. I sunk to my knees at the finish. His outstretched hand meant I had to reciprocate. Barely able to muster an intelligible word, I offered up a wheezy, 'thanks.' My time: 44 minutes 54.5 seconds.

If you can't do it in training, then how do you expect to do it in a race, he said later. Well, he was training; I was close to killing myself. I learned a valuable lesson. From then on, I put my head down and trained longer and harder.

By the spring of 1983 I already had an unconditional offer on the table from Plymouth Polytechnic. Then, to my surprise came an invitation to have interviews at Exeter University. My application had been made with no real belief that I would hear from them again. I was so sure that I would be out of my depth amongst all the bright young things from privileged backgrounds. Hooray-Henrys were on the march and descending on places like Exeter. The university had long been rated amongst the top in Britain and believed to have the highest percentage of Oxbridge *rejects*. I was sure that I must have slipped through the net.

Of course at 26 years old, I may just have been part of their required quota of mature students. Together with a growing notoriety in the press as an athlete with Olympic ambitions, my promise to work hard if given the chance to study there was both sincere and honest.

I had a series of good race results leading up to the latest bi-annual World Cup finals hosted this time in late September by the town folk of Bergen in Norway. One of the best results was a seventh placing over 30kms in a 12 nation competition in Milan ahead of amongst others, Mexican, Raul Gonzalez, one of the world's greats. There were also wins on the track over 3000m and on the road over 20kms in London's Victoria Park. The latter result was both pleasing and disappointing. It was there that I was allowed by unprepared race stewards to go off course whilst leading early on. Walking the extra distance before being told to double back and rejoin the tail of the competing field was an avoidable mistake that inadvertently added more than two minutes to my finishing time of 89 minutes 42 seconds. This meant that I narrowly missed qualifying for the inaugural World athletics championships in Helsinki later that summer.

Sunday October 2 1983: The day that I moved into Halls at university *and* the day that I had the first of seven club six mile league races held at Dawlish – each held on alternate Sunday afternoons leading up to Christmas.

That morning there was just enough time for Mum to drive me to St Lukes College, get a key from the porters' lodge, find the student accommodation that I had been allocated, dump my bags down in my new room on the second and top floor of Nancherrow House, say a brief hello to a few early arrivals already ensconced in the large Victorian building, begrudgingly say why I was in a rush, and depart again for the short drive to club mate Peter Jennings' home in Exeter.

Mum needed to return home while Peter and I left for an afternoon meeting up with our walking friends at the Dawlish Cricket pavilion – a place used routinely by us during our annual racing days for changing facilities and for the post race cup of tea and sticky bun.

The usual gathering of walkers varied from a handful up to a dozen or more. The range of abilities was such that in order to spice things up we started our respective six mile walks at different times – the slowest led off first with the others handicapped by an agreed time according to predicted finishing times. I would invariably set off a distant last. The aim of the yacht handicap system was to encourage those in front to stay ahead by walking faster with the desired end result being that all finished within a minute or two of each other.

So long as I had a successfully fast walk, I was quite happy to be beaten by any of our slower club members, some of whom would start up to half an hour before me.

There was nothing as formal as a starter's gun here. Whichever friend or spouse was willing and available generally determined who would set you off with the press of a stopwatch. Today it was the turn of Richard Pannell, one of my best and most important of friends. Originally down to walk, his knee had been playing up. One by one, with the immortal words, *are you ready…GO!*

Starting from outside the glass fronted pavilion, the annual six mile circuit followed a route that wound its way down towards the Dawlish Warren sea front, a point at which it was best to ignore any finger pointing and bemused looks on the faces of pedestrians and late season holidaymakers. Continuing on, the road ran adjacent to the Great Western line that saw trains periodically thundering past in the blink of an eye. More than once I had been scared witless by drivers tooting their whistle as the rush of carriages shot alarmingly close by.

By the time the village of Starcross was reached it was usual for walkers to be on the receiving end of varying levels of banter from the beer drinking locals standing outside the pub. Comments ranged from friendly encouragement to down-right abusive insults. It was at this halfway point that I felt I probably suffered the most.

Unwitting spectators were treated to a succession of anguished sweat sodden faces each with obvious determination as they trundled pass. Whether there was any real appreciation of speed differential between myself and the others was open to conjecture. I may well have been operating at a swift sub-seven minute mile pace; but, as was likely at this halfway point, I would not only still be behind our next fastest walker, Edmund Shillabeer, but also still significantly behind *plucky Brenda* and *fat Jim with his dodgy hip.*

The more vocal of those amongst the pub drinkers were often keen to remind me of my failings with encouragingly typical cries not unlike:

'C'mon mate, get yer ass in gear. You're way behind.'

'You've just missed the last bus.'

'Speed up boy and you might catch that last guy…he's there, just across the bridge.'

Either appreciatively encouraged or thick skinned bruised, we would all follow the S-bend route that would take in the harbour bridge at Starcross before turning back along the A379 road and the three miles of long straights and arching hills back towards Dawlish.

With each passing quarter mile silhouetted walkers would come into my view. Spotting the occasional glance over a shoulder would invariably cause an increase in arm pumping action and one final desperate effort to stay ahead. Turning away from the main road and sighting the playing fields leading back to a pavilion finish could not come quick enough for most.

Driving back to Exeter that day, I was satisfied with my 41 minute 28 second time as was Pete Jennings with his 59 minute 23 second effort particularly as he had finished 50 yards ahead of me. Softly spoken, tall dark and languid, Pete was married to the lovely Sue. The offer of a hot meal back at their place that evening was gratefully accepted. Truth was that I felt reticent about my impending life as a university student and anything that might delay going back to my new home was welcomed.

It was gone seven when I walked back into Nancherrow. I was at the foot of the stairs when I heard the approaching sound of chattering female voices and the man who I had met briefly on my earlier arrival. As they descended I readied myself to meet half of my new housemates, four young women and Mike Judd, who like me was another mature student.

Top floor bonding appeared to have been swift in my short absence. Partway through telling what would become one of many amusing anecdotes, Mike already had his new friends laughing. Loudest amongst the captive group was the girl with a mess of long blonde corkscrew curls whose choice of bobby socks and stripy dungaree jeans reminded me of those clothes typically worn by Andy Pandy on playschool TV. In a show of womanly sisterhood she was locked in arms with her new roommate, another attractive teenager and someone who struck me as overly keen on being noticed – that is if, thrusting herself forward swishing her long auburn hair and flashing eyelashes provocatively was anything to go by.

36

The most enigmatic smile belonged to the girl in a tasseled studded denim jacket and the only black female amongst the group; in fact, Aphinia would prove to be one of only two *black* students of the 500 or so attending St Lukes during my first year. This revealing statistic would have no apparent adverse affect on the confidence of this tough girl from Bradford. That said, on first impressions it looked something of an oddity seeing her arm in arm with the most conservatively attired one amongst them. Unquestionably pretty, the girl in the loose fitting cardigan, upturned collar and knee length skirt looked more suitably dressed for tea with the vicar rather than a student night out. The green bomber jacket, white t-shirt and baggy blue jeans worn by Mike would grace the halls of Lukes frequently over the next three years.

Standing six foot two, he had a receding hairline and a mischievous grin that suggested a wisecrack was never far away. Fairly apt, as he was the spitting image of Phil Silvers, an American actor probably best remembered as Sergeant Bilko. I smiled at the thought, particularly when he pushed back the spectacles slipping down his nose.

'You look quite pleased,' he said. 'How'd the walk go?'

'Good thanks,' I replied. No sarcasm, thus far. In fact, I was relieved and pleasantly surprised that it was a sensible question. It was probably the *last* sensible thing he ever said to me in what would turn out to be an unlikely lasting friendship.

Mike nodded. 'We're going across the road to the bar in the common room for a drink,' he said. 'Fancy joining us?'

'Yeah, go on,' said one of the girls. The others concurred.

'Huh, maybe later,' I said.

They left while I walked on up stairs towards room 201. There was no mistaking it. Pinned on the door, a newspaper page headlined, *MAGNIFICENT MADDOCKS*...and below it, a black and white photograph of me in walking action together with a local paper report of my race in Bergen from the previous weekend. The report said how I had finished 9th in the 50km race in a new British record time of 4:02.37...23 seconds inside the qualifying time for the 1984 Olympic Games in Los Angeles. Scrawled in capital letters across the top of the page in red biro ink were the words, *IS THIS YOU?*

Trainee teachers constituted the vast majority of those students living in halls on the St Luke's College campus. Mike Judd and I on the other hand were in that small minority of *Lukies* who would be required to make the mile and a half journey across town to the main site in order to attend our lectures. Given that our respective degree courses both included reading sociology, his combined with psychology and mine with law, we were destined, metaphorically speaking, to be partially joined at the hip over the next three years. Had I known it from the beginning it would have been a particularly disturbing prospect.

Any thoughts on that first Monday of an early morning training session were abandoned in favour of breakfast in the Lukes cafeteria. Found towards the east side corner of the campus' main quadrant, wafts of fried bacon greeted us as we walked through the double doors of a bustling canteen. Glancing around there appeared to be a predominance of track suited PE students, a number of them identifiable as rugby players, if only by their beefy size and first signs of cauliflower ears.

Whilst in the throes of gathering up our cutlery, I heard voices directed at us.

'Mike, Chris, we're over here.'

Waving frantically, our four housemate friends were seemingly keen that we joined them. We had yet to make the acquaintance of the other six girls roomed below us on the first floor. That invisible division would ultimately remain throughout the forthcoming year. In time, they would prove to be the more cultured half of the house, where words such as *phew* and *gosh* were commonly spoken, words that I previously thought were only said in the comics I read when I was growing up. In due course I learned to appreciate that not all undergraduates at Exeter were from affluent backgrounds with snobbish airs and graces.

By some fortuitous twist of fate I would share a floor with group of new students that were so obviously unaffected by privileged surroundings. And so it was that without any real harm done, tame rules were there to be broken. Unwritten rules like those that dictated students did not deface the menu white board set up behind the cutlery trays. Which of our four girl friends wrote *MAGNIFICENT MADDOCKS is here* remained a mystery to me. My embarrassment was temporary, as was the innuendo behind the scribbling that perhaps suggested to some of the green eyed, red blooded males that the new guy on the block may have stolen a march on them with regard to the houseful of young fillies over at Nancherrow, known affectionately as the Ranch. The notoriety was brief, but covertly I enjoyed it while it lasted.

With the contented satisfaction that comes with a full stomach, Mike and I enjoyed a leisurely cycle ride to the main university campus. Neither of us had arrived with a car. Mike simply saw no reason to drive from his home in Cambridgeshire. My beloved old chocolate brown six-seater Wolseley 18/85 bought cheaply from eldest brother Patrick would remain in dry dock until I could afford the necessary £350 for repairs and a new MOT. It was a relief to know that I had been awarded a full three year educational grant from my local authority. However I was one of many students affected by an administrative hold up that meant a delay in the distribution of our first term cheques. Any new books would have to be bought from my meager savings.

Cycling towards the fringes of the redbrick campus I felt a sense of wonderment and privilege. With the bikes padlocked to the first available spare railing, I glanced up and around. It looked so big. A few deep breaths and we were on our way. First stop, joining the assembly of 2000 freshers in the Great Hall where a succession of course tutors would each make their brief welcoming speeches. Mouths were agog during the closing address from the student union president.

'You probably think that three years is a long time. Well, it's not. Let me tell you this. It will fly by. This is a great place. Make the most of it…'

Mike and I filed out with the masses. Energized with hope and expectation, the early days on campus were met with a sense of foreboding whilst coming to terms with our new surroundings. For now though, it would be a time of endless queuing, reams of form filling, and meeting faculty tutors.

We found some relief from all the formalities in Devonshire House. There, numerous tables were manned by second, third and fourth year students each trying to catch the eye of impressionable faces in their efforts to entice new blood to join their respective societies. Astronomy, Debating, Poker, Book club, Geography, Christians in Sport, the choices seemed endless.

'No!'

Mike was not prepared to take no for an answer, 'Why not?'

'I do not want to join the Mature Student's society.' I said. 'And that's final.'

'C'mon, if I am you might as well.'

'Look, if you want to join some old farts society, then that's up to you. I'm 26, you're 27. The trouble with you is that you're getting old before your time. I want to blend in.'

'What, with that hairstyle?'

'At least I've got some hair, and it's fashionable.'

'Maybe in the '70s. Were you in Showaddywaddy once? *Under the Moon of Love*, you were one of the backing singers, weren't you? Hey, you could join the music society. You look like a man who knows how to play the recorder.'

'Look,' I said, 'I'm not fussed about joining anything.'

Mike Judd had an innate gift to irritate and make me laugh in equal measure. Right then, the former gift was edging it. Over my shoulder, he had spotted the two stick thin young men manning the athletic club table. 'Hey, there you go,' he said. 'They look a bit desperate. You might get in there.'

Against my better judgement I followed him through the throng. As we approached, the taller of the two men started a conversation with three girls.

Mike stepped forward and spoke to the other. 'Hi, my name's Mike.'

'Hi.'

With a wave of the hand, Mike beckoned me in closer. 'My friend here might be interested in joining your team. Let me introduce you.'

I offered my hand. 'Hello,' I said. My handshake was reciprocated with a firm nod of the head.

Mike interjected, 'This is Cliff Maddock. You might have heard of him. He's quite famous, you know. Sorry, I didn't catch your name?'

'Keith!'

'Well, there's a coincidence. You two have the same name.'

'What? I thought that you said his name was Cliff?' The kid's agitation levels were already up. He looked at Mike. He gave me a cursory glance. 'Sorry, are you...?'

'Mike interrupted again, 'You recognise him, don't you? Yes, this is Keith Maddock, the famous walker.'

The kid looked completely bamboozled. 'Sorry, I was going to ask if you were first year students. Should you be here?'

I leaned forward and said, 'Sorry mate, maybe we'll think about it and get back to you.' I looked at Mike with my best pissed off look and said, 'C'mon, let's see if we can get those concert tickets now.'

'Okay.' Mike turned to the kid, winked, and showed him a thumbs up and said, 'Good to meet you Cliff.'

'Keith.'

'Yes, of course. Get in touch if you want to talk. You'll find us at Lukes. I'm his manager. Remember, Chris Maddocks is his name...famous walker.'

The sneer on the kid's face said it all. He looked like he had just been slapped about the face with a wet kipper.

Mike stepped away from the table, looked at me and asked, 'Are you alright?'

'You twat!'

'What? I told him who you were.'

A chap from the athletic club did eventually get in touch. Thankfully, I don't think it had any connection to that sorry incident. Interviewed for the student union magazine, I was happy to answer questions about being an undergraduate, what it was like to be a race walker, and most pointedly talk about my Olympic ambitions.

Training was minimal during that first week. The cinder track at Clifton Hill was a short convenient stroll from St Lukes' campus. It soon became apparent that during regular office hours the track was virtually unused by other athletes. Exeter Harriers had their club nights, and the adjacent dry ski slope was obviously underused if the shoots of sprouting weeds were anything to go by.

Joining me on Wednesday for a short thirty minute track session was Pete Jennings who had driven the few miles from Killerton Gardens where he worked as a National Trust estate manager. With Saturday's race in mind, plans were agreed between us for our rendezvous time with friends traveling up from Plymouth.

Thursday afternoon, it was Mike's turn to join me at the track. Donning the same kit he had previously used at Cambridge rowing regattas back home, he attempted to run alongside me until his lumbering 14 stone frame began to object.

I forged on ahead and walked the 25 lap 10km distance in 43 minutes 33 seconds. There was considerable debate afterwards as to how many times I had actually lapped him. Three I said; two, he argued. Not in dispute was his crumpled state. His vow to get fit again would have implications that meant I was destined to see more of him than I might have wished.

That evening we were perspiring again as we joined two thousand other students packed in to the Great Hall for the Fresher's Ball. It was hot, it was noisy. It was going to get a lot sweatier before the end. Accompanying us, Aphinia and excited friends could hardly contain themselves.

Mike had been less than enthusiastic when we bought the concert tickets. As far as he was concerned, Gary Glitter did not quite cut the mustard. Well, it might have been 10 years since I remember buying *I love you love me love...*but felt vindicated when it when straight into the charts at number one.

The girls were obviously there just for a laugh. And so they did when the Glitter Band entered side of stage some holding guitars aloft like warriors brandishing their sabers. The whoops of cheering and foot stomping continued as each band member strutted towards their microphones in what looked like at least four inch heels all sartorially attired in a variety of sequin spangled coloured jump suits with shoulder pads a mile wide. This was glam rock at its best.

My initial fears that 99% of the audience would not know any of the lyrics were allayed as soon as the drummer took his seat and started to thump out their intro beat while the remainder of the band strummed opening chords whilst repeatedly chanting *C'mon, c'mon, c'mon, c'mon...*

The floor beneath our feet immediately began to vibrate as the place rocked with seemingly everyone joining in, leaping on the spot and air punching. True, the lyrics were not difficult to follow. Completely tone deaf, my best efforts thankfully could not be heard amid all the noise. With thick dry ice descending centre stage, we did not have to wait long before the main man appeared.

Arms spread high and wide, his heavy mascara emphasized an eye-popping glare. It was pure theatre. Looking like a giant oven foil ready turkey at Christmas in five inch platforms he belted out, *I'm the leader, I'm the leader, I'm the leader of the gang, I am...* It was brilliant. Shouting along with him, Mike was a leader, as were the rest of us. Gary had everyone one of us in the palm of his hand.

Okay, it may not be too clever to say it now, but back then we really did enjoy hearing him sing, *Do you want to touch me...*

GG slowed things down later and serenaded us all with *Remember me this way...* Well, I for one will fondly remember it as one of the best concerts ever for unadulterated fun filled madness. None of us were to know how things would change decades later.

Two days on, my voice was still hoarse when I toed the line with 175 others at the start of my next race. The annual Chippenham to Calne six-mile event had long gained a reputation as Britain's premier town-to-town road race.

Through the decades most of the best walkers in the country had tested themselves over these Wiltshire hills. The course record had long stood to 1964 Olympic 20km Champion Ken Matthews. A special gold medal had been struck for anyone who could better it. Finally, after 25 years it was beaten in 1982 by Welshman, Steve Barry. He did it in the same year he won Commonwealth Gold in Brisbane, Australia and lowered the record to what seemed at the time to be an unassailable 41 minutes 22 seconds.

A precedent had been set. A new special gold medal was commissioned by the local organisers, few of whom I guess would have anticipated it being claimed so quickly.

Well, when I finally pulled clear of 20 year old Phil Vesty at the four and half mile point on the longest and steepest climb, I knew that I only had to hold my technique and concentration, and a famous win was mine.

As was the tradition, a brass band could be heard playing from the middle of Calne's memorial square in readiness for walkers nearing the finish. Led by the jolly sounds of trumpets and big drums, I turned off the main road and on towards the finish line. Standing by the race time keepers, the town Mayor was there ready to hang a medal around the winner's neck. Moments after breasting the tape I accepted the outstretched hand and medal as I slowed to a stop.

Beating a rising star by 47 seconds was reward enough, but it was with incredible satisfaction that I was later presented with that special gold medal for my time of 40.02.

Back in Exeter I had to get my head down to studies. Fortunately I felt I had a bit of a head start given my A-level passes. At least that's what I thought at the time. Law lectures in contracts were just about within my range, as were aspects of theories and methods in sociology. The sociology of Italy I was less sure about.

I doubt anything could have prepared me for my first tutorial with the rather debonair Mr Poole. Floppy hair, tweed jackets and an assortment of cravats were his style.

Perhaps the six others in my group felt the same, I'm not sure. For an hour or so we had a nice convivial introductory chat, the degree course, and what might be expected in the three years ahead. We were told that our lecture timetable might appear sparse but no one should be lulled into a false sense of security. If there were gaps, we would be expected to fill them with a lot of private study. My thoughts drifted quickly to the endless possibilities for loads of preferred daytime training before, between or after lectures. I would just have to be organised and disciplined with my own private study, even if it meant burning the midnight oil and foregoing much of the infamous student social scene. Before I had time to feel at all comfortable, alarm bells rang in my head when Mr Poole suggested that we should be aiming to read course books at a rate of 40 pages per hour. Forty pages an hour? That sort of number usually took me at least a week, and that was supposing I could stay awake. The final bombshell hit right at the end.

'For your first essay, I'd like you to write…'

What? I felt a hot flush coming on. The horror was probably shared given the number of dumbstruck faces that I found myself surrounded by. What did he mean…our first essay? We had not even had a lecture yet. How could we possibly write an essay on a subject that we have not even had some tuition in?

I was not alone in having to scramble for a pen and paper to write with. As Mr Poole dictated, so we furiously wrote: *Cavour to Craxi, the inheritance of the Risorgimento. Discuss.*

Discuss what? I did not know what any of those words meant, let alone discuss anything about them. Mr Poole assured us that if we went to the library and sought out the relevant books, we would be able to produce the appropriate answers. We had two weeks.

I eventually cobbled together a four page essay and scored a *remarkable* A-.

Of course this was the first of a conveyor belt of requested essays. I found it hard. My training up towards Christmas and the end of term suffered. While I adjusted to these new demands, it was as much as I could do to find the energy and enthusiasm to walk up to 10kms. The cinder track across the road was convenient for a quick 25 lap session. Mike occasionally kept me company, as did the girls who joined us once in a while if only to have a laugh at our expense. Race results were holding up but I knew that it was only a matter of time before my fitness would wane and the speed and strength would fall away.

A letter from the BAAB (British Amateur Athletic Board) informed me that I could expect to receive help from a newly formed Olympic action unit led by influential athletic officials, Frank Dick, Andy Norman and John Le Mesurier. I was excited. The feeling would not last. Apart from being advised in December that I should do the Spanish Open 50km championships in March, and that I should do just enough to beat other GB walkers in order to secure Olympic selection, I failed to see what extra help I actually got.

I was also frustrated that I was being advised to do another 50km race. If I performed poorly, it could undo the good that had already been achieved by my recent world top 10 placing in an Olympic qualifying time. It's not rocket science to understand that it will take longer to recover from walking a fast 50kms than it does the 10 seconds or so for sprinting 100m or even running middle distance events like 1500m or 5000m races. It is more reasonable to compare it to the marathon. Due to the extreme demands on the body, runners do not expect to do frequent marathons before major championships.

One thing was for sure, I had to get my car back on the road. I needed to get away from the congested city roads and out into the countryside environment more suited for the necessary long hard miles of training. There were only so many times that I was prepared to rise at dawn and walk the same uninspiring network of car-lined streets within the immediate vicinity of Nancherrow. I quickly learned that starting much after 6am was simply out of the question. Work traffic was horrendous. In fact, once the steady flow of polluting engines had begun, repeatedly walking the 1.5km figure-of-eight circuit that I had devised was tantamount to entering a dodgecar rally.

Try telling any young person to voluntarily get up at 5.30am, particularly when some think there is only one 5.30 in a day. Ordinarily this was not a problem for me. I was used to getting up early…had done since I was a kid when I started out on my first paper round. Even during school holidays, I would routinely take Mum tea in bed before I went off training. This was normal for me. By contrast the life of a typical university student appeared to be more akin to work quite hard, play hard, play late, lie in bed for as long as possible.

With 10 young women living in Nancherrow, the house was a proverbial honeypot for visiting bees where hormones and testosterone regularly clashed. Stuck right in the middle of it all, by the end of the first 10 week Michaelmas term I was all but partied out. Quiet nights were a rare treat. Social gatherings in other rooms often evolved into spontaneous parties, and when they did it was naïve to hope for an early night's sleep. One such night the sounds of music and laughter coming from a room across the corridor meant my head was again buried beneath the pillow. Against the odds I managed to drift off to sleep until woken by a scraping sound. My slightly opened sash window was being levered up.

Now some might call it ingenuity, while others could call it sheer audacity. I called it a bloody cheek. The locked door downstairs had not deterred one red blooded, sex hungry character from trying to get in – at least, not where there was a fire escape to scale. Trouble was, that fire escape led right up to my bedroom window.

I only saw the large shadowy figure for a matter of seconds. Stepping through, he placed one foot on the bed, whispered, 'Excuse me mate,' and was across the room and out through the door before I could comprehend what was happening.

Though no excuse was ever needed, the end of mid-term exams was time for another celebration. The doors of Nancherrow were thrown open for the biggest toga party I had ever seen. For most it was a happy drunken affair. Clive thought otherwise. Before our rather unsavory encounter this particular student had barely registered on my radar. I wish I could have said the same for him.

When he stuck his face in mine, I initially thought it was a joke. It was well past midnight with the party beginning to break up. All I wanted to do was go to bed. Clive, who I had some notion was a rugby front row forward, spoke first.

'You must think your something special, don't you?'

I had no idea what he was talking about. I was more sure about his garlic breath. I pulled back and said, 'What! What are you on about?'

Clive pushed his forehead against mine and said, 'Wearing all that fancy kit – you think you're something special, don't ya?'

Any bemused smile quickly dissolved into a hardened stare. 'No,' I replied. There was an unbearable silence. I was not going to back down. I thought this ape could probably beat the crap out of me, but I was most definitely not going to back down.

This ridiculous stand-off continued for what seemed like several heart thumping minutes until one by one the girls intervened and coaxed Clive to step back and leave. He had by all accounts taken some exception to the *offensive* sight of seeing me around Lukes wearing any item of GB athletic kit no matter how small or insignificant the motif. That, I thought, should have been the end of the matter. Not quite.

The following morning I was in bed, in one of the girl's room sipping tea, reading the Sunday newspaper. I had another afternoon race at Dawlish scheduled and was not being picked up by Peter Jennings until 12noon. Julie, Sue and Sarah were mooching about, each scantily attired in their nightwear. It was still too early for anyone to care that the room had the look of a post-party tip. Through the opened bedroom door, I heard a voice from down the stairs. Two of the girls left to investigate.

A moment later one dashed back in and breathlessly said, 'Clive's here. He wants to see you Chris.' I glanced up from the sports pages. 'He wants to apologize,' she said. 'Do you want to see him?'

Squished next to me, Aphinia lifted her head from under the covers and mumbled, 'This should be interesting.'

I took a moment to think. Did I want to see the twat? How bad does this look? I am in bed with a friend. Absolutely nothing untoward has happened, apart from me catching up on the football results. Worst of all, I am surrounded by girls in various states of undress *and*…I have a GB athletic vest on.

'Yeah, all right,' I said. 'Show him in.'

Clive was in and out in no time. I imagined for him, every second of that apology was sheer purgatory. I doubt the poor chap had reached the bottom of the stairs when the girls could stifle their laughs no longer. The ear piercing cackles might have been more painful than if Clive had hit me.

Mike appeared at the door. Yawning loudly, and wearing only boxer shorts, he said, 'What's going on? Have I missed something?'

A few nights later, ball gowns and tuxedos were the dress code for the traditional St Lukes' end-of-term formal dinner in the plush surroundings of the Giraffe House. The food served on silver platters by smartly dressed dinner ladies was great; too good I would suggest for some unappreciative students. My heart went out to the ladies once the evening meal descended into a food fight as it would be they who would be left with the almighty mess to clear up. Order restored, it was onto the post-dinner entertainment with an inter-house trophy to be won. Little more than 10 minutes was given over for any necessary costume changes before the show started in earnest.

Bawdy rugby songs and feeble comedy sketch routines would prove no match for Nancherrow's spoof rendition of Summer Nights from the musical Grease. Our cause helped, no doubt, by the fantastic party atmosphere created by the laughing, cheering and a sing-along grand finish.

Aphinia revelled in the part of gang leader Danny, the role made famous by John Travolta. Aided by a backing sound track, Mike flipped up the collar of his borrowed leather jacket and along with girls making up the rest of the T-Bird greaser gang with considerable aplomb they all aped the chorus, 'Tell me more, tell me more…'

The Nancherrow girls had taken great delight in raiding their wardrobes for anything that could be perceived as clothing worn in the 1950's by the schoolgirl clique called, The Pink Ladies to whom Sandy Olsson deferred. When she sang of her candy coated love for Danny, it was me who had the unenviable task of emulating the lovely Olivia Newton John. With my long hair scraped back by an Alice-band I was squeezed into a colour coordinated skirt and cardigan. Fast forward a few years, and think of Queen's drummer Roger Taylor in their 1986 video, *I want to break free*…and you have an impression as to what I looked like. It was embarrassingly good fun.

The last day of the first term was by contrast a complete drag. It took me four hours to write that methodology essay. I may have left it to the last minute, but it was a burden lifted from my shoulders when I handed it in. I am sure that the sense of release from any immediate study commitments contributed to my good walk at Calne the next day. Jimmy Ball, much to his chagrin, had long got used to finishing second in most of our races in the South West. So it was this time. A minute and a half behind was no disgrace when I was in the mood for another course record previously held by Steve Barry. Winning the annual Pewsey Cup seven mile road race in 48.01 was very satisfying. It was just what I needed to spur me on to train extra hard over the forthcoming four week Christmas break. This was an absolute necessity if I was to be ready for that 50km race in March.

Fueled with big meals from Mum's home cooking, I averaged 100 miles per week. There was nothing scientific about the type of road sessions. Day after day I simply went out from our home and walked the hills around surrounding villages covering anything from 10 to 20 miles each day. Each walk was preceded with a 25 minute routine of warm-up stretches and hundreds of press-ups and sets of 80 sit-ups in the corridor of our family bungalow. So used to this, if anyone had to pass whilst I was puffing through with a set of press-ups or twisting into an improbable position they would simply step over or around me without so much as a nod or a wink.

After training and a soak in the bath, I'd recover by walking the dog. Catching up with old friends in town was something to look forward to, but only if I had time and had done required revision studies. I made a point of seeing my old coach, Jack Snow. It had been three months and by now I was deciding all my training and racing programmes.

My attitude going into 1984 was one of resolute determination. I would be tough on myself, I would be focused. The first term at Exeter may have introduced me to a whole new world, one in which I loved being a part of. But my primary goal was to grab the chance to become an Olympic athlete. It was within my grasp and I knew that I would be a fool to let it slip away. Yes, I loved being a university student. And for that reason alone I would study as best I could. In racing terms though, Villanova in Spain was the next big target with March 17th the date firmly imprinted on my mind. The five races I had scheduled before then were viewed as fast training sessions under competitive conditions.

Looking back on it now, it was almost certainly too much. Good or bad, I was making my own decisions. I guess most athletes might be horrified at the prospect of three 20km races and two six milers' before an important mid-March long distance race? Well, I was feeling fit and strong and at that time it did not unduly faze me.

First race up was our club 20kms at Dawlish. No real pressure amongst friends though all of us were probably affected on the day by strong headwinds making it more of a grind than a racing pleasure. Recording an 88.42 was still a good start.

Six days later, I lined up with 500 runners on the soon-to-be completed bypass linking the M5 motorway to North Devon and did 86.41 at the 20km mark en route to walking the Tiverton half marathon in 90.55. It was a straight forward out and back route that saw me overtaking masses of faster starting runners during the return half. Not all the support and encouragement that I received was fantastic. In fact I was mildly surprised and amused at the irritation of some as I ghosted pass.

'Hey mate what are you doing? This is a running race…'

'Oh hell, I thought I was doing alright until I saw him…'

That same day I was driving back to Exeter for the commencement of Lent term. I had my Wolseley back on the road and determined to use it in order to drive out to suitable country roads and miles of anticipated hard training.

The three hour mid-sessional law exam in the Great Hall on Monday morning was a relief to get out of the way. Exhausted by exam fatigue and the physical efforts of the race the day before, I decided to leave training until the evening.

Stepping on and off pavements, shooting across road junctions, avoiding pedestrians, tooting cars and the occasional stray cat or dog, eight times around my street circuit in 57 minutes was a sharp reminder as to why I had to get out into the countryside.

Once my lecture and private study programme had clearly been mapped out on my room wall chart, I was able to pencil in the maximum time I could put to my training and pinpoint all the key races; I treated it like a military operation, one I surely did not want to fail. I met club-mate Pete Jennings in his smart office at Killerton House. With his help over coffee we devised a suitable road lap of seven undulating miles, a part of which went within shouting distance of his window and past the wide expanse of National Trust gardens. It meandered away on through an English hamlet called Poltimore and an assortment of thatched cottages, bungalows, period properties wrapped with a heart-warming feel and a succession of sweet aromatic farmyard smells beyond. It suited me perfectly.

The drive out from the Ranch or from the main campus to the start point could take between 10 and 15 minutes but it would be worth it. Come Sunday I had trained there five times and notched up another weekly total of 100 miles. Not wishing to miss out on the action, my self-proclaimed manager and house-mate Mike Judd, thought he should test this new circuit if it was indeed going to form the basis of my training ground for the next three years. Bike or no bike, I considered it unwise. He was adamant.

The gradient pulling out of Poltimore was modestly steep but undoubtedly long as Mike became all too aware after the completion of the first circuit. The great oaf was sweating more than me. It may well have been a cold winter's day but he surely regretted the choice of jeans and padded bomber jacket as he floundered a distance in arrears whilst climbing that hill for the second time. It had been several minutes since I last heard his breathy exertions. Though I had to power my arms and shoulders in order to dig deep to keep my strike rate up, I could not resist a fleeting glance over my shoulder to see what was happening behind. It was not the best time to laugh, but the sight of that distant lump on a three gear bicycle out of his saddle wobbling from side to side almost had me in stitches.

The occasions when I could train with other athletes of a similar standard were few and far between. On those rare times when it did happen, I would travel considerable distances for the pleasure. Seriously underfunded by our athletic governing body, national squad get-togethers for race walkers were infrequent and in recent years held on weekends at comparatively low cost locations like Aldershot army barracks.

Facilities were rudimentary and the food plentiful but basic. For a group of a dozen or more young ambitious men led by National Coach Julian Hopkins, all we really needed was a place big enough to meet, eat, sleep, talk and go walking. Our knowledgeable leader in classroom time would impart the latest international information at hand while the rest of us played our cards close to our chest. When I was home with my club mates I passed on practical coaching advice and hoped that they might improve even if only a little. The feeling at national squads was quite different. There were too many of us who wanted the same thing. Sure, we were friends, but we were not all prepared to share our thoughts on individual training regimes for fear that one or the other might get the upper hand.

In many respects it was like being part of the secret service…no one completely trusted anyone. Everyone was economical with the truth about what they were doing back home. We all wanted to be in a three or four man GB team competing in the next International walks competition, we all wanted to qualify for the major championships be it at a Commonwealth Games, Europeans, the next

World Cup, the World Athletic Championships, and most of all, we all most definitely wanted the ultimate prize of a place on the Olympic team.

Training alongside men who were as fit and as fast as you was the best thing about national squads or at least that was the impression that everyone tried to present when out knocking off the miles together. The chat during the early stages of a typical 20 mile Sunday morning road session was convivial enough. It would change once someone upped the pace and tested the others. The key at this point was not to appear unduly stressed and to maintain a comfortable breathing pattern even if your lungs were burning inside. If you were one of the poor saps that succumbed and dropped away before the end it was best to have a ready prepared reason (excuse) in the communal showers. It was ridiculous of course. How could we reasonably be expected to meet on a given weekend and be at the same level of fitness? That sort of simple rationale did not come easily to any of us when our competitive urges took over. I for one often went home from these squad weekends with some sort of strain or injury because I had done more than I was capable of at the time. I had too much experience now to make that mistake again.

I suffered defeats in my next two races. Second to Ian McCombie over 10kms on the track at Brighton was no disgrace, as was my third position over 20kms on the Isle of Man at the end of February. Both Phil Vesty and Martin Rush were in Olympic contention and my time of 87.14 was good considering that I was still racking up the miles in preparation for the Spanish 50km race. A win at the Bournemouth Piers' six miles in 41 minutes 49 seconds was on the back of a final 100 mile week of training.

I more than halved the training during the next seven days of tapering down. While most other Exeter students readied themselves for a mass exodus and a four week Easter break at the end of Lent term, I packed my bags for a weekend trip to Spain.

I met the majority of the traveling British party at Heathrow airport. Julian acted as team manager to a group that included trusted kit and drinks man Tony Perkins, two race judges, and a total of 10 senior and junior male and female walkers. There should have been three other senior men in the team. After travelling independently, and for reasons best known to them, they only caught up with the rest of us late Saturday night when we were already roomed at our Villanova hotel. A *breakdown in communications* they called it. Whatever the details of that mix up, the three decided not to race the next day due to fatigue. I could not concern myself with that business. I had a race to do and no kind of unwarranted distraction was going to help.

The following day it was great to see our 19 year old Tim Berrett win the junior 20kms in 89.38, half a minute ahead of Sweden's Stefan Johansson. I could only pay scant attention to it because it was a race staged during the longer 50km event. Held in the heart of the town amongst tall apartments and a variety of shops, roads were cordoned off for the series of morning races. The faces of Jose

Marin and the charismatic Jordi Llopart were stars in Spain and rightly dominated the advertising posters following their recent medals won at European championships and Olympic Games. Spectators lined the 2km circuit and duly made themselves heard. To be a part of it was brilliant, particularly as I held second position behind Marin until around 35kms. Llopart had stopped a few kilometers earlier.

It was too good to last. Feeling sick, I bent over double and threw up the lemon drink until not only my sore stomach felt empty but in turn so was my energy stores. One by one they filed past, Lars Ove Moen from Norway, Alcade from Spain a man who I had beaten in to second position in Paris in 1980, Roland Nilsson from Sweden and Jose Pinto from Portugal. USA's Dan O'Connor had me in his sights until I rallied and picked my pace up again. I had worked too hard to let it all slip away.

Marin was serene and triumphant and won in a world leading 3.50.12. The other Europeans followed in quick succession. Pinto was the first of the leading walkers to fall the wrong side of the four hour barrier, I was the next but...4.02.00 was enough, just!

Before our flight home, some sightseeing around the city of Barcelona helped ease the physical pain of the day before. I had another Olympic qualifying time in my bag of dreams. Only time would tell if those dreams would be realised. The answer came more quickly than I thought.

Three weeks on I accepted the invitation to train for two weeks with a group of walkers and other British Olympic athletic contenders at the La Santa sports resort in Lanzarote. I stayed overnight at Ian McCombie's flat in Blackheath and moved onto Gatwick airport with him and Paul Blagg the next morning where we met up with more familiar faces from the walking squad.

Stepping off the plane it was good to feel the warm breeze so typical of the Canary Islands. This was a trip that I had known about only for a short time. It was exciting. I felt as if I was living the high life and it was going to get even better very soon. Along with several others, Julian Hopkins was an earlier arrival. He was there outside the airport ready to greet us.

Catching my eye Julian smiled and walked purposefully forward with an outstretched hand and said, 'You're in. You're in the Olympic team. You've been selected.'

No matter how many times or how many different ways he said it, I could hardly comprehend the magnitude of what it all meant to me. Tears welled up for sure as we shook hands.

I said 'thanks' more than once. My mind was a kaleidoscope of emotions. Bells were ringing, a choir of voices singing halleluiah and then, a wonderful peace, a wonderful feeling of contentment. If only I could have shared that moment with all those nearest and dearest to me. I know that I had worked hard for it and achieved what was necessary to be in this position, but until it was confirmed I had taken nothing for granted. Moscow hurt. This news was the perfect antidote.

I savoured every moment on the island. We trained well. I got free physiotherapy treatment for all the aches that would ordinarily go untreated, not least the latest ailments including a sore knee and left groin strain. I met new friends, beautiful people, introduced to more athletes and saw some great sights. The 100 strong camel train that meandered up the volcanic hill to the peak of Fire Mountain and its lunar surface, was a photo opportunity that the national press did not miss, a copy of which I later added to my scrapbook.

The Press were long gone when we made the descent deep underground into the illuminated tunnel and caves of Los Verdes. Opening up to a breathtaking 45 feet high cavern that stretched at least that much across and maybe more, the myriad of colours within the molten wax-like rock was something that you only see at Christmas on a dark wintery night and where every echo and whispery conversation is amplified. In those rare moments of serene silence it was possible to hear secretions of individual droplets from the moist walls around like a slow dripping tap into a tin bucket.

We had been walking for a while when our guide held a hand up and signalled for us to stop. We waited for a few moments to allow a large silhouetted group of chattering tourists who were approaching to pass on by. Once the last of the stragglers had disappeared our guide gestured for us to move on around the corner.

Without exception each jaw dropped in our party of 12. Stretching out ahead was the most amazing deep crater that looked passable only by creeping sure-footedly around either edge should anyone feel brave enough to do so. My extreme fear of heights meant that there was no way on earth I was going to volunteer.

Ian McCombie stepped forward as did two of the more excitable girls. The guide smiled. Apparently three would be enough. I didn't know the girls but I did not want to see them hurt, and as for Ian, well I wasn't sure whether I should be impressed or think him recklessly stupid by risking any kind of injury.

A deathly hush fell as they moved to the edge of one side of the crater and shimmied forward with their backs to the wall. Thankfully they were sensibly cautious as each followed the lead of the guide. The rest of us were encouraged to inch closer to the edge and gaze down deep down to the bottom. My heart was in my mouth. Before I could step back to a position of relative safety, the guide picked up a stone and told us to watch and listen. With bated breath, we did so. For one second I thought about putting my finger to the button on my wrist stopwatch in order to time how long the stone took to hit the rocky base.

No doubt for some theatrical effect the guide paused for a moment before he gently released the stone into the air.

Plop! The splash as the stone hit the water's surface was minimal, the wave of ripples instant.

'Wow!'

'Ooh...God!'

'Ah, that's amazing.'

Amongst the multitude of guffaws, laughing and spontaneous clapping there was plenty of incredulous acts of air punching and swearing, some of it from me. It was indeed, quite amazing. We had been completely fooled by the reflection from the ceiling to the shallow pool of crystal clear water below.

Mine, was just one of a sea of smiling faces that emerged back into the bright daylight energized all the more for the hard work ahead.

Back home in England, training was relentless. Races came and went. The commencement of Trinity term meant that exams needed to be endured, the last of which was completed at the end of May. It would be all of one month before the results were pinned up on the foyer walls of the Amory building. In the meantime, there was no let up in classroom study as second year work was set by our various tutors. There was some down time where we allowed ourselves to relax. The warm month of June meant that the nets were raised within Lukes quadrant and grass court tennis began in earnest. Mike and I had some *titanic* five set duels with Julie and Sarah that were great fun. If games were reduced to three sets we invariably lost and were less enjoyable. I blamed him. He blamed me.

June 26th, the day when I braced myself to look at what I had achieved with the five law and sociology first year papers. I went back to my room and pulled out my training diary and simply wrote...*FAB*! I had passed the lot. If I thought the day could not get any better, well I was wrong, it did. It was there in all the papers, the full British Olympic athletics team. Of course I already knew my name would be amongst those selected, but it still felt great to see it in black and white alongside so many famous names, illustrious names like Steve Ovett, Sebastian Coe and Daley Thompson. The team numbered 75 in total. I was the only 50km walker named, while Ian McCombie, Phil Vesty and Steve Barry made up the full complement of three qualified 20km walkers.

In the South West region I was just one athlete from a handful of others from a range of different sports who made up the British team. I met with both TSW and BBC television crews for up-dated new film. Newspaper and photograph meetings were agreed at frequent intervals, as were radio chats with Radio Devon and Devon Air. I was flattered by all the attention. Being told early on by journalists that I had a natural fluency on air whetted my appetite for more. It also meant that I invariably looked forward to appearing on camera or speaking on the radio.

I knew however that in terms of the national press, I was just another name on the team list. An indeterminate order of subjective importance and merit between athletic events put sprinters and middle distance runners in the executive board room, whilst the likes of me and my fellow walking team-mates swept up after the board-room had been vacated. Anytime in the national spotlight tended to be short-lived. In my six years as an international walker I had never known it any other way. Long before my time, in 1964 four British athletes won Olympic gold at the Tokyo Games; all but one was awarded an MBE in the Queen's New Year Honours lists. It took nearly two decades of lobbying before Ken Mathews, winner of the 20km walk, was afforded the same honour.

I had my inoculations for tetanus and polio at the surgery on main campus, yet took some warped satisfaction in returning home to Tiverton and revisiting my old family GP who two years earlier suggested that my racing career was possibly over because of my injured back. To be fair, he was more than happy to give me a general medical and sign a few declaration papers to that effect. Picking up my made-to-measure Olympic formal uniform from Hepworth Tailors in Exeter was good. Perhaps even better was traveling to Hamilton House in London to collect the remainder of my Olympic gear, including tracksuit, racing kit, sunglasses, even toiletries.

The final training session before departing for the USA was a 36km road walk on some of the steepest hills around Cove. I was pleased. Two hours 55 minutes, and that included the time lost whilst I threw up my drink within a few miles of finishing at Mum's home. The dogs had come scampering up the driveway barking incessantly until they reached the wrought iron gates separating them from me. Breathing heavily with hands on knees, sweaty long hair hanging like rat tails limp around my chin, they would have to wait patiently for a friendly pat on the head. The vomiting I could have done without, but in the 70 degree heat it was the kind of hard walk that I wanted as a last confidence boost before leaving for Heathrow airport later in the day.

PART THREE

Part three. Becoming an Olympian: Los Angeles 1984

Flying out on a 747 jumbo jet I was one of a party of 70 members of the British Olympic team that touched down in Los Angeles 1500hrs local time. Beyond the 10.5 hour flight was a further three hour coach journey to Point Loma Nazarene University in San Diego. Rooms at the religious student college had been vacated for the summer and adapted for use as the official GB training camp.

With daytime temperatures hovering around 85 - 90 degrees it was baking hot outside. Paired inside with Steve Barry we considered our temporary accommodation to be absolutely fine, perhaps a bit basic but comfortable. When the time was right, athletes of all disciplines would move back to LA in readiness for their respective competitions. The entire British team ran close to 350 people and with team officials, medics and coaches that number rose to well over 400.

I already knew from the team administrative pack that I would be at this holding camp for around 10 days. It was team policy that athletes would only be transferred to the Olympic village at UCLA no more than a few days before their respective competition, and for that reason numbers at the camp would diminish with each passing day. As the 50km walk was scheduled for the penultimate day of the two week long Games I reluctantly had to accept that I would not only miss the opening ceremony but also miss all of the first week of events. This included a multitude of sports that in other circumstances I would have loved to have seen live. So, if I wanted to view favourite events like the swimming, gymnastics, boxing, or any of the cycling then I would have to find a television screen like most other folk. It didn't feel right, but that's just the way it was. I had every hope that I would at least see live athletics as those events always started at the beginning of week two.

I had been at the camp for exactly one week when I ventured to honour a promise made to a journalist a few days prior to my departure. Appreciating the fact that there was an eight hour time difference between California and England, the live radio link up to Devon Air via a telephone call from me would be made at 15 minutes past midnight precisely.

A summary of what private media contacts were permissible had been outlined in the administration pack. I had already spoken to team management and sought further assurances that my proposed bit of radio reporting with local media people back home was okay and within the spirit of reasonable broadcast communications.

At the agreed time I got into position. I decided to use one of the two public kiosk telephones near the tartan track. Not wishing to disturb those wishing to sleep I considered that this was a safe distance away from any twitching ears. Illuminated only by the dim glow from a nearby streetlamp, I had a quick read through my one sheet of crib notes before making the call.

Asked…'So, Chris, what's it like? How is the training going, and tell us about some of the people you have met.'

This was a 10 minute slot and I had proven more than once before that I am more than capable of suffering a terrible affliction of verbal diarrhoea. This was perhaps one such occasion.

'…Well, the college that we're using for our training camp is not unlike Exeter University, perhaps a bit smaller. It's very green, surrounded by trees. Buildings are spread over quite a big area. There are loads of sports facilities; in fact right now, I am standing by the track that I've already used several times for short sprint sessions. Because it gets quite crowded with all the other runners, jumpers and throwers using it, I've also been off campus with my three other walking team-mates and found an out 'n' back coastal path to use for our longer walks. It's beautiful scenery, quite hilly, overlooking the bay. It's tough though because it really is so hot. Even right now I'm only wearing T-shirt and shorts and it's after midnight and it is still in the mid-60's and very humid.

'When I first arrived there was already a lot of the team here. I think some have been here for more than a week. Of course I recognise most of the people on the athletics squad but in terms of a being on a major championship team, I'm really a new boy. It was nice that the first person that I bumped into in the corridor when I was trying to find my room was David Moorcroft. We said *Hi* to each other. He asked me how things were going.'

I was confident that the journalist would know that Moorcroft was the world record holder for the track 5000m. For that reason I chose not to elaborate and hoped that the majority of the radio listeners might at least know he was one of the stars in the athletics team. Truth was that I was bowled over that any famous athlete should know my name at all. That brief encounter put a spring in my step as I walked on through the corridor.

'…After that I dropped my bags in my room. I didn't have any difficulty finding it because I knew that I would be rooming with Steve Barry though someone had replaced my nametag on the door with *MADMAX* written in biro. I later found out it was one of the other walkers Phil Vesty who has insisted on calling me that ever since and encouraged others to do the same. Well, anyway, I went for a bite to eat in the cafeteria and first person I saw was Allan Wells, the Olympic 100m champion. He invited me to sit down with him and his wife Margot. We had a good chat which was fantastic. Although I have to say that Margot was not too impressed when I naively asked Allan if he had had a chance to get out and see any of the sights. You see, she nearly chewed my head off and said that the only thing her husband was going to see was the training track and the Olympic stadium.'

The radio journalist interjected with a chuckle and said, 'Well, I guess he is extremely focused.'

'Yes of course, but most athletes have I think gone out sometime in their spare time and seen what there is to do and see around here.' Abundantly aware that I was in full name-dropping mode I ploughed on. 'A few nights ago I was in a communal room with a group of guys watching TV sharing my pizza with Zola Budd. I know that she's young but she seemed genuinely excited to talk about the tourist things that there was to see around here.'

Zola was arguably the most controversial member of the British team. Her story had been all over the news in the months leading up to the Olympic Games. A white South African by birth, she was only on the team by virtue of a having British born grandparent. Her British passport was acquired with indecent haste many argued, simply because she was a renowned world record breaking runner and therefore a prized asset to the British team. South Africa was excluded from Olympic participation because of its apartheid policy, and so in spite of her great running exploits, sometimes in bare feet, she had no means by which to compete until a daily newspaper came forward and helped speed up the acquisition of the necessary passport. She became a very public political pawn. When it came to the women's 3000m final in Los Angeles she was up against many good runners including Mary Decker, 'the darling' of the American public. It was ironic that Zola literally got tangled up with her when they were contesting the lead. I would be in the stadium at the time and witnessed one of the highlights and lowlights of the Games when Decker tripped and fell to the floor and ultimately out of the race with Zola subsequently fading to 7th amid a chorus of boos. It was horrible yet fantastic to hear, and in my opinion quite unjustified. I thought it was a racing incident that got blown out of all proportion because of the famous characters involved.

'…And last Sunday I was sat around on the grass at a low key athletics meeting chatting to Steve Ovett. Like me he had trained earlier in the day and was enjoying seeing some of our team-mates using the competition as a final warm-up before the Olympics. He had been out and about was relaxed and most importantly said he was very fit.

I don't know if Steve went to San Diego zoo, but earlier today a big group of us did and it was fantastic. San Diego is a seaside community and Sea World is just down around the corner. We had a few hours there last week and saw walruses, seals, sharks, and the killer whale they call Shamu who did lots of impressive ball tricks with his trainers in the aquarium. Oh and a few of us also hired an open top jeep and nipped across the border into Mexico a couple of times to look around the shops in Tijuana. The second time we had a crash.'

'Really!'

'Yes…only a small one. We accidently went through a set of red lights and hit another car. The other driver got a small bump on the head, nothing serious. The police were called but let us off with a warning. To be honest we were quite relieved.'

'I bet,' said the radio journalist. 'Chris, your race is next week. We understand you will have two very special family supporters there that will be cheering you on.'

Aware of the possibility that this question could be raised, I had already decided that I was not prepared to tell the *cow story* again no matter how much the radio jock appeared to like it during our previous on air interview. I had said then how happy I was that my Mum and my brother Peter would be supporting me in LA. I was not about to repeat the circumstances by which they were able to *afford* the expensive trip. I thought it made a good story at the time but as a result of my loose tongue it unduly worried my Mum that certain uninvited people might come knocking on her door making demands. I had said how a herd of cows from a nearby farm had strayed from a nearby field onto her property and wreaked havoc with their hooves on her garden. The farmer's insurance company coughed up £750 in compensation damages. Mum got the gardens repaired on the cheap and used the insurance money towards her trip to the USA. For his part, Peter, who in spite of only being 20 years old, proved so resourceful that he immediately began planning their trip and through friends made it possible for them to stay free of charge in LA.

For the sake of my Mum I kept quiet about the stampeding cows and if necessary I knew that I had enough left on my crib notes for a suitable deviation. A glance at my watch also suggested that time was running down anyway.

'...Yes, I guess you mean my Mum and my brother Peter. They are staying with some American friends in Los Angeles. I don't think it will be possible to see them until race day. But I am really pleased that they will be there. They know that I have got to stay focused anyway. I've got one last longish session of about 23 kilometers tomorrow morning. Alan Storey our marathon coach is going to run the first half with me and Phil Vesty, one of our other walkers is going to walk the second half. Steve Barry and Ian McCombie, the other two British walkers left for the Olympic village in LA yesterday. I think it will be quite quiet around here after tomorrow because I know the last big group of athletes is leaving. Phil and I are traveling in a transit van with a small group on Thursday. I have to say that it was a bit of a surprise when the team management agreed to allow him to leave as late as possible. His 20km race is on Friday evening and all being well I will be there cheering him and the others on. Then it's down to me at the end of the week...' Done! By my reckoning the ten minutes were up.

Quietly underscored by music, there was time only for one or two reciprocated pleasantries and a final good luck wish. A wry smile crept across my face as the latest number one record was faded up as we said our goodbyes and Stevie Wonder sang...*I just called to say I love you.*

There was little love going around when Phil and I were shown to our new room in a high tower block within the UCLA Olympic village. Door closed behind us, bags down, I was fuming.

'This is crap!'

Now I was as big a fan of the great middle distance runner Said Aouita as the next person, but I did not want to be sharing an accommodation block with him, nor the rest of the team from Morocco or any other athlete from Qatar, Saudi, Egypt or any other Arab country that may have taken up temporary residence in Sproul Hall. This feeling had nothing to do with racial prejudice or any other political motivation. This was all about my feelings of victimization, feelings of being expendable, feelings of us walkers being less important than other members of the British team who were all in another block of flats across the way. We had been told on our arrival that there was no room for us to join the rest of our team. It would only be for one night we were told, after that Steve and Ian would be moving out of South Units where the GB team was based and joining us, as if that extra piece of information was going to appease me. It did not.

I tried to keep my intense irritation under control while I was in Phil's company. He was young, he was a friend, and he had to race the next day. I went alone to speak to team management. The likes of Mary Peters and Lyn Davies did try to ask me to calm down, but unless they helped by being proactive to see that we were moved out of a potentially dangerous situation and treated with the same respect as the rest of the team I was going to continue my protests. Other British athletes arrived after us. None were moved into Sproul Hall. It was suggested that I was overreacting. I felt patronized. The four of us would remain segregated from the rest of the team in their more deluxe surroundings for the duration of the Games. As for us walkers, well I guess we got accustomed to our smaller, noisier, more uncomfortable abode. True, no one lost their life, no bombs went off, nor were we ever threatened. Speaking just for myself, that was not the point. I had to get over it.

Things looked brighter the following day. It was late afternoon the sun was still high in the sky as 39 of the world's fastest 20km walkers filed out of the awe inspiring Los Angeles Memorial Stadium and headed towards the two kilometer road lap on Exposition Boulevard, little more distance away than a strong baseball throw. I and hundreds of other fans followed in slow pursuit.

'C'mon, Phil,' I shouted. 'Well done Steve, that's good Ian,' I bellowed as hard as I might.

By the time I made it out to the road lap, the field was well strung out. I found shelter from the rays of the sun under a shop canopy and watched with delight as the walkers all sped past with each successive lap covered in a little over eight minutes. I ventured forward to shout for those men known to me and of course for the Brits who were all operating at sub 90 minute pace.

Well inside the top 10, the leading American Marco Evoniouk ensured that home supporters had plenty to cheer. The Mexican fraternity went crazy for Ernesto Canto and Raul Gonzalez who vied for the lead with Italian and reigning Olympic Champion Maurizio Damilano.

It seemed no time at all when roadside supporters like me who either had accreditation passes or tickets to the Coliseum had to make their way back to the stadium if the finish was going to be seen.

I made it back into a seat on the east side of the stadium close beneath the imposing peristyle tower that carried the Olympic torch and flanked by double peristyle arches. Sweating like a pig, I marveled at the spectacle of seventy thousand others rising to their feet and greeting first Canto then Gonzalez in quick succession ahead of Damilano each in a time a little over 83 minutes. Phil was fantastic in a commendable 13th position just four minutes after the winner. Ian did well in 19th and Steve who struggled with a knee strain was 24th.

It was customary for most athletes to *let their hair down* after competition. While the Brit walkers hit the town that night I managed to find refuge for one night only in a spare bed in Peter Elliot's room. Affable and quietly spoken, the Yorkshireman's 800m heat was a day or two away so he was more than happy to share his time with me.

In conversation it was interesting and sometimes uncomfortable to exchange thoughts on the evolution of athletics and other Olympic sports from one with intrinsic amateur status to one that was beginning to embrace what could be described as an era of semi-professionalism. Indeed part of the success of these Olympic Games was driven by the proud boast from organisers that they would be the first to make a financial profit, estimated in millions of pounds.

Certainly in Britain, these were the early days of *shamateurism* where old Corinthian values were very quickly eroded by a new attitude that put arbitrary values on individuals and their events. If it was deemed marketable, it came at a price on an unfathomable sliding scale that saw so-called minority events like mine clinging to the slippery end. It was difficult not to be envious.

I had been an international athlete for six years and never received any financial payment for a race or for an appearance at a race. It is almost laughable to even think that I might have done so. I was after all a race walker, even more pointedly, a British race walker. I will not pretend that had it been attainable I would have happily accepted some financial recompense for all the time and hard work.

The only means by which I knew how to acquire additional funds for training was through laboriously filling in application forms to the national Sports Aid Foundation. I had done this for a year or two. Every pound spent had to be justified whether it was for special food (I never really understood what was meant by *special food*, unless it meant having a juicy steak once a week for a treat?...whatever, I wrote £10 per week on the form and hoped it might help my application), racing shoes, petrol, or anything else that was considered essential for training and racing. It was awful. It was demeaning. But, for a few hundred pounds it had to be done, it all helped.

I wanted to be the best that I could be, but without the financial resources to travel and train with superior foreign athletes and coaches it felt like an improbable dream.

It is probably true to say that good extensive publicity is an essential commodity if the paymasters are ever likely to come knocking on your door. The problem for the British race walker was that national media only paid us lip service, something quite unattractive to any potential sponsor or personal agent trying to seal the deal for his athlete.

With frustration, I had to concede that I competed in an event that in Britain at least, was as amateur now as the day I started. Officially all athletics up to this point was still amateur; unofficially, the 'stars' in the so-called glamour events were allegedly receiving financial payments in one form or another. Terms such as, *the brown envelope* and *under-the-counter* payments involving hundreds even thousands of pounds were apparently being made to athletes. Allegations and denials were commonplace. Whether or not money is the root of all evil, I don't know. I do believe that the developing situation caused divisions and resentment and it was likely to get worse until such time that the sport became more open and honest.

It is probably naive to hope that the playing field in sport competition could ever be level. Talent augmented with good preparation is essential. The thing is that good preparation often costs, and costs big.

The following morning Peter received more physiotherapy treatment to his injury while I loosened up on the grass with stretching exercises and no small amount of yawning before my 10km session on the UCLA track. We heard all about the so-called best hot spot in town for visiting athletes. Apparently, if you were willing to leave the closely guarded confines of the Olympic village and make your way through the hordes of autograph hunters standing outside, then Baxters' pub/restaurant was *the* place to be. I put it out of my mind until Ian had timed me through a good walk in 43.10. After that satisfyingly hard effort in 85 degrees of heat, I thought there was no harm in checking it out in the evening.

We probably looked like extras from the set of Miami Vice when we strutted down through the village towards the exit gates of the Olympic village. Ten of us decked out in casual clothes all displaying varying levels of reddish flesh each with respective passport style accreditation tags dangling around our neck with the strong advisory message ringing in our ears that it should be worn at all times, particularly if going off site.

I soon realised that bearers of an accreditation tag, no matter how unknown that person may be, was liable to be mobbed at the gates. It was brilliant. I had never signed so many bits of paper in such a short period of time. I am not sorry to say that I milked it for all it was worth even if I had to hot foot it after my mates who had disowned me once they had had their fill of furious scribbling and smiling for the cameras.

Once outside Baxters, our special VIP entry courtesy of the beefy door staff was met with some understandable resentment. The looks of disdain as we bypassed queues of local men and women had to be ignored. I for one felt mildly embarrassed.

Crowded inside, it was heaving with fit chattering bodies amid loud indistinguishable music. It was a revelation to be in a pub and be approached by so many beautiful women. Like picking your favourite candy in a sweet shop, the choice was gloriously outrageous. I was under no self delusion that the *babe magnet* hanging around my neck could be taken home and have the same effect in the Lukes bar. Enjoy it while it lasted, I thought.

I supped my glass of orange juice and was amazed that someone as lovely as Alicia was prepared to spend so much time talking to me. All hair and teeth, I may have struggled to hear much of what she said in her strong American accent, but did not fail to note that she was prepared to take me out on another night and see some of the sights around LA. With that improbable date swirling around in my head I left early with Peter and headed back for the village.

Monday was an unbelievable evening of athletics under floodlights in the Coliseum. I sat in the stands in an area reserved for accredited athletes and soaked up the atmosphere as I saw USA's Carl Lewis win gold in the 100m sprint. It was a good night for the British as gold was won by Tessa Sanderson in the women's javelin, silver for Coe in the 800 metres, and bronze medals for Kathy Cook in the women's 400m and for Fatima Whitbread in the javelin. In the men's 10000m run Mick McCleod crossed the line third for a bronze medal that would later be upgraded to silver once the disqualification of Finland's Vaino for a post race positive drug test was confirmed.

The mood amongst the British camp was soaring. Any lingering personal issues I had over our accommodation were put to one side. This was unique and even I was not so stupid as to let it spoil what was so obviously a once in a lifetime experience. Tuesday was a rest day on the athletic schedule. Along with the majority of the team I enjoyed the bus trip to Disneyland where we got a chance to be kids on all the rides before an evening back on the UCLA campus listening to the Beach Boys in concert…simply wonderful.

Ian was again on the stopwatch in the morning as I pushed through another 25 laps on the track. Phil stretched his aching limps by joining in with a few laps of pace making and helping me to a time of 43.52. Plenty of bodies loafed by the pool in the afternoon. Those, like me who had yet to compete, were easy to spot by the predominant choice of sun hats and gravitation to any shaded area. With each passing day, more and more athletes were slipping out of their tracksuits and by night making their way down into town. I joined the developing throng of *Miami Vicers* only as far as the other side of the exit gates and through the mass of eager autograph hunters. There, much to my pleasant surprise was Alicia sitting in her red convertible, smiling and waiting for me. I looked nonchalantly at my drop jaw mates as if this was a regular occurrence. I sat in beside her, said hello and waved cheerio to my gawping friends. I probably failed miserably but still tried hard not to look too smug as we pulled away.

On a sultry warm evening, the cruise around Santa Monica and Venice was blissful, James Bond without the martini. At the very least it was a great way to relax before the biggest race of my life.

0700hrs, Saturday August 11 1984. I made my way from the village to the athletic stadium. It was already 80 degrees Fahrenheit and rising: The forecast was for the hottest day of the Games so far. Steve, Ian and Phil tried to make light of it before the start.

'You'll be alright,' one said. 'Just think, four hours and it will all be over.'

'Yeah,' another said, '...And we'll have the beers lined up at the finish.'

Cometh the hour, cometh the man: 0800...The first five laps around the track was quick but not so fast that any of the 31 starters broke from a tightly bunched pack. My legs felt heavy, a sure sign of nerves. Experience had at least taught me that. I felt nervous, nervous that this was going to be so hard that I might fail. The 10km track walks gave me the confidence of speed, but that was only one fifth of the full 31 miles ahead of me. Thoughts came flooding back of my final longish training session back in San Diego. In the stifling heat I remembered hanging on for grim death towards the end in order to maintain my pace, and that was for a walk that lasted a little less than two hours.

I shook myself back to the present. I had to concentrate I had to finish and finish well. What would make that desire even more enticing was to return to the roar of a full stadium. The pace heated up as soon as we filed off the track into the tunnel leading out towards the road. I had to banish the feelings of disappointment at the sparseness of the crowd inside the stadium. With no other athletics scheduled that morning until ten o'clock my expectations of a big send off from the start were of course totally unrealistic.

My spirits were lifted by the sight and sounds of Mum and Peter calling my name from the fringes of Exposition Boulevard.

'Well done champ,' Peter called.

My brother, ever the optimist I thought as I caught his and Mum's eye with a weak returned smile.

The clock ticked over, time passed. The leading walkers blazed a trail ahead of me and any early fanciful thoughts of a fairytale medal faded with each passing lap. The oppressive heat after more than two hours ground me down. I had covered 25kms but my energy levels were dropping like a stone. At the 28km point my stomach muscles that for so long had been tightening by the minute finally contracted and, reminiscent of a woman in labour I emitted the most prolonged groan as I bent double, letting go of the first of several floods of undigested drink. In full public view on the most important racing day ever, it was pitiful. It was horrible.

From a distance I heard Peter scream, 'C'mon, forget about it. Keep going...' And so I did.

Beyond three hours of relentless walking in 95 degrees, I was slowly but surely dying in the heat. There were others similarly struggling and with some calling it a day. As bad as I felt, it was a humbling sight to see a walker like Maurizio Damilano ahead of me reaching for refreshment at the official drinks station and tumbling through the tables in apparent dehydrated exhaustion. I heard cries of anguish and felt for the great man as a frantic flurry of people leapt to his aid as I went pass. His plight was over, while mine still had some way to go.

Meanwhile, Raul Gonzalez was ultra-smooth as he glided past me for the second time and well on his way to a new Olympic record. Some distance behind in second, Sweden's Bo Gustafsson was taking full advantage of more fancied pre-race favourites falling by the wayside.

Though my sponge sodden head had dropped and the stride length shortened, my arms were still pumping back 'n' forth in some desperate hope of forcing more pace than the body and mind could muster. So sore were my stomach muscles that if I was going to be sick again I doubted much more could come up. In my peripheral vision I could do nothing about the increasing frequency and presence of persons in white coats watching me closely, not necessarily as fans or supporters but as I strongly suspected as another targeted patient to be dragged limply into the sanctuary of their portable medic cabin. Mindful of this, Peter had run alongside behind the spectator barriers shouting at me to keep going, imploring me to try and catch either the American or Chinese walker a short distance ahead. I was in desperate survival mode and thoughts of catching anyone was not on my radar.

When the inevitable actually happened, Peter's alertness proved crucial. 'Leave him alone,' I heard him scream. 'He's alright.'

I was on my knees and vomiting. The three or four medics that had descended upon me immediately backed off without actually laying a finger. Had they done so, my race would effectively have been over; technically disqualified for physical assistance. At that moment it might have been kinder to have put me out of my misery and shot me. I guessed Mum might have been close by. I was sure that it was her voice that I heard whimpering something incomprehensible.

I did not look across at Peter, but as sure as hell I heard him.

'C'mon, get up,' he said. 'We haven't come all this way not to see you finish this damn race. You haven't got far to go. 'C'mon, get up and get back to that stadium…'

I rose to my feet, took as deep a breath as my crushed chest would allow and started walking again. In spite of everything, I was in sixteenth position. There was one man behind me: Jose-Victor Alonzo Alonzo from Guadalupe. He presumably had a worse time of it than me, if that was possible?

I completed the final two road laps and headed back towards the stadium. In all the circumstances it was too much to hope for a truly uplifting finish that might have made all the pain worthwhile.

When I did eventually emerge from the tunnel onto the track it was good but not great. The temperature had risen to 100 degrees Fahrenheit. In any other situation, upwards of 30,000 people scattered in large pockets around the stadium generously applauding your progress to the line would and should have been an unbelievable experience. But, in an arena that could hold more than 90,000 my heart felt as if were at least two thirds empty during those closing moments.

1.	Raul Gonzalez	Mexico	3.47.26
2.	Bo Gustaffson	Sweden	3.53.19
3.	Sandro Bellucci	Italy	3.53.45
4.	Reima Salonen	Finland	3.58.30
5.	Raffa Ducceschi	Italy	3.59.26
6.	Carl Shueler	USA	3.59.46
7.	Jorge Llopart	Spain	4.03.09
8.	Jose Pinto	Portugal	4.04.42
9.	Manuel Alcalde	Spain	4.05.47
10.	Ernesto Canto	Mexico	4.07.59
16.	Chris Maddocks	GBR	4.26.33

Back home, I pulled out the note stuffed inside the large jiffy bag. It was from my old mate Richard Jarman. *I recorded as much as I could,* he wrote. *I missed some of it because a lot was on in the early hours of the morning. I didn't see anything on the 20km walk. They only showed about 10 minutes of your race, some of it is on tape 4. Hope you like it. Rich.*

Six video tapes: 18 hours of BBC Olympic coverage. Tape five was marked, *mostly athletics, including the finish of your walk.*

I thought it would be a while before I had the time to watch all the tapes but could at least review the 50km walk quickly enough and rationalized that it was more than the usual 30 seconds to look at. As for those other people who either knew or recognised me in the street, they were perhaps less familiar with the BBC's usual negligible attitude to showing race walking on television and as a consequence were not always quite so magnanimous.

'I stayed up all night. Why did they only show a few minutes of your race?'

'I popped out made a cup of tea and missed it.'

'They showed the 100metres loads of times, day after day, from every conceivable angle. Bloody hell, there's only so much that you can say about a race that lasts for 10 seconds.'

'They showed every step of the marathon and hardly anything of your race. Why?'

Occasionally, I heard a more heart-warming flip side. 'Hey Chris, I saw you on the telly…it was brilliant.'

By and large, it was brilliant. The memories will live with me forever and a dream fulfilled to be able to call myself an Olympian. Had I not finished my race I am sure I would not have felt the same. It was disappointing that I could not reproduce my best level of walking when it really mattered but in the extreme weather conditions this was unlikely anyway. Ordinarily this level of acclimatization would take a very long time to achieve, many weeks and months over a number of years. I was up against many top walkers from around the world who had been preparing long term with coaches, scientists and medics.

It was evident that athletics as a sport in Britain and around the world was changing. Standards in all events were rising and likely to do so at a rate with greater degrees of professionalism. Appropriate facilities, money, science of training, acclimatization in heat and at high altitude with frequent year round squad training were all part of a more professional approach. Added to that, looming dark in the background a sinister undercurrent of suspected drug use aiding performance levels would continue to muddy the waters.

I was flattered to attend not one but two civic receptions held in my honour. The first was at Tiverton town hall, the second at Dawlish. Both were surprisingly grand affairs that I enjoyed immensely.

Though I am a little ashamed to admit it, at the Tiverton function there was a lot of people there that I simply did not know, including a couple of Olympic gold medalists who perhaps I should have known. Tony Nash – one half of the legendary Nash & Dixon partnership won the two-man bobsleigh at the 1964 Olympics and Bertie Hill won equestrian gold in 1952. By all accounts more Olympic stars had been invited but had sent messages of congratulations with their apologies for absence. Important to me, Jack Snow with other members of Tiverton Harriers was there as were Mum and Dad, together with my Nan and granddad.

With all guests gathered around, Mayoress Mrs Dot Harris presented me with an inscribed glass tankard given to me by the town of Tiverton and a coat of arms from the French twin town of Chinon. Her husband the Mayor, Mr Jack Harris said, '...It had been a magnificent achievement and that the whole of Tiverton, the county, and the country had been proud of him. It was very well done indeed, and next time Chris, bring us back a gold medal!'

I obliged by joining in with the laughs that helped conclude his brief speech. My plans were only to race for two more years by which time I would be 29 years old and ideally retire at my peak hopefully with a good performance at the Commonwealth Games.

If anything, the civic reception at Dawlish Manor House was an even grander affair where aside from my attending club mates, even more unknown people were present than before. The Mayor, councillor Douglas Mugford in his speech referred to the town's successful nomination of me as Teignbridge Sports Personality of the Year when he said, 'The very fact that you went to Los Angeles and did so well shows it was a very wise and good selection.' Accompanied by a round of applause he handed me a town plaque and said that I had helped put the town on the map. I was pleased if he was pleased. The BBC had indeed mentioned Tiverton *and* Dawlish in their extensive coverage of my race.

Edmund and Eric Shillabeer used the occasion to present me with a special commemorative American silver dollar and with a giant *congratulations* card made by Ed's son Andrew and signed by all those present that evening.

I have since looked back through my scrapbooks and seen newspaper photographs of these gratifying occasions and read through the reports. It amused me to read that in response to a question as to whether I would take part in the *next* Olympic Games in Seoul, South Korea, I answered with certain understated vagueness that, 'I hoped to maintain my motivation...'

My motivation when I took to the track at Birmingham on September 22nd was to break British records again. It may have only been six weeks since I felt close to death when I crossed the line in the heat and humidity of Los Angeles, but I had recovered well and trained hard. Bob Dobson's 50km track record of four hours 11 minutes 11 seconds had stood for 10 years.

Quite understandably, the thought of walking 125 laps of a 400m athletic track would seem to some to be complete and utter madness. Why do it? I guess it's another example of that old, *why climb mountains thing* – because it's there!

Of the 25 walkers that started that day I guess all of us could have done without having to contend with the gusting wind and squally autumnal showers. This was more like typical British weather and a far cry from the extreme heat and high humidity that contributed to my racing demise in LA. This race also offered me an opportunity for some form of redemption. I started fast. Walking close to 13km per hour pace, it was no time before I moving out wide into lanes two and three in order to lap the back markers who were moving at a rate closer to 10kms per hour. I was on a mission, not only did I want to break the track record, but in my mind and heart I wanted a sub four hour mark to my name. For three hours it looked on the cards. I had passed through 95 laps and covered in excess of 38kms. Then it happened. Yes...I was sick again. Not like last time, where it was in front of those hundreds of unfortunate Olympic spectators in close proximity and roving TV cameras, but out on the far side of the track. At least some dignity was preserved by the fact that I was 100m away from the melee of time keepers, race judges and lap recorders whose view of my predicament was almost certainly obscured by the infield hammer cage. Of course I was only alone for a matter of seconds. I would have liked more time, but my friends, husband and wife team Peter and Kim Buxton was having none of it.

Imagine for a moment that you have your head down the loo. You feel ill, and...? Well, the gory details can be spared. One thing is for sure, you do not want company; you do not really want to chat about it, not for a while at least. Worst of all, no pictures!

Pete and Kim pleaded with me to stop wasting time and to get going again. Mum busied herself by taking photographs for posterity while I managed to pull myself together and resume walking at a reasonable pace, but only after the third or fourth retch and a soak with a saturated sponge over my face.

Considerable momentum and time had been lost. In the end I finished nearly 20 minutes in front of second placed man, Barry Graham. My *consolation* time of 4.05.48 meant that I also bettered seven other British records en route.

Prior to the race I was unaware of these intermediate records. I learned afterwards that I missed by only a fraction the distance record of 26.1kms set by Ron Wallwork in a two hour race held at Blackburn in 1971. Thereafter I achieved new figures for 30kms, 20miles, 35kms, 40kms, 30miles, 3hours, 4hours, and finally the most important one in my eyes, the 50kms.

It amused me later to read a letter in a magazine written by an old boy who was known to have been a fine walker in his prime. He was amongst those who had taken part that day and whilst publicly congratulating me posed the question: *I estimate that I was lapped 40 times; can I claim a world record?*

It was fortuitous that like the year before, starting a new term at Lukes was particularly satisfying given that it was on the back of another good well reported 50km race result. No longer a new boy, I had manipulated a relocation of room through administration staff to the biggest room in Nancherrow. With its expansive bay window overlooking the garden, it was palatial by comparison to the room I had before. The previous term I had already weighed it up against arguably the only other contender to the crown of best room in halls by visiting one about to be vacated by Richard Hill, a fourth year PE student and incumbent England rugby union captain. It was good, but not good enough to force a move out of the Ranch.

Like me, Mike Judd also opted for the assurances of guaranteed warmth and provided hot meals by choosing to stay in halls for a second academic year. All our other old housemates departed for the promised land of fresh digs and independence, or as it would ultimately prove, varying levels of squalor, baked beans and spaghetti bolognaise on special occasions. Filling the void left by the girls of year one, half a dozen young sportsmen and half a dozen young non sportswomen. It was a good mix. My desire to train hard around my studies was immediately respected.

One abiding memory from my race in Los Angeles was one that I took into training and repeatedly re-ran over and over again in my head. The image of Raul Gonzalez walking with fluidity and a style was, to me at least, a picture of poetry in motion. Until then I had not seriously considered what it was about his style that was so different to mine. On reflection, my style was one of gritty and dogged determination powered by strength in the shoulders. His was seemingly powered by an apparently effortless grace of leg speed that could only have derived from years of practice and miles of concentrated effort under the watchful eyes of top coaches.

Some weeks later during the aftermath of the latest annual Chippenham six mile road race, I sat in the crowded changing rooms at Calne leisure centre graciously accepting the plaudits of bodies in various states of undress and sweatiness. Not only had I finished ahead of Phil Vesty for the second year in succession but I had also done so with a super fast winning time of 39 minutes 31 seconds. I was already allowing myself to think that the hours of visualization in training trying to emulate the mighty Gonzalez was coming to fruition. The feeling was short-lived.

A face appeared around the door. Alf was a dear old friend and a respected walking judge.

'Hey Chris,' he said, 'You don't know do you?'

I looked up and said, 'Sorry, know what?'

'You were disqualified not long after that big hill on the A4 around the four and half mile mark. One of the judges called your number, but as you carried on, he thinks that you probably didn't hear him.'

My head dropped. I felt as if I had just been kicked in the stomach. I was obviously going to need more time perfecting the Gonzalez walk.

I continued to train well and study hard. Come December and the end of Michaelmas term I looked forward with relish to some fun and relaxation at the next concert in the Great Hall. Until that was, the headline act pulled out at short notice citing how the lead singer was too busy, involved in a particular charity song for the Christmas singles market. Maligned by many, I was amongst those who were less than enamoured with this news. Without a hit record in years, The Boomtown Rats were hardly the hottest band in town. By the time they rescheduled in February, Bob Geldof had assumed the status of pop royalty, and when he and the Rats took to the stage and sang, *Do they know it's Christmas?* those original lukewarm tickets could not be exchanged for love nor money.

February continued to be a great month. I won the Isle of Man 30kms in a fast 2.11.09 beating both Ian McCombie and Phil Vesty. With the retirement of Steve Barry the three of us were the established top male walkers in Britain. We met up again along with several other walkers and scores of other international athletes at a British team training camp in Acoteias, Portugal shortly before Easter.

Acoteias to all intents and purposes was a leafy green holiday camp, frequented by sporty types making use of good facilities in near guaranteed warm conditions. It was here that I first met a young teenager who was destined not only to become one of Britain's best ever female walkers but someone whose racing career would have some parallel with mine.

Lisa Langford was just 17 when I saw her coach Charlie Bean trackside, stopwatch in hand, calling times whilst putting her through her paces during a 400m interval session. Dark, lithe and attractive she may have been, but there was also a steeliness about her that was evident from the outset. In her sights was another walker, a man who had been out there for almost three hours during which time sprinters, hurdlers, throwers, even distance runners had come and gone, their respective training sessions completed. The *mad walkers* you see were traditionally a rare breed of person on the athletic team that sometimes was best ignored almost to the point of being invisible. Why indeed would anyone want to walk 100 laps of any track at any time let alone in the middle of the day?

Mad dogs and Englishmen applied to characters like Paul Blagg. By reputation, he was a hard-nosed no nonsense policeman in the Met back home. And here, he may well have been bullish enough to ignore the occasional clatter of a hurdle toppling over or the grunt of another throwing implement being thrust into the air, but male pride was surely dented when Ms Langford kept gunning him down during one of her sprints? I sat on the grass highly amused at the spectacle and hatched a plan to challenge this girl to a 5km time trial. Of course she rose to the bait.

With Charlie's blessing I had assessed what I thought she was capable of and with respect I thought the exercise would be fun for me. The rendezvous date was set for three days hence by which time word had spread. On a gloriously balmy evening a tidy gathering assembled on the banked grass and watched her follow my strict instruction to stay locked on my heels and not to worry about the fast pace. She may not have been too charmed by the extra attention the challenge had caused, but I know she enjoyed the chance on the thirteenth and final lap to pull out of my slipstream and move ahead just before the finish. Her reward was an unofficial British junior record of 22 minutes 47 seconds.

With breathless sweaty excitement I think she tried to say how happy she was with the walk. I had already bluffed my way through several earlier conversations not least because understanding her staccato West Midland accent was proving difficult for this slow burning Devon lad. Given time we found a way, particularly when I later took on responsibility for her coaching up until 1989.

After just eight days at the camp I cut short what should have been a two week trip in order to keep my promise to support a 20km race in Bournemouth. It was sponsored by the Royal Mail and tirelessly organised by George Williams, a man who I knew was trying so hard to raise the profile of race walking in the area. The clash of dates, though unavoidable, meant that Ian and Phil were amongst those that thought I was daft to return home early merely because I had made an unnecessary promise.

For me it did not feel quite so simple. I already knew that George had used my name to promote the event and felt that I could not let him down. Little did I know it at the time, but that curtailed warm weather out-of-competition training camp would be the last I would ever attend.

I was pleased for George that in all age groups there was 215 entrants, which was a multiple number of walkers that ordinarily competed in his hometown. I believe he had hopes that if he could help start a revolution of interest in his area then other race directors might replicate his efforts around Britain, whereby a resurgence of walking might be possible. His thinking was similar to the one that helped create the running boom by Chris Brasher and John Disley from the success of the first London marathon in 1981, where in excess of 6000 runners took to the roads. George's reasoning along with other like minded people was sound. Prior to 1981, the number of entrants in marathons could often be counted in double digits.

With the pressure on to justify my top billing I was pleased and relieved by my win at Bournemouth in 87 minutes, three ahead of Roger Mills. The first prize of a portable black and white TV was the best I had won until then and a welcomed addition to my student room. Considering the rising sums of money up for grabs in the increasingly popular running world this was relative peanuts by comparison, but it was at least a start. Indeed, the four man winning team from Coventry each had an identical TV set to take home; in terms of financial value this was of astronomical proportions by contrast to the usual award made to a British walker.

Alas, I heard that Mick Smith and the lads all had their TVs stolen from the back of the car whilst on a refreshment break at a motorway service station on their journey back to the Midlands; a case of easy come, easy go…

Fortunately I managed to drive back to Exeter without any similar mishap. Rather than go home to Tiverton for what was left of the Easter vacation, I met up with Mike Judd and moved into the rented house temporarily vacated by our girl friends from year one. We thought that we would try and stay on top of our studies by choosing to work near library resources.

It may have been free accommodation, but so cold was it that we invariably put a coat on when we went inside. It was dark, it was horrible. Turning the pages of a book proved particularly difficult when gloves were left on. Tracksuit and socks were a necessity in bed in order to avoid the risk of hypothermia. If I thought it was bad, it was about to get worse.

Supported by standing on one leg, I was doing a series of leg swinging exercises when I accidently kicked a chair. The pain was all the more excruciating given how cold my feet were. Mike of course thought I was making a fuss about nothing until the x-ray revealed a fracture.

Unable to train properly, my strict routines crumbled to the extent that I failed to study effectively. Such was my irrational knee-jerk reaction and worry over my loss of fitness and concern about impending exams that I told people I was considering retiring from racing. These comments were picked up by a number of walk officials when I was seen at Battersea Park watching a Southern track competition in the summer. Although my head was all over the place, some suggested that I should consider taking a *sabbatical* until I felt ready to train and race again. The weeks of silly statements, procrastination and finally a u-turn meant I was not in fact ready to quit after all.

For that reason I clearly stated that I wanted to be included in either the four men 20km or 50km World Cup teams to race on the Isle of Man in September. In spite of reliable assurances, my desire was rebuffed without rational explanation. Old wounds from my Moscow Olympic exclusion were reopened. Once again, I felt there were few that I could genuinely trust on matters of international selection. It was of little consolation that I reasoned it was the team's loss as much as mine.

I had five more races and five more wins plus one weekend helping Edmund before the World Cup came around. To say I had it easy assisting my friend during his long walk on the track at the Garrison athletic stadium may be true, if put into context with the work done by other personal aides that day on September 14th. I did after all *only* have to provide him with drinks, food, sponges, ointments and verbal encouragement for 250 laps. Once he eventually pulled away from his nearest rival Bob Dobson and completed 100kms in a new British record time of 9 hours 41minutes 54seconds, I was able to collapse in a heap on the back seat of our car and enjoy some fitful sleep.

Other aides did not have this luxury as some were consigned to more work, helping their men and women continue on for a full 24 hours of track walking. On other occasions at different race venues, Ed opted for the same challenge. Soon after a scrub down he was seen on this occasion revelling in his success by drinking at the bar and bopping away in a trackside marquee that was pumping out music for all the other competitors carrying on through the dead of night.

Edmund's powers of recovery were legendary. There was no evidence of fatigue whatsoever, when he joined me and five of our other Dawlish club mates two weeks later for our long drive north to Lancashire and ferry trip across the Irish Sea to the Isle of Man.

On the sunniest of days it felt like a summer cruise on a millpond, with hundreds of others basking on deck as we made our way over on the six hour crossing.

The races that took place on the streets of St John's were fantastic to watch. East German, Hartwig Gauder won gold at the Moscow Olympics and it was his experience that was enough to lead home the USSR's Andrey Perlov in a tight 50km race, while Jose Marin beat Maurizio Damilano by a mere second in the 20km race. Ian McCombie was the first of the British in 20th position. In the women's 10km event, Chinese and Soviet women shared the top four places.

The open 10km walk for all those walkers there supporting the main World Cup events, was a good opportunity to try out the course and feel even more part of the weekend of racing. Whilst I might have felt that I had a point to prove to the British team selectors, there was little I could do about Norway's Erling Anderson. He was too strong for me on the day, yet settling for second position still allowed me to hold my head high. By late evening however, my chin was on my chest. I was drunk. Three drinks or more would invariably do it. And so it was, after gate-crashing the official World Cup post-race festivities in the Empress Hotel, we sang *you'll never walk alone* with anyone who cared to join in. Though it was great fun, if I had a hat I would surely have doffed it in deference to the Soviets. Their reputation as unbelievably fit athletes seemed at odds with their remarkable ability to out drink all-comers if vodka was within easy reach.

Leaving hand in hand with a Danish girl, I recall walking through the hotel foyer and having to circumnavigate a mob of baying men surrounding two others lying on the floor in an arm wrestling challenge. Through the melee I saw Richard Pannell taking on all-comers, and smiled. I knew how strong he was.

They had no chance, I thought. I heard later that he remained unbeaten.

A bracing walk under the stars along the promenade beach in the early hours was lovely as I made my way back towards the Strathmore Hotel. The chance to clear my head and think did not last long however. Coming across a large group of other familiar weary-legged walkers, I refused to get drawn by a barrage of suggestive lewd comments.

It felt like my head had only just hit the pillow before Edmund was coaxing us all to get up and gather our bags. It was probably no more than we deserved that the dark skies and choppy waters during our ferry trip home was as unwelcoming as the headaches that we took on board. Richard at least had the consolation of knowing that he had won more than enough in the casino to pay for his entire contribution to the trip. While he treated himself to a plateful of fresh kippers, the rest of us hung our faces overboard.

I have been lucky enough to meet some wonderfully genuine people throughout my athletic career. Before his move to the USA, Ian Brooks had shown some promise as a young international walker before injury cut short his progress. A few years my senior he was tall, ebullient, an intellectual who was never short of an encouraging word. Some years later he would play an instrumental part in my participation in arguably one of my career defining races. Before that however, and in his post race Race Walking Record report of the 1985 and 37th annual staging of the Chippenham to Calne six miles he wrote:

On a delightful day with a welcome sunshine, Chris Maddocks fairly glistened with class as he dominated the opposition to win with supreme authority in a very fast time of 40.20. Chris now approaching his finals in Law/Sociology at Exeter University is intent on preparing himself to meet the considerable challenge of Dave Smith, Australia, and Canadians' Francois Lapointe and Guillaume LeBlanc at the Commonwealth Games in Edinburgh next year. A mentally prepared and physically fit Chris Maddocks would be a potential medallist and it is to be hoped that he is ready for the trial in April.

This particular Chippenham win was all the more satisfying because I shared the success with my Dawlish club mates who all contributed to us winning the team trophy. Behind me, Ed finished 7th, Stuart Phillips 9th, Andy Bainborough 22nd, Richard Pannell 23rd and Ian *Chopper* Alford 66th. As a group this proved to be our best ever result. In addition to the award of individual and team trophies we each collected a foot long block of pork pie courtesy of the race sponsors; when in Wiltshire, when in England. Wonderful!

The inspirational words written by Ian Brooks helped motivate me further. Six more races before the end of the year saw six wins including two sub 40 minutes six mile walks and a track 20km 85.11 on December 29th.

Meanwhile, I had a new group of housemates at Nancherrow. All males meant there would at least be no immediate feminine distraction for my final year, particularly when my new next door neighbour was Phil Rudd, a Welshman who for some inexplicable reason seemed to attract the ladies. Sure, he was quite muscular and far from bad looking, yet he made no effort, was nearly always unshaven, and probably personified scruffiness. If it was an apparent rugged charm that appealed, then anyone foolish enough to make an advance was usually in for a rude awakening.

Now I accept that when eating I am less than keen on sharing my chips with anyone. There are times when an exception to this general rule may apply such as when an attractive student might flirtatiously lean across the dining room table and try to pinch one or two. Then, and perhaps only then, the sacrifice may well be a price worth paying? It's reasonable to assume that Phil Rudd did not share my reasoning when presented with this very dilemma during one supper in the Luke's canteen. His response to the seductive theft was met with universal derision.

'...Oh, that's disgusting!'

'Oh my God, you're horrible.'

I had never previously seen anyone repel a chip pincher by spitting all over his plate and then carry on eating with a victorious grin on his face, completely unconcerned by the instinctive reaction of others on the table. Phil Rudd was a man's man who loved sport, and apart from his studies did not appear fussed about much else.

A post-graduate PE reading mathematics, Rudders played rugby, a scrum-half who idolized the likes of Barry John and Gareth Edwards both of whom adorned his wall. Accessed through a robust fire door, our two rooms could be found in the unventilated corridor of the east wing. Like me, Rudders trained most days. Unlike me, he washed his kit at best only once a week. So long as it was dry it could be reused, he'd argue. And argue we did.

No matter how many times I complained about the wretched smell of his jock strap and rugby shorts dried to a crisp on the radiator in the corridor, he always found it too funny to take me seriously. In the end I resolved to taking deep breaths, have my room key at the ready and shoot through the fire door and hope for the best. We at least made our peace in the weights room where we combined our efforts by doing some great workouts together.

Rudders had taken up the room vacated by Mike Judd who had moved up the road to try something different in his final year. Mike unsurprisingly liked Phil who he said had a certain panache. I believe Mike simply liked him because he appealed to his own more basic instincts and, most important of all, because his lack of hygiene irritated the hell out of me.

A new quartet was made up by second year Phys.Ed student, John Murphy. *Murph* was a fanatical road cyclist roomed in the west wing whose four hour cycle rides on Wednesday afternoons helped keep me inspired during that final year at Lukes. Many a time I would sit in his room exchanging thoughts on my latest 43km walk on the roads around Killerton and Poltimore whilst he lovingly cleaned his bike for the umpteenth time and told me all about his scenic rides to Torquay and back.

Mike had his football. My self-proclaimed manager should have had my best interests at heart, and yet it did not stop him cajoling me down to Duck's Meadow playing fields one Sunday afternoon to help make up the numbers and play in an inter-Mural league match between Scum and Shitface. The Meadow was so big at least half a dozen matches could be in play at any one time. Played in a quagmire, we waded through the mud and won 5-3. The victory came at a price. My post-match strains were such that my training was compromised for days and ensured that I would not allow myself to be swayed by *Hoofer* Judd to kick a ball again no matter how much fun it was.

Aside of my exam finals, the primary target for 1986 was the Commonwealth Games 30km race in Edinburgh at the end of July. We all knew that the first three Englishmen across the line at the trials in April would be selected. Unlike qualification for other major championships this would be as cut-throat as the American system of athletic team selection – first three across the line at the trials is selected, no argument. No past form would be taken into account, no qualifying times, no account given for being ill on the day. Plain and simple, I had to be ready.

I trained meticulously and early race results indicated that all was going well until one disappointing *blip* in March.

February 2:	Brighton track 10kms	1st 41.58
February 15	Basingstoke 10miles	1st 67.51
February 22	Salisbury 10miles	1st 67.47
March 8	Bournemouth Piers 6miles	1st 40.11
March 16	Spanish 50kms, Madrid	DNF
March 22	National 10miles, Redditch	2nd 67.11

I travelled out to Madrid with Richard Pannell. It was a mistake from the start. He was injured, I was ill. It was only because I had worked so hard and felt so fit that I was prepared to ignore the flu-like symptoms and *give it a go…*

On my occasional visits to Plymouth, Richard would routinely forsake his own training and work like a Trojan in order to help myself and Edmund with refreshments and encouragement during our long walks on the roads around Dartmoor. He was as tough as they came, so it was a surprise to meet up with him when he so obviously was in pain. The plaster-cast on his arm was there to protect a broken wrist, all as a result of an accident whilst at work on a building site a few days earlier.

I have no doubt that we looked a pitiful sight when met by a party of seven other Brits from the walking fraternity at Heathrow airport: Richard in a sling and me sniffing feebly into a handkerchief.

The race for me was certainly a wasted opportunity. With an early morning start and a flat well surfaced course of 2.5kms with sweeping bends and world class opposition, it had all the ingredients necessary for fast times.

The weather was cool and clear. I went through 5kms in 23.04 with Les Morton and Paul Blagg on 23.38, Dennis Jackson on 23.56 pace. I passed through 10kms in 46.27 and maintained this speed up until 20kms by which time the effects of my illness were dragging me down. By halfway my paced had dropped off, with the clock showing 1.59.33. The leaders had long pulled clear when I finally stepped off the race circuit three-quarters way around the 11th parkland lap.

Devoid of all energy, I sat with my head in my hands feeling sorry for myself. A race official helped unpin my race number. It took a while before I could summon the energy and enthusiasm to stroll on around the circuit and walk over towards Richard, who in the meantime had been busy at the designated table for the British walkers assisting David Rosser and Tony Perkins by handing out drinks and verbal encouragement.

Richard glanced over his shoulder and saw my listless approach. Like the dripping sponge held in his hand, his body momentarily sagged. He stepped away from the table, offered up a wry smile and asked, 'We guessed you'd dropped out. You all right?'

'Yeah, Okay,' I said. 'How's your arm?'

'Yeah, Okay,' he replied.

There was little more that could be said. We were both fed up.

Richard perked up and said, 'Hey, that Norwegian chap looks fantastic. He really is a brilliant walker, he looks so smooth. On that last lap he started to get away from Llopart. And Les, well he looks like he might be on for a sub four if he can hold it together.'

That was the killer blow. Already feeling weak and powerless, that shot across the bows was fair warning that not only had I failed that day, but it could get a whole lot worse if Les Morton were to achieve something that for so long I had wanted to add to my racing CV…to be the first Briton to walk 50kms in less than four hours.

With the race well into its final quarter it was only going to get tougher for those still going. For that reason this was a time to be nothing less than supportive. I cheered when I could, no matter what nationality.

Yes, Erling Anderson may have been in a different league walking a superb 3.49.00 just one minute ahead of Spain's Jorge Llopart, but for purely selfish reasons my mind was on things to come.

I waited impatiently around the finish gantry bracing myself to swallow the bittersweet pill of someone else's success. Chattering race officials went about their business exchanging information, calling out times to those with more laps to complete, and occasionally throwing me a dismissive glance that suggested that I should move further away. With one eye on the digital clock and another on the far corner, I watched as one by one, leading walkers appeared from behind a long line of trees at the top of the road and made their final dash down towards us at the finish. First appearing like matchstick silhouettes the strained sweaty effort on each face became ever more obvious the closer they got. Forty-five seconds I estimated it took each of the first few to cover that last push for the line.

I joined the applause that greeted each finisher. When the digital clock finally ticked well beyond 3.59...I relaxed until, seconds later, the white vested number 31 came into view.

It was not difficult for me to understand Les Morton's awkward smile as he approached the line. He was about to achieve something very special but with that extra slice of time removed, a history making performance had just slipped from his grasp.

Les finished in a time of 4.00.47. He had improved my British record by over one minute. Pushing my way through the throng I did my best to be one of the first to congratulate this most genial of Yorkshiremen. Before long I was also offering my hand to Dennis, another really good guy and a man who in the twilight of his racing career came home in personal best time of 4.03.08. Paul Blagg slowed in the second half and eventually gutted out a 4.15 finish.

Given that the best long distance walkers in the world had long mastered the four hour barrier, it would be all too easy to scoff at the best British efforts to do the same. However, as I have mentioned before, whilst most leading British walkers continued to train in isolation, many of our foreign counterparts enjoyed the benefits of good coaching in squads home and abroad, utilizing the most advanced scientific facilities.

Most successful endurance athletes, including walkers used warm weather training camps and felt the benefits found way up in the mountains at high altitude camps where the body learned to adapt to training with a lack of oxygen. The effect of training in the rarified thin air of altitude meant muscle metabolism was beneficially altered by an increased number of red blood cells in the body with their oxygen carrying capacity. This extra concentration of blood cells enabled them to develop a competitive advantage over those like, me, Les, Dennis and Paul who more routinely trained at sea level, at home, alone, or at the very best, with a few like minded friends.

Of course we had sampled a total of maybe two or three weeks warm weather training over the previous couple of years. It was good, but only a start. Les was a Sheffield welder, Dennis, a postman, Paul, a policeman, me a student. Altitude training would remain a pipedream for most British walkers for the foreseeable future.

I had to put the disappointment of the Spanish race behind me. For that reason, I was pleased to get back home, start to feel better by mid-week and race well the following weekend even if it did mean that I tasted defeat to Ian McCombie who won in 66 minutes 35 seconds.

That national one-two would prove ominous. Ian McCombie was obviously in great shape. There was only five weeks to the Commonwealth trial and I felt there was only so much that I could do to improve in that time.

At a cost of £30, I *hired* a room at Rowancroft Court from a second year student who was vacating it for the Easter vacation. I think he was more than happy to get the money if for no other reason it helped him with his train fare home. For study purposes it suited me that St Lukes campus felt like a mini ghost town during vacation time. Mum visited on my birthday and brought me a cake with candles. While in the evening, Mike and I went to the cinema to see the new Michael J Fox film, *Back to the future*. Other than that, it was hours of revision study and training.

The first two weeks I averaged 100 miles per week. The third I tapered down so as to be ready for what I hoped would be a fast 20kms on the track at Leicester. As it turned out, I felt lethargic but still managed a win in 87.49 almost a full lap ahead of Phil Vesty who did 89.17. I was really hoping for something closer to 84 minutes. Richard Pannell spent much of the time driving home trying to convince me that everything would be all right if I eased back on my training. This was the kind of sound advice that I was never very good at taking. However, for once I did listen, if only because I was increasingly concerned about a hamstring strain that had developed during the track walk and because I generally felt so knackered over the next two weeks in the lead up to my departure for Edinburgh.

Where Edmund is involved, travel plans are seldom simple. Dare I say it, even convoluted? You see, he had competed in Hungary the previous weekend, a 50km walk that he had done in 4hours 28 minutes, and was traveling back from Budapest on the Thursday. Andy Bainborough and I agreed to leave on a coach and meet up with him in Birmingham. From there we would drive onto Middlesborough where we would grab an overnight stay at the home of an old buddy of his. It may have meant eight long hours on the road but, to be fair, it worked fine.

The three of us left the following morning and via an invigorating one hour break strolling along Hadrian's Wall, we finally arrived at Meadowbank stadium around 5pm. We changed into our training kit and did a series of sprints totaling 6kms. We eventually made it to our B&B around seven.

Who actually booked the room is unimportant. Edmund was the senior one amongst us and it was felt that he should have the single bed. That left Andy and I needing to share the double. It may well have been perfectly all right for Morecambe & Wise, but for us, two 29 year old men sharing a bed, somehow did not feel quite so right. An occasional stray foot apart, the proverbial roll of barbed wire down the middle did at least keep us separated for most of that quite uncomfortable, yet very funny night.

In the morning Edmund looked a rare sight fussing as he always did when he was trying to find something in his kit bag. I never knew a man who could cram so much incidental stuff into a confined space. Stood in slippers and stripy pajamas with his back to us, his hot water bottle already cast to one side, he looked like a character out of Brideshead Revisited minus the teddy bear tucked under his arm. Leant over the single bed ferreting through his bag, he was quietly cussing to himself, presumably unaware that Andy and I were lying on our backs, heads resting on our pillows smiling whilst watching him in the half light.

'Ed, what are you doing?' I asked.

Without looking around he said, 'Looking for my brush…Aah, there it is.' Turning his attention to the large antique wood framed mirror standing atop the mantelpiece he promptly set about brushing his wispy thatch into place.

Andy, who had even less hair than Edmund, piped up, 'You look beautiful Ed. Going anywhere nice today?'

Edmund looked at his watch. 'Breakfast is in half 'n' hour. I don't want to be late. You two had better get up if you're joining me.'

I slipped my legs from out under the duvet and sat up on the edge of the bed. Andy spoke again. 'I suppose from now on its okay for me to say that I've slept with the Olympic walker, Chris Maddocks.'

Of the three of us, Edmund's laugh was probably the loudest.

Andy Bainborough had been a good mate for about 10 years. He was a gardener with the council back in Exeter and a recent churchgoer. Occasionally, he'd come around and see me in Nancherrow. Impossibly shy around girls, his visits during my third and final year became more frequent. With few academic qualifications, I admired his ambition when he said that he had started evening classes at the local college in order to try and get a maths 'O' level. I asked Phil Rudd if he would give him a hand with his homework.

Rudders agreed to help Andy but worried sick when he realised that he had forgotten much of the basics at that level of maths, a level that in a few months time he would be working at a private school where he had provisionally secured a teaching position.

Although not as quick as Edmund, Andy had competed in a number of ultra-distance events including several 100 mile races, the best of which he completed in less than 22 hours. On one particular occasion I enquired how his latest effort had gone.

His deadpan reply was priceless: 'Oh, I was okay for about 40 miles, but then I hung on for the next 60!'

Come Sunday's race, it was me that was hanging on. Ian McCombie was on sensational form. From the moment the starter's gun fired in the Meadowbank Stadium he bolted to the front. I managed to peg him back before we walked off the track and headed out and along Portobello road towards Cockenzie and the halfway turnaround point.

Side by side for close to an hour we raced, neither prepared to concede an inch of ground. It was clear to me he was more comfortable than I was. My lungs were burning up while he seemed to be breathing within himself as we moved along at top speed probably close to 9mph. He may have sensed my discomfort because he certainly made his move at the right time. With the slightest injection of extra pace he was away. The gap between us ever lengthening, there was nothing that I could do about it, not even with the encouragement of a familiar voice from a passing car.

'C'mon Chris, you can catch him.'

I looked over and caught a brief glimpse of Mum, who was hanging her head out of a car window, her usual quaffed blonde hair blowing every which-way. She had hitched a lift with a race official and was doing her best to see as much of the race as was possible. Prior to that fleeting moment, I had only the time to briefly speak to her before the start of the race at 10am. Very bravely, she had traveled alone overnight on a coach from Exeter to Edinburgh only arriving minutes before.

Ian was around the arc of road bollards at halfway and heading back in my direction while they still looked like pin heads in the distance to me. Walking fast in opposite directions, we barely glanced at each other as we passed. I thought that unless he faltered in the second half, the best I could do was retain my current position and guarantee my spot on the England team.

Heading back, I sized up the gaps between me and the chasing walkers: Phil Vesty, Mike Parker, Paul Blagg, Martin Rush, with increasing gaps to Dennis Jackson, Barry Graham, Darren Thorn, Andy Drake and Les Morton. I managed to reserve some breath in order to shout across the central reservation and offer words of support, first to Edmund and then Andy Bainborough.

I pushed on and was more than pleased when I finally made it back into the stadium without my pace dropping off and losing position. Ian sportingly was there on the track by the finish line applauding me. He had pulled so far out in front that he had time to towel down and put a T-shirt on before I re-entered the stadium.

Mum, bless her, had made it back to the finish in time and her first thought was to commiserate with my loss. I assured her that it was all right, that she should be happy because I was happy. When you lose to a better man on the day, particularly one that had just walked a world class 30km time, then you just have to say *well done* and be satisfied with your own performance.

Twenty year old, Martin Rush walked in for third and did fantastically well for someone so young. Ian's team-mate Paul Blagg was the first of the leading finishers to suffer the heartbreak of missing out on a Commonwealth Games team place.

1st	Ian McCombie	2.07.56	*New British Record
2nd	Chris Maddocks	2.11.53	
3rd	Martin Rush	2.13.29	
4th	Paul Blagg	2.15.44	
13th	Edmund Shillabeer	2.31.13	
27th	Andy Bainborough	2.55.41	

Ten O'clock Tuesday morning, so tired was I, so dull was it that I was barely able to concentrate on the industrial law lecture. I could see her, there down at the front of the stage, standing behind the lectern gesticulating, her mouth may have been moving but lord knows what she was saying, I wasn't listening. It was safe to say that I was hardly in a receptive mood to hear anything more about trade unions, industrial strikes or company contracts.

All too often the Moot Room with its tiered seating and wood panelling felt so stuffy. We were surrounded by windows and hardly any appeared to be open. There must have been 60 or more students in there that morning, most of whom choosing to keep their coats on, and if not, a scarf wrapped jauntily around their necks. A coat, a scarf, what is it with these people, I thought. A different heating mechanism, I guessed. I was in t-shirt and jeans, and would have been down to my boxers if I thought no one would object.

It was the start of Trinity term, my last as a student at Exeter. My mind was on other things, training, the races I had planned, and that coaching session on Thursday with a group of first year PE students. For the life of me I could not recall how I allowed myself to get talked into doing it. Mr Edgecombe, the head of the PE department could be very persuasive. In truth, our paths seldom crossed and yet, in this instance he assured me that it would be all right. I did not share his confidence. Sure, I had plenty of experience from invites to schools and clubs over the years where I had been asked to talk about my racing career, offer coaching tips and give some tuition in the art of fast walking, but that was to young, impressionable kids who more often than not were quite excited by the chance to meet an international athlete. Talking to a bunch of undergraduates, who I thought were just as likely to take the piss, held little appeal.

St Lukes' playing fields, 3.15pm, Mr Edgecombe stood back after wrapping up his brief introduction, where he cited the considerable achievement it had been for me to have become an Olympic athlete and that I was *one of the hardest training athletes* he'd ever known. The suggestion that race walking may be harder than running provoked a few furtive sideway glances and wry smiles.

Immensely flattered, I took up the reins. Grabbing the attention of 30 young PE students could have been difficult. Instead, I was able to share a joke, explain that for some, trying to walk fast for the first time might feel awkward, to a few it may feel surprisingly natural, and for others nigh on impossible. I looked around. Those shifting uneasily on their feet perhaps feared they might be amongst the ones falling into the latter category.

Surprisingly, there was no shortage of volunteers when I asked if two from the group would run alongside me. I proposed to give a three lap demonstration walk and allow everyone else to stand back, watch my technique and see how it compared to the running action of their friends. I pointed out that they should see with each rapid stride my feet skimming low to the ground and how my knee virtually locked straight on forward heel strike whilst the toes of the rear foot stayed in contact with the ground. I hoped they would also notice the very different technique of good runners in full stride with their high knee lift and high heel flick back. I said that fast walkers could walk at a rate of around four strides per second.

I first had to deal with the usual comments like, *Yeah, but how fast could you run? Are you tempted to run when the judges aren't looking? How fast do you walk? Wow, that's almost as fast as I can run...'* The latter quip had long been a bone of contention, particularly as some inquisitors have an over-inflated view of how fast they can actually run. Almost anyone who for example, thinks that they would be able to run 10kms in less than 45 minutes or a half marathon in 90 minutes without having first done some regular training is usually deluding themselves.

Seen side by side, a walker and a runner going at the same speed never previously failed to impress. And so it proved this time.

The three minutes 54 seconds that it took to walk the 900m was not the quickest time possible for me, but it was hard enough on a parched 300m grass track with its fair share of divots. I tried to disguise just how hard I was pushing, preferring to appear as if I was *coasting* at speed by exchanging a few nonchalant words whilst on the move with the volunteer runners. Thankfully, by the end of the three laps their heavy breathing suggested that a reasonable degree of effort was necessary on their part in order to keep up with me.

I gathered my breath, turned to the group, smiled, and said, 'Now it's your turn. If you line up here, I'll call the start and we'll see what you can do.'

The reactive banter subsided and led by an enthusiastic few jockeying for a good position at the front, the majority filed in behind, the more reluctant ones shuffled forward seemingly happy taking up a rearguard spot.

'Are you ready...?' Reminiscent of the school sport day cross-country run when, like it or not, limp bodies suddenly became taut, poised for that all important command. I suppressed the urge to laugh. 'GO!'

They were off. Striding away, it was an amusing yet pleasing sight, all hip swinging, all thrusting elbows and bums. No one seemingly wanted to be left behind as each and everyone walked the first lap with spirit and whilst the gaps quickly opened up between the fastest and the slowest, the 900metres was eventually completed with considerable gusto.

By the end, the spread of times ranged between five and a half minutes and six and a half minutes. The comments that followed were all too common:
'Blimey, that was hard.'
'Ooh, my shins hurt.'
'Mine too...'
'Aagh, I've got a stitch.'
'I finished in front of you.'
'No you didn't...'

Mr Edgecombe stepped forward. 'Be quiet now.'
I was impressed and I told them so.

It was kind of ironic that only a few days later I should be race walking in front of students again, only this time with more serious competition and many more watching. In my three years at Exeter I did little to involve myself with the athletics union. With no recognised race walking section there was no real incentive to attend their training sessions. I was however quite happy to don the dark green vest and try and score good points for the team at the annual university track and field championships. At Crystal Palace in 1984 there was no disgrace in narrowly losing out to Phil Vesty, whereas last year a certain broken toe prevented any participation. This year's event at Derby was my last chance to win.

It was never likely to be easy once I saw two other international walkers just minutes before the start. Seven and a half laps of the track equated to three kilometers, a relatively short distance that would hold no fear for either me, Tim Berrett or Andy Trigg. The same probably could not be said for most of the other dozen or so students limbering up. Amongst all the twisting, stretching, and toe touching, a few appeared genuinely nervous as if they were about to do an exam for which they had done no revision. Others ignored the catcalls of their watching friends and tried some last minute cramming by marching at speed down one length of the track. Two I noticed seemed totally unconcerned, choosing instead to enjoy the last few puffs on their cigarettes before the call of the starter.

The buffeting wind contributed to me sharing the lead with Tim and Andy for the first four laps by which time we had already lapped the remainder of the field. From that point on, Andy slowly slipped back as Tim and I lifted the pace for a deciding thrash to the finish.

Strung out around the track, the other walkers were eventually lapped for a second time. As for the *two clowns* right at the back, they were in my sights for a third time as I finally broke clear from Tim just before the sound of the bell signaling one lap to go.

Instead of enjoying the final 400m victory lap I resolved to vent my pent up frustration caused by the two back markers ahead of me. On our penultimate lap my attention had been drawn to a commotion on the far side of the track, where I saw a spectator scampering across the track before ducking under the spectator rails and lost amongst the watching crowd. An ice-cream each had been delivered into the hands of two walkers who appeared to be playing to their audience by holding their gifts aloft like some prized trophy. Call me a killjoy, but I was having none of it.

They might as well have had targets painted on their backs as I gritted my teeth and accelerated towards them. Like some demented fool, I was quite prepared to barge straight between the two of them and inflict as much pain as was possible. Perhaps it was the sound of my breathy exertions from behind that caused one to flinch, but joy upon joy, I was within striking distance when they suddenly

So young, so naive; I actually believed Dad when he said knicker-bockers were all the rage

Alf Tupper – my inspiration in the early years

I was quite upset after losing my entire marble collection in a winner takes all game

My James Bond gun may have lacked real bullets; it did however make a shockingly loud noise

Me at 14 years old with just one mile to the finish of the Tiverton 50 miles

Pictured with my sea cadet teammates after I had won my first ever competitive walk

Aged 18, at the fifth attempt, I finally win the Tiverton Youth Centre's annual 50 miles

Club photo call for Tiverton Harriers in 1977. I'm standing towards the far right next to coach, Jack Snow

Modelling my first ever
GB tracksuit in 1978

Showing off some of my trophy collection in 1979

Central London 1980 – British Olympic 50km trials. Spot the
Union Jack shorts.

East Devon College 1981 – the year I was robbed of victory in the sausage eating contest. I'm the one in the check shirt.

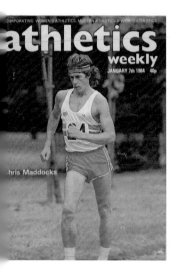

Athletics Weekly – the 'bible' for every athletics reader. Proud to be on the front cover.

Dad reading an interview with me in that 1984 AW magazine

Mum showing gritty determination during one of my
training sessions

On the ferry to the Isle of Man in 1985 with l-r Andy Bainborough,
Ed Shillabeer, Ian Alford, and Richard Pannell.

Accepting the applause after finishing fourth at the Edinburgh
Commonwealth Games.

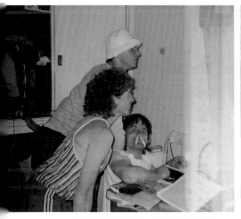

Neither myself, Mike Judd or Phil
Rudd (pencils up the nose) ever
discovered the name of the topless
lady sunbathing in the garden next
to our Nancherrow home

Andi Drake and I in Central Park,
New York after finishing first and
second in a 5km road race.

The National 35km cup won for the second time in 1988

Up with the leaders during the 1989 World Cup 20kms
at L'hospitalet, near Barcelona.

parted, leaving the smallest of gaps for me to bulldoze through. As I did so, in one sweeping movement, I vigorously swung back my arms kung fu style and connected beautifully with their ice-creams. As I tore on around the last half of the track towards my finish, I hoped some of the cheers I heard may have been for a particularly messy result to that little passing confrontation.

The laughs were more genuine when it came to preparing for the traditional end of year, St Lukes' summer ball. Tuxedos and ball gowns were the order of the day. Some of us had made do in previous years with collar and tie, not so this time. We had heard about this old lady down the road who specialized in providing students for such occasions.

A Victorian house we were told, in the basement, where there would be so much to choose from. If only any of it was any good? One thing was for sure…it was an Aladdin's cave in there. One giant wardrobe it seemed with clothes hung on rails in every conceivable cavity, from architraves, on the back of doors, slung dispassionately over chairs. Boxes of shoes, row upon row of shoes on rickety shelves. The overpowering whiff of mothballs added a hedonistic flavor to our jungle like hack through the array of vintage wear.

'You look like a bag of shit,' Mike Judd proffered. He stood there in his socks, no trousers, squeezed into a black dinner jacket, possibly with the widest lapels I had ever seen, wiping the tears from his eyes. He tried to repeat his less than qualified appraisal of my appearance. 'Maddocks, you look like a bag of…'

'Everything alright my dears?' asked the old lady. Her sudden reappearance had Mike biting his lip. She had gone out of the room in order to find a dress shirt that she considered would be a suitable match to go with my choice of tux. How long she had been in the room before she reappeared was difficult to tell. Phil Rudd and John Murphy were out of sight but evidently still around, somewhere in there at the back trying on double-breasted jackets. Their sniggering laughs had barely stopped since they disappeared out of view 15 minutes earlier. The old lady looked at me with a warm, possibly insincere smile. 'Now, that does look good on you,' she said. 'All it needs is a nip 'n' tuck here and there.'

I ignored Mike's dismissive snort. While he turned away to blow his nose, I was more concerned by this lady's professional judgment. To be fair she was only trying to help and I knew that I was a bit of an odd shape. Medium height, wide shoulders, a barrel chest, 32 inch waist, no hips to speak of, skinny legs, I did look a bit of a cheese wedge with tentacles.

The jacket did indeed fit well across the shoulders, buttoned up it was loose, very loose, in fact it was so baggy that it must have once been worn by a portly man whose only regular exercise was to the pie shop. Certainly the trousers that accompanied the jacket would need to be taken in. My Mum could do that, and it would save on any alteration costs. The well-heeled shoes, a product no doubt of the 1970's offered extra height that would not go amiss if a smart appearance was ever likely to be achieved. Unlike Mike, I did not want all the fancy extras and rejected the dress-shirt with frills and saw no need for the white scarf and silk cummerbund. He did and called it a look of sophistication, a sartorial eloquence that I could not conceivably aspire to and that if it was good enough for agent 007 then it was good enough for him. I thought that he looked more like Brooke Bond than James Bond, and he might as well have chosen a black bow tie that twirled. Determined to have the last word, he said that he was so impressed with my final purchases that he considered that for a grand total of £33, I had been fleeced.

The four of us left there with our carrier bags of choice, achingly richer for the experience. We had until our respective exams were done to decide if we dared be seen in public wearing our *new* suits. The mere thought of it saw us laughing at each other all the way back to St Lukes.

Three years of reading law and sociology was condensed into two more weeks of exams. Finally, three hours after starting a paper with questions on criminology and deviance, the pen was laid to rest. The relief was immense. In contemplative silence I got up, left the Roborough reading room avoiding eye contact with any other student on the way out, looked to the skies, smelt the fresh air and went for a long stroll on my own. I had a lot to think about.

Degree or no degree, I had no immediate plans how best to use it. Aside of all the studies, my primary focus had always been on training for races. The Commonwealth Games walk was less than two months away. As a potential last race, that surely fitted with my long held goal to retire somewhere near the top whilst I was still in my 20's, still at the peak of my fitness. Thereafter, it would be a good time to get on with the rest of my life, get a good job, earn enough money to buy a nice house and perhaps settle down.

Deep in thought, I saw other students but spoke to no one as I meandered along wooded paths past Berks halls through the oldest most historic parts of the university. It was easier to have plans when they were still a distance away. The three years at university had bought me time to delay any commitment to the future. That time was almost up.

Because I had spoken about my intention to retire by the age of 29, I felt a bit of a phony even thinking about racing beyond Edinburgh. The fact that I had competitions lined up before and *after* the 30km race did not sit well with my conscience. Of course no one was holding a gun to my head; I was not compelled by what I had previously vowed to do. I knew that I had friends who saw no reason for me to stop racing, at least not while I was still physically capable of getting faster.

Edmund Shillabeer and Richard Pannell had already suggested that I might move to Plymouth, and between them they would help set me up with rented accommodation, find part-time work and for me to train for one more shot at an Olympic Games. In one sense the idea appeared attractive, perhaps even conveniently so, and in another sense I wondered if I could face up to another two years on minimal finances and a rudderless career path. I asked myself a lot of questions and as Mike Judd liked to remind me, I quite predictably came up with no clear answers.

Mum had done wonders with my dinner suit. With an air of elevated confidence that smart clothes help exude in seconds, I joined my mates and the throng of 500 cocktail, champagne, beer swilling students all dressed to the nines on that balmy summer's night at St Luke's. Canapes and barbeque food filled the air with sumptuous smells. Strewn with bunting and balloons, marquees, music and glamour, the campus was transformed by a variety of live bands playing pop, jazz, folk even classical. Illusionists, hypnotists, magicians took their turn to entertain.

It proved to be quite a night. During the earlier part of the evening it was nonstop entertainment. Exiting one marquee, ears throbbing by an assault from over amplified drums and guitars, we ate chicken wings on the move whilst walking diagonally across the grass to a crowded lecture theatre where just in time we saw one hapless innocent on stage munching on a raw onion as if it were the juiciest of apples. I laughed and cringed and wondered what damage might have been done to the poor sap's taste buds once he was snapped back to the present.

It was probably all too smug of us to think that it would only be Mr Onion Breath who by his reckless deeds might have severely compromised his chances of attracting a willing kissing partner. As it transpired, he would not be the only unfortunate soul that evening. At least Mr O could blame any lack of post-party action on the hypnotherapist. I, on the other hand, was more desperate to divert the responsibility.

'I don't believe it,' I moaned, 'not even a sniff. It's your fault.'

Mike Judd scoffed, 'Don't blame me. Have you looked at yourself in the mirror? You look like Shirley Temple in drag. Besides, you must have known that it was not going to be your night when that bit of posh totty you always fancied only asked you for a drink because she thought you were one of the waiters.'

It was three in the morning. The party was all but over, bar the faint hum of music emanating from dimly lit rooms and by a few canoodling couples and whispering persons milling about sharing a last drink under the stars. Walking around in our own romance free zone could partially be attributed to the wasted time chatting in the common room with a bunch of post-grads that we hardly knew long after the jazz quartet had packed up. It was a merciful release when we finally walked out of there, free to yawn unreservedly.

Too tired to think straight is really a poor excuse for the regretful incident that followed. Aided only by the light of the moon we approached the exit gates of the campus. Tucked up neatly in a corner of the grounds was a familiar glass boxed trailer, concealed only partially by bushes. I had to squint in order to see it. I wished now that I never said anything.

'Do you see that?' I asked. 'Wasn't that thing hooked up to a van earlier, you know, when we bought an ice-cream a few hours ago?' Furtively, I walked forward, Mike followed. It was a criminal act and for that I owe an apology to the unknown owner who presumably left his goods mistakenly unlocked.

We were in and out of there so quickly, just enough time to lift the lid of the freezer and for our greedy eyes to marvel at the treasure trove within. We grabbed and filled our pockets with as many Cornetto ice-cream cones as we could manage before making a hasty retreat back to the sanctuary of the Ranch, just across the road.

Ascending the stairs, muffled voices could be heard from behind more than one closed door, though we saw no one as we headed for the fire door leading to my room. Instinctively I took a deep breath and filled my lungs as I pushed through.

Mike was less prepared. 'Oh God, it stinks!'

'Shush!'

We had not seen Rudders for hours, and didn't know whether he was in or out. My fridge-freezer proved too small to take so many cones, so in a state of hushed dread it was up to the top floor and along the corridor to the communal kitchen where the fridge's freezer compartment was crammed full; what we could not squeeze in we left in the main body of the fridge amongst the out-of-date processed cheese, a part bottle of curdled milk, and two cans of lager. Fearful that our *swag* might not survive too long in its new hiding place, we set about eating what we could; three each was just about the maximum we could manage.

Mike licked his chops and slid away into the night back to his house. The mad excitement of it all quickly evaporated once he was gone, leaving me feeling sick with worry. He returned the next morning by which time rumour had spread that the police had been called in to investigate a late night theft. I had already been questioned by two conniving housemates who had stumbled upon the incriminating evidence in the kitchen. Their silence was bought in exchange for the few surviving frozen cones squeezed in the freezer compartment. The remaining mush was reluctantly washed away down the sink from whence no more was heard. I have never stolen anything since.

I had enough time over the weekend to emotionally recover from the self inflicted late night trauma, lift the worst of the chocolate stain off the lapel of my dinner suit that I'd chosen to wear for the drive to Tiverton. It was my Mum's birthday and I wanted to surprise her with an unexpected visit and a bouquet of flowers at Hodges menswear where she worked as a retail shop assistant. Because the local press had already been in touch with me about wanting a photograph to go with latest race reports, I thought I could kill two birds with one stone by agreeing to meet their photographer in the high street outside the shop.

Lee Flaws had taken my picture on numerous occasions previously. The fact that he was an old flame of Mum's in their innocent youth only became apparent to me years later. A quick sneaky glance past the mannequins into the shop was enough to tell us that subject to anyone else entering we would not have to wait too long for the customer within to leave. His departure moments later, was our cue to enter.

Mum's squeal of delight made all the clandestine planning worth it. She had grown used to my general scruffiness and could not remember the last time that she had seen me looking so smart. The flowers were an added bonus as was the opportunity to say hello to Lee before he left. I stayed long enough for a cup of tea and to be introduced to the Manager and the few customers she served whilst I was there. She said she would cook dinner if I agreed to go across town and surprise Nan and Grandad with a visit at their bungalow.

Once that deed was done, I completed my round of social calls by detouring to see my sister. Jane thought it was hilarious that I was prepared to be seen in town in the middle of the day dressed in a tux.

I was in more comfortable Bermuda shorts and t-shirt by the time John Murphy showed up at Mum's home that warm mid-afternoon. He had cycled the 20 miles from Exeter and stayed long enough for a chat and debrief on his night at the summer ball before resuming his training ride back to St Luke's campus. He left shortly before Mum arrived home. While John was around I had given minimal thought to the absence of Toby, Mum's partner. They had lived together for more than two years and been an item for some time before that.

Mum did not know how to serve up a small meal. Combined with the fact that I was possibly the biggest, slowest eater meant it was quite late when I put down my knife and fork. The two of us had chatted quite amicably about the day, her first signs of her arthritis, my time at Exeter, and my next few races leading up to the Commonwealth Games. There was something else that she was not saying.

'What's wrong Mum?'

'Nothing.' The tear rolling down her cheek belied her response.

I had hoped to drive back to Exeter whilst it was still light. A faulty headlamp bulb on my car needed replacing. I prayed that no police would spot this indiscretion while I mulled over and over again the long conversation with Mum about her personal problems with Toby. I was upset because she was upset. They had been arguing and were considering splitting up. He was a good guy, a simple gentle type that worked hard all his life doing various manual jobs, a man who had travelled nowhere but offered Mum stability and help at home. There was little that was dynamic about him but I believed that he loved her, and I thought it was reciprocated.

In no fit mental state to train the next day, I rested before my appointment in the city centre *Next* department store in order to be measured for my formal Commonwealth Games blazer and slacks. In the intervening hours I sat down and wrote a long letter of advice to Mum. What did I know? I tried to emphasize the positive things in their relationship, at least anything I knew about it. Just how much of my letter was my selfish fear of my Mum alone, as opposed to her saying that she no longer wanted to live with someone who did not excite her, or demonstrate a willingness to do anything out of the ordinary. Although I always knew that Mum could be the most loving of people, who was equally obsessed with caring for a lifelong menagerie of pets, she was also someone who I knew could be feisty and argumentative. Like all of us, they both had their faults.

I have no idea if my letter made any impact on the two of them resolving their problems. It was never really talked about again. As it turned out, Mum and Toby would stay together for the next 21 years until his cancer-affected death at the age of 71. Though seriously afflicted by then with her own health problems, she never failed on a single day to nurture him during his declining months. I was so proud of her.

Mum would not have wanted her problems to adversely affect me. So, one rest day was all I had.

I parked up in the lay-by near Killerton Gardens and steeled myself for a fast walk that would help clear my head and get me right back on track. One hour 57 minutes and 22 seconds later, 27kms was done. The pitch 'n' putt golf that afternoon on a municipal course just off Topsham Road with Mike, Murph, Andy Bainborough and Rudders was a great way to relax again and enjoy the encouraging words of good friends.

'Maddocks, you're crap…you won't find that ball again.'

The final few weeks at university were an odd affair. With no lectures to attend, no members of staff to see, no one telling us where to go or what to do, it seemed as if until the exam results came through, biding our time was a virtue. It was okay to play more golf and tennis, train as hard as I wished; actually say *yes* to a few more late night dinner invitations with the girls before we all went our separate ways. Even then, the long goodbye would not be complete for a further three weeks when officially and metaphorically we would indeed be shown the exit door.

With the benefit of hindsight, I realize that for most departing students their thoughts turned to planning the next chapter in their respective lives with hopes of a career path laden with dreams and aspiration. My thoughts usually extended no further than my next big race. When my degree result came through, I felt a warped justification in prioritizing my racing ambitions. When it came to matters of academia, I rationalized that I had to work hard just to be average; but my pass was below average. A crushing disappointment that felt as wrong as it felt unfair. There must have been a mistake I argued. Around my training I had worked diligently and did well with my course work. I made sure to make that point to the increasingly elusive members of department staff, all to no avail. Exam results were what mattered and none would be reviewed.

Whether it was something done in desperation, I don't know. Until we made the appropriate enquiry neither Mike nor I knew exactly where the career development officer's office was on campus. I sat down. Mike Judd pulled up a chair immediately behind me and stayed silent.

Exactly why he went with me neither of us can remember, only that he seemed to be ever present during those three years, and so why not? To us it seemed natural, whereas to others, including the bespectacled man before us it probably appeared rather unusual to say the least. We were not after all, teenage children looking for professional advice with the guiding hand of an attending parent, but two grown men who were probably not that much younger than the man asking the questions.

'How can I help you, Mr Maddocks?'

It was not an unreasonable question. My answer on the other hand was something else.

'Well,' I replied, 'I've just got my degree result. Not great, but I do have an important race this weekend in Plymouth and an even more important one in Edinburgh in a few weeks time. Oh, I should say that I'm a race walker. After that I am thinking about moving to Plymouth where I will have to think about what I am going to do next...' Beyond this I do not clearly recall what I said, only that I spoke for an indeterminate amount of time going off on all kinds of tangents. I believe that I may have veered back to career aspirations with the mention of journalism and vague references to the legal profession before clouding relevant issues by wandering off course again by returning to my racing goals. '...It's difficult to know what to do for the best.'

Once I finally decided to stop talking, there was a deafening silence. It was broken only by the merest hint of a suppressed snigger over my shoulder. I'd completely bamboozled the poor man. So convoluted was my answer, even I had no idea where I had gone with it.

Agreed that I had a lot of thinking to do, I was quite satisfied with a firm handshake and the man's best wishes for the future. I rose from my chair and walked out grateful not to make eye contact with the bowed head of my friend sat directly behind me.

Naturally, once we got outside Mike Judd was less forgiving, or at least he would have been if he could have stopped laughing.

The event in Plymouth over the weekend was a triumph. Richard Pannell rightly accepted the plaudits as the principal organizer. His thorough preparation work over the past year was evident from the start of the Saturday evening International women's 5km and 10km track races between Great Britain, Norway and Sweden until the end of the men's national 35km city centre road event on Sunday morning.

Like George Williams with his promotion of walking races in Bournemouth the previous year, Richard made the rallying call to all our club members to help him stage a great national championship that would attempt to rival anything that was happening in the running world at that time. Through business sponsorship, thousands were raised. His promise to local council authorities was that if they helped him stump up more funds then *Plymouth* might be a part of a revolution to raise the profile of race walking in Britain.

Richard somehow managed to organize accommodation for competitors and officials at the notoriously famous *Grand*, a hotel with oodles of grandeur that provides the most spectacular of views overlooking Plymouth Hoe and the English Channel beyond. He also got the cooperation of the police, whereupon the city centre was closed for what would be 17 laps on a circuit that went up and around Royal Parade and promised TV coverage and on-course race commentary from an open-top double-decker bus. I provided what I hoped would be 60 minutes of taped music aimed at inspiring the walkers in front of good crowds. *The Walk of life* by Dire Straits, *Walk Tall* by Val Doonican, *I'm Walking* by Fats Domino, *We are the Champions* by Queen, and *Simply the Best* by Tina Turner did it for most, but not it seemed for my so-called friend, Lisa Langford.

Half way through the 35km race I was in the midst of a hard fought battle with at least six other men who had at some stage contested the lead, when the music changed to Spandau Ballet singing *True*, a ballad of nauseating sugariness. Lisa had evidently by the start of its third airing heard enough of my rolling tape. I was not happy, but with a race to complete I needed to get on with the job in hand.

Beyond the 25km point, the leading group had whittled down to three. I was needing to grit my teeth just to stay in touch with Mike Smith and Daz Thorn, two young men from the Coventry walking club who were five maybe six years my junior. The reduced level of training during the weeks leading up to and including my exams had left me short of endurance strength.

Daz glanced across at me and must have sensed how much I was straining to hang on. He injected more pace and pushed on ahead. Mike Smith fell back behind me at which point I thought I would do well to retain second position.

By 30kms my legs were shot. There were only three laps to go and I was getting fantastic vocal encouragement from those who still saw the chance of a *home* race winner. Daz was only 40 yards ahead and apparently beginning to wilt. I responded to the raised level of cheering by first catching and then passing him before going on to win in 2.47.54, a win that gave me my first national road title. Mike finished second, Daz slipped back to third just ahead of a clutch of walkers from various other midland clubs until Edmund broke that sequence by coming home in seventh with his best ever time of 2.58.04.

Afterwards there was a real buzz amongst all the athletes, helpers and supporters at a civic hall reception where the talk was of new beginnings for race walking; if this kind of city centre racing was repeated up and down the country, a boom in popularity and status was really possible. The Mayor of Plymouth reiterated this when he presented prizes and spoke enthusiastically about what a great day for the city it had been.

Brief highlights were shown on local TV the following day, and there was a good spread in the newspapers. The efforts by Richard Pannell, assisted by Edmund and his father Eric Shillabeer, helped convince me that with their kind of help and energy, a new start living and training in Plymouth could be just what I needed after the Commonwealth Games.

From the peak of Arthur's Seat, the panoramic views of Edinburgh city were breathtaking. It had taken Andy Bainborough and I little more than 15 minutes of easy walking to ascend the grassy slope that at its summit, 800 foot up, overlooked Dunsapie Loch. I hadn't seen Andy for six days, not since the eight hour journey I made with him and his friend John on the train from Exeter to Edinburgh via Newcastle. While they began their package holiday that included watching events at the Games, I had moved into Pollock Halls and Cowan House where I was accommodated with the rest of the English team.

It was seven-thirty in the evening. Andy flipped up the hood of his fleece and shivered. The cold blustery wind peppered with spots of rain was not what either of us had expected, much like the earlier part of my day.

'It's true,' I said. 'I had lunch with the Queen and Prince Philip, and Edward was there as well. I was only a few feet away on another table. I could almost hear her talking.'

'What was she saying?'

'I don't know. It was noisy in the refectory, probably the most packed that it's been since I've been here. It's just like a school canteen, only bigger.'

We glanced around the wild highland landscape. Familiar landmarks caught our attention. In the distance, the huge medieval grey stone of Edinburgh Castle was easy to spot, Princes Street was distinguishable by its length through the heart of the city, and Meadowbank, the stadium where we had already seen medals won in the first days of athletics competition. There was plenty to talk about.

A lot of events had undeniably been weakened as a result of a boycott by a large number of African, Asian and Caribbean countries. Once again I was saddened by politics and sport getting so entwined that the real losers were those athletes qualified to take part and denied the right to do so, largely by decisions of their respective Governments.

This time, of the 59 countries that were due to take part, 32 boycotted the Games in protest at the Margaret Thatcher government's attitude to its sporting links with South Africa, a country so affected by apartheid. As sad as that was, no known top walkers came from those countries boycotting the Games and therefore unlikely to have any bearing on the outcome of the men's 30km walk other than perhaps the number taking part. The withdrawal of Australia's David Smith on the other hand would.   I had previously got to know the two-time Olympian and witnessed him doing a super-fast 10km track time trial a few days earlier. I stood in awe, along with many of his teammates, who like me stopped their own training routines and watched the latter stages of an incredibly fast 38.40 walk. So it was a shock when I heard the reason for him pulling out a day or so later was a respiratory virus and fever. This was confirmed the following morning when he failed to turn up for an obligatory pre-race medical for all competing walkers.

This development would have tactical consequences for the race. When the matter was raised, all 11 walkers seemed cagey and reluctant to say too much more about it. Everyone was playing their cards close to their chest.

I walked back to Cowan House deep in thought and immediately started a full range of stretching exercises and a few hundred press-ups and sit-ups and considered my race tactics. Smith was a renowned fast starter and had been a virtual certainty to set the pace.

The significance of his withdrawal was predictably raised again by Harry Gration later that afternoon when he asked me, Ian McCombie and Martin Rush questions for a BBC pre-race recorded interview. Sitting side by side, we looked uniformly smart in collar and tie and our England team blazer last worn at the Meadowbank stadium during the opening ceremony. It was Ian, a recently qualified solicitor and arguably the most articulate one amongst us, who spoke first on the matter. He summed up the Smith question by saying that such was the standard of the other walkers the race was likely to be super-fast anyway.

Immediately after the interview we were away and boarding one of a convoy of buses headed for Holyrood Palace and a very special royal garden party.

Within minutes of taking a seat on the bus, a woman was up at the front on a microphone and calling for our attention. She emphasized to all the athletes that the evening was likely to be a unique occasion for most of us, a chance to meet the Queen and other members of the Royal family, that we should enjoy ourselves but only speak to any of our Royal hosts if first spoken to. The point was reiterated until enough nodding heads suggested that the right protocol was clearly understood.

To say it was an *evening* party was stretching the imagination. Arriving at six, we had been told to return to our bus by seven-thirty sharp. An hour and a half was all that we had to mingle amongst several hundred other British athletes, eat a nibble, quaff a drink and hope that you might snatch a word with a passing Royal.

I can only assume the same message had been conveyed on the other buses. The sight of suited and booted athletes pouring out and rushing away towards the surrounding grounds of the magnificent 16th Century royal residence like headless chickens, suggested that many perhaps thought the *first come first served* rule applied. I chose instead to step out and walk with Ian at a more sedentary pace, mindful of conserving energy for the next day. I was as keen as the next person to engage in a treasured chat with one of our hosts no matter how brief it might be.

In and out of crowded marquees we walked, ambling across manicured lawns catching fleeting glimpses of a Royal amid throngs of craned necks and smiling faces. The sense of history and occasion was not lost on us, but with less than 30 minutes to go our aimless maneuvering had got us nowhere. I saw our chances of a Royal chat slipping away.

'Right, that's it,' I said to Ian. 'We've got to make this happen. Follow me.'

Ian protested. 'No! Remember what that woman said.'

'Bugger that. C'mon, let's go.'

'No!'

I made a beeline for the nearest crowded gathering, Ian was in my slipstream still muttering his protests. I muscled my way into a melee of athletes readying themselves to speak to Prince Philip. Ignoring the disgruntled objections, I had rationalized that it was dog eat dog time. Ian meanwhile had sidled up next to me.

The Prince passed with not so much as a word. It was a setback for sure, but I was determined to try again. Ian protested yet stayed close.

Prince Philip moved on into a marquee and like stalkers we followed. Calculating his possible exit point, we strategically positioned ourselves and waited. Minutes later…bingo!

I can't really remember what was said; something fairly innocuous I think about the event we were doing, and then it was over. I think Ian was satisfied that we had bagged at least one Royal chat. Of course I was pleased, but with the clock ticking felt as if we had just started.   Amid a scrum of people inching its way towards us, Prince Charles came into view with Diana at his side.   We stood our ground. My heart was pounding as they came closer.

Diana appeared to be in animated conversation with someone as she slowly passed by in front of me.   It was so frustrating, but I resisted the strong temptation to interrupt. Prince Charles was a stride or two behind and similarly about to exit the marquee without even exchanging eye contact. Inexcusable it may have been, but I extended my hand across his torso in a manner difficult for him to ignore.   The Prince graciously saw fit to shake it, though probably unprepared for the firm grasp that I then had on him. Like a fish hooked on a line, I continued the handshake whilst reeling him in. Caught, he said hello and wished both Ian and I luck for our race. I was feeling impossibly smug and on a mission to top what we had just done. Nothing could excuse the next act of foolhardy audaciousness.

We stepped out of the marquee. Heavy spits of rain meant those that had gone prepared were moving about under their umbrellas. A distance away I saw a number of beefy looking men in dark suits walking either side of a familiar person carrying a particularly large umbrella.   I felt a surge of excitement as I strode on like a nuclear missile towards its next intended target. Ian held back.   He must have feared the worst. Moments later and without hesitation, I ducked beneath the large umbrella and came face to face with The Princess Royal, Princess Anne, offering up a toothy smile and saying, *hello, I hope you don't mind?*

Unlike her bodyguards, she barely flinched.   Deadpan, she very civilly suggested that my action was not a good idea. I immediately pulled back and apologized. The twitchiness of her bodyguards should have been warning enough, but her relaxed demeanor kept them at bay for those crucial seconds that ended with her returning a wry smile and moving on.

Perhaps I should have felt some shame? Instead, high on adrenalin I wanted more. Ian's reluctance to follow me was understandable, for in the space of a few minutes I had become a loose cannon, but, follow me he did, and by the time we boarded the bus to return back to Pollock Halls I am confident his share in my reminiscences are both good and excruciating in equal measure. Indeed, the final encounter was conceivably the most memorable one that neither of us is likely to forget.

In response to my question, the Queen had said that due to her other commitments, she was unable to watch our race. I asked if she might instead present the medals to the winning walkers, and that if she could, it would be a *great gesture* appreciated by super-fit athletes. Her busy schedule meant that it was not possible, and for that she apologised. Sat back on the bus, conversations were frenetic with boasts and counter-boasts over who had got to speak to which Royal. By contrast we kept our thoughts to ourselves and listened to the cross-fire of animated chat. I ignored the directive that a Royal should only be spoken to if spoken to first, and for that reason did not raise my head above the parapet for fear of being subjected to cries of foul play. I don't think either me or Ian were prepared to risk any sort of criticism so soon after our mad half hour of great fun.

It was the last day of July. An almighty burst of torrential rain had seen everyone diving for cover just as I and the other 30km walkers were being led out on to the Meadowbank track in readiness to race. Waiting for the repeat command to move on out of the concreted tunnel had delayed our stage-managed grand entrance by several minutes, enough extra time for the nerves to really build. Finally, after several long minutes, the downpour subsided and the call was made.

'Okay everyone, we're ready to go.'

Led by the same official who had made the call, we walked out in single file, each athlete accompanied by a young aide at our side carrying a bag primed to take kit from us once we were stripped down ready to race. The noise that greeted our appearance on the track was truly uplifting. There was no hope of spotting a familiar face as they would have been impossible to distinguish cowered beneath row upon row of umbrellas. At that moment I could only imagine where my Dad and Margot and other family and friends might be, whether beneath the myriad of colour or somewhere out on the roads.

Once the flurry of loosening up sprint walks had been done, we were called to starter's orders and on the fire of the pistol set on our way. Spontaneous applause accompanied a lap of the track that was done at a pace over 14kms per hour. It was a fast opening gambit by a breakaway pack that saw me tucked in behind the two Australians and Ian McCombie with two French Canadians a few strides back. I felt strong as we left the stadium and set out towards Portobello and roads adjacent to the Firth of Forth in the direction of Musselburgh before passing through Prestonpans and turning back at Cockenzie.

We had covered little more than a mile when the heavens opened up again. Against a swirling wind, I gritted my teeth, injected more speed and decided to really go for it. Immediately I pulled out a small gap. Fast footfall on wet tarmac heard from behind confirmed that I had not got too far away from Ian. Without needing to look around, I knew the other pace setters were also not far adrift by names called from supporters along the route.

Given the pouring rain, I was amazed at the number of people either side of the road watching our progress and shouting encouragement. By five miles, Ian and I had settled into a joint lead with Australia's Simon Baker a short distance in arrears with both Willie Sawall and Guillaume Leblanc within striking range.

Breathing heavy, I was feeling the strain. My ambition had got the better of me. Ian surged ahead. He was soon joined by Baker who passed me in the blink of an eye. By the halfway turn at Cockenzie I was lying third, over 20 seconds in arrears with Leblanc closing down fast.

Approaching the 20km point, in the far distance I saw that Baker had eased ahead of Ian who in turn appeared to be faltering at the same time that Leblanc was passing me. I was so distracted by foot pain that the Canadian ghosted past without me able to raise even a token spirited fight back. The rain had saturated my feet and softened the skin so much that I felt blisters forming with each stride. The encouragement from the sidelines was virtually constant. Mum, Edmund, Andy Bainborough, Phil Rudd, friends from Tiverton each and everyone bellowing words that implored a strong walk towards the finish. Within sight of the stadium, the rain finally relented allowing the sun to make a brief appearance before it disappeared behind the clouds again.

Turning away from the road towards the stadium entrance I was in an isolated race position, feeling both tired and relieved.

I have always thought it a cliché to say that fourth is the worst of all competitive finishing positions. Surely to finish fifth, sixth, 27th or lower is worse? I most definitely wanted to win a medal and the large crowd that cheered me all the way helped alleviate some of the lingering disappointment I was feeling as I approached the cluster of timekeepers at the finish.

After crossing the line I shook hands with the three men who had finished ahead of me. I then made my way around the track in order to recover my breath and soak up the atmosphere as other walkers arrived back in the stadium, their faces seemingly etched with pleasure and pain. I was about to leave for the changing rooms and a much needed hot shower, when I heard a familiar voice. It was a poignant moment for both Mum and I when we shared a big trackside hug.

Perhaps less than 30 minutes later the significance of my near medal miss really hit me. I was inside lying on a treatment table when I heard a fanfare of music signaling that another medal ceremony was about to commence. On a TV monitor I caught sight of officials leading out a line of three walkers towards the medal winners' podium. The introductions were made and the medals presented. Simon Baker was a worthy winner and when his national anthem piped up I felt a sense of shared pride tinged with an aching heart.

Afterward I heard a simple anecdote that illustrated the type of sportsmanship that still makes me proud to be a part of the race walking fraternity. During the second half of the race, Ian McCombie saw Baker drop his drinks bottle at a feed station due in part to the rain adversely affecting his bespectacled vision. Ian told reporters that he tried to help by upping his pace so as to catch up and offer the bottle of juice that he had collected for himself. The typically selfless act may have contributed to his undoing, first by the rash change of pace when he was himself struggling to hang on, and secondly by the bottle being returned with most of the contents drunk, leaving little left for him! No hard feelings were expressed.

1.	Simon Baker	Australia	2.07.47 (Games Record)
2.	Guillaume Leblanc	Canada	2.08.38
3.	Ian McCombie	England	2.10.36
4.	Chris Maddocks	England	2.12.42
5.	Willie Sawall	Australia	2.14.29
6.	Murray Day	New Zealand	2.15.11
7.	Martin Rush	England	2.16.01
8.	Steve Johnson	Wales	2.21.05
9.	Graham Seater	New Zealand	2.22.48
10.	Steve Partington	Isle of Man	2.23.02
	Francois Lapointe	Canada	disq

PART FOUR

Part four: A new beginning in Plymouth 1986

Moving into that first floor flat above the bookmaker's betting shop in Armada Street was a bit of a culture shock. Empty, soulless, plaster crumbling off the walls, it stank of cigarette smoke. Suffice to say that it was in a poor state of repair. On the plus side, it was up to me and Richard Pannell to make it habitable to live in. An old buddy of his owned the entire property and said that if we did the first floor refit he would pay for all the costs and for a period of time it was mine rent free. Problem was I have always been completely talentless when practicable dexterity is called for. Richard on the other hand had the necessary DIY skills and with me as his jobbing lackey we set about the renovations. Because his family plant-hire business was struggling at the time, he had more time on his hands than he would ordinarily have wished. His misfortune was my good fortune and though money was tight for everyone, over a period of months the work at the flat was finally done.

For a time, I slept on a second-hand sofa bed that I had bought from a charity shop for £20. The weeks of living in dust and general filth was eventually replaced with what I thought was half decent accommodation. Given a free rein to choose the decorative order, I have no doubt that by the time I moved out a year later, the first thing requiring changing by any discerning new occupant would have been the black ceilings and the Ferrari red doors each with their metallic gold trim. As for the black and white floral wall paper, well, I thought it was terrific until I saw the exact same in the Peckham flat used by the Trotter family in TV's Only Fools and Horses.

It soon became apparent that living on my own, in a less than salubrious part of town where I knew no one, was an experience that I did not enjoy. Returning each day to a one bedroom flat that continued to smell of grubby ash was also disheartening. The evenings at least were broken up by the part-time work at Edmund's veterinary surgery where I helped in the dispensary, answered the telephone, and generally assisted with the variety of pets brought into his busy practice for treatment.

I was shown new training routes, some good, some dangerous. For the sake of minimizing wasted time and travelling costs, I persisted with the latter until a near fatal accident was warning enough that I should stick to suitable quiet country roads; more about that later.

Becoming a new member at the Plymouth Health Studio was a godsend. Located in the leafy suburbs a short stroll from the surgery, Edmund had been a regular visitor for years. He initially paid my fees in return for extra bits of work at the practice and introduced me to some great people where enthusiastic training was the norm. Though small and dated by comparison to modern state-of-the-art health clubs, it was a perfect place for me to train and socialize. I learned that it had originated as a council owned post-war single-storey breeze-block building. Its use had gone through several reincarnations until it became an established gymnasium in the 1960's.

I discovered that a number of the older clientele prided themselves on being founding members. Arguably its greatest claim to fame was the visit by a youthful Arnold Schwarzenegger during the early days of his body building career. A photograph marking the occasion hung in the reception office. This was perhaps apt as Tony, the current owner, organised body building shows in the area. He did his best to keep the gym clean and tidy although the building's tired exterior was matched inside by an array of aging fitness training equipment that included multi-gym apparatus, stationary bikes, a rowing machine and a treadmill.

Perhaps most important of all, the club's friendly atmosphere was evident as soon as you walked through the door, though it might be true to say that membership included an unwritten rule that any sensitivity to verbal abuse be left on arrival at the reception desk. It suited me fine.

I soon established a three day a week routine at the gym where I would train up to three hours at a time doing floor mobility exercises, pumping iron and occasionally walking on the treadmill. Because I covered hundreds of miles on the road and track it was not always necessary for me to do more indoors. At the back through the saloon-type swing doors past the sun-beds and changing rooms there was a Jacuzzi and a sauna. Though use of these facilities proved a wonderful bonus over time, it wasn't quite so at the beginning.

Unlike the three men sharing the sauna with me, I was fairly new to the pleasures of using a sauna when a certain old boy persisted in adding another ladle of water to the hot coals.

With only a towel covering his modesty, the big hairy man lying naked on the top wooden tier merely grunted his dissatisfaction.

Richard Pannell likewise was unimpressed. 'Good God Percy, what are you doing? First you chuck on too much of that bloody eucalyptus oil, and now more water. I can hardly breathe. Are you trying to kill us?'

'Sorry.'

Had I the strength I might have laughed.

Richard shook his head and looked at me. His eyes were blood-shot, his face dripping in sweat. 'Go on mate. You were saying about the French race.'

Go on? The grains of sand from the egg timer on the wall had all but filtered through. We had been cooking in that sauna for nearly 20 minutes. Even my light silver crucifix and chain that I had worn irreligiously around my neck since 1978 was beginning to scorch my neck. Prior to the heavy gym workout, I had already done a long morning road session in record time. I was feeling tired even before I stepped into the big wooden box, now I was reduced to a state of pathetic weakness. What energy I had left would surely be needed to negotiate the step down from our perch and get out as soon as possible for a cooling shower.

I also needed to be mindful not to further aggravate the sore hamstring muscle that had continued to bother me for weeks and required several sessions of physiotherapy treatment. At least it had successfully helped me carry on churning out successive months of good training with satisfying race results until that disappointing track race at Brighton in September.

'What more can I say Rich? My pace judgement that day was awful.' I slumped forward, buried my sweaty face in my sweaty hands and groaned. The memory of those 50 laps came flooding back. It may have only been a two-sided 'B' International match against France, but I so wanted to impress at what was my first selection for the Great Britain team over the 20km distance.

Starting fast, I had shot to the front and built up a big lead that saw me reach quarter distance in 20.41. I had already lapped the entire field bar one. From that point on my pace gradually slowed. The 88.07 that I eventually clocked was good, but I was very fit and should have walked several minutes quicker.

Richard needed no reminding of my little prank at the prize presentation dinner that evening and the stir that I caused. For so long I had been criticized by a number of important British walk officials, not least for my apparent scruffiness. As my student status could no longer be used as a plausible reason for my apparent offensive dress sense, I had hatched a plan for what I thought might be an amusing riposte.

The directive was for informal smart casual wear. Only my room-mate, Phil Vesty knew that I was deliberately leaving my entrance to the last possible minute. I walked in, heads turned, people laughed, some shook my hand. Like some prized peacock, I walked on smiling knowing that I was completely overdressed, wearing a dinner suit. The dismissive look on the faces of my usual critics was priceless. I might not have got away with the stunt had my race completely turned on its head. A fact of which, Richard was keen to remind me.

He wiped the sweat from his eyes and said, 'But you won it. At the end of the day, you got maximum points for the team, and that was the most important thing.'

He was right of course. Richard often was. I knew that I was lucky to have him and Edmund as two men I could confide in and get intelligent, well thought through advice. I was not always prepared to listen. Too often, I was glass half empty where they were most definitely glass half full. My other race performances at Dawlish had reflected some of the super fast training sessions that I had been knocking out on the rural roads around Dartmoor and those more precariously done on the traffic-laden A38 dual-carriageway leading to and from the Devon and Cornwall borders.

In each of the six mile club races I had consistently walked fast times around 39 minutes 50 seconds, and when we staged the South West Open 10km Championship in November I was way ahead in 41 minutes 13 seconds. I won the Chippenham to Calne '6' again, the Belgrave '7' in London, and best of all, the Pewsey Cup '7' at Calne in Wiltshire.

There are occasions in all athletes' lives when they look back and can say there was a day when just about everything about the performance went right. So it was that December day when the sunshine made it a perfect afternoon for racing the Pewsey '7'.

The first two miles I was content to walk at the front at around seven minute per mile pace shoulder to shoulder with Jimmy Ball. Tall, lean, blond haired, he was a younger man from the Southampton club who so often found himself walking in my shadow at races.

Starting fast, once we had got beyond the few farms where the roads were left notoriously slippery by copious deposits of cow pats, I turned on the afterburners and surged away from Jimmy.

It is a truly wonderful feeling when you feel so fit and unafraid to go at full speed and fearless of slowing in the latter stages. I pressed and pressed, motoring through those country lanes, only bothered by the occasional glare of the sun as I turned corners. The final push to the line was a joy. I am convinced that had someone stepped forward and said keep going until you have done 20kms, I would have done so just to prove that I could have turned that unofficial British all-comers seven mile best time of 45 minutes 29 seconds into an even more significant metric performance. It is all hypothetical of course, but does at least allow the likes of me, glass half empty, to have the occasional speculative leap of fantasy.

In fact, for one brief moment when we were rudely interrupted in that sauna, I might have been excused for thinking that I had indeed leapt into some parallel universe.

'Hey, Chris,' Edmund said, as he pulled open the door and leaned in.

'Oh God!' I jolted upright and accidently elbowed Richard.

'Ouch!'

'Whoa!' Edmund clung to the door handle and veered backwards, his nostrils no doubt assaulted by a hot blast of eucalyptus. He ignored our initial disgruntled groans and eyeballed the elderly man sat on the top tier behind us at the back and said, 'Percy, you've done it again, you daft old...'

I interjected, 'Ed. What the hell are you wearing?'

Edmund ignored Richard's laugh and with characteristic eagerness said, 'I just got it. I've been walking on the treadmill – testing it for comfort. It's a bit tight. I'm wearing it on behalf of the CPL when I do the London marathon.'

The big hairy man tilted his head and mumbled, 'Well, I'll be damned. It's Postman Pat's black and white cat. There's a saucer of milk outside. Now, shut the bloody door, will ya. Some of us are trying to sleep!'

Standing six foot in his trainers, Ed Shillabeer's craggy facial features and oversized nose was framed neatly by the hooded cat suit topped by fluffy triangular ears sent to him in gratuity by the Cats Protection League. Obligingly he stepped back and slammed the door shut.

Richard and I knew Ed all too well. So, it was with only a degree of incredulity that we sat there and watched him peer back through the steamy porthole in the door. I assumed that he must have gathered the tail up in his hand because he produced the white tip of it and held it to the side of his face.

He said, 'I think I might need a larger size. And, I'll probably have to safety-pin this to my hip. I can't have this flopping around my ankles.'

Too hot and bothered to listen to more, I said, 'Ed! Now's not the time.'

I saw him tug at one of his cat's ears and pull off his hood.

'No, of course not,' he said. 'Okay, I'm off now. See you both, tomorrow morning? Usual seven o'clock start?'

'Yes.'

'Yeah, okay.'

Edmund and I had established a routine of training together in Central Park on certain days of the week. We used a measured one mile lap of wide parkland paths that went up through a long avenue of trees and around the Plymouth Argyle football ground and on past acres of rolling green playing fields. Six or seven laps would be typical for us at that time of morning, and because of our different speeds, he walked in one direction, I walked in the other. Richard occasionally joined in, either with a shorter training session or a stroll with his dogs and an opportunity to watch our progress and holler abuse if necessary.

Edmund stepped away from the porthole. We heard him call back.

'Good. Oh, and one other thing. If you want to have a laugh, go and check the Jacuzzi. Jim's in there, belly-up again.'

The image of a big fat man asleep next door floating in the Jacuzzi, possibly drunk, was not enough to encourage me to want to step out. Dehydration was another thing all together.

Training was hard, it had to be. I treated it like others would treat a job. Sometimes it was enjoyable, other times it was monotonous and felt like sheer drudgery. But ambition to be the best you can be is an intoxicating stimulant. I would forward plan my Monday to Sunday sessions months in advance whilst taking into account the proposed races throughout the year, targeting the big championships. Dreams of competing at a second Olympic Games drove me on, particularly when I was feeling down. A breath of fresh air was Lisa Langford. She had called me and asked if I would coach her. When she came to visit, and when I visited her, I was organised.

Our weekends would be a mix of speed work, longer endurance walks, technique analyses with references to the best available video coverage of top walkers, and race planning. For her there was no foreseeable opportunity to compete at an Olympic Games, at least not then. In fact it would take until 1992 before she and other female walkers would benefit from gender equality and be presented with a first chance of becoming an Olympian.

Prior to 1984, women ran no further than 3000m at the Olympic Games, remember that's equivalent to running less than two miles. Incredibly, from that point onwards it went from one extreme to another with the introduction of similar race distances for both men and women. The first ever women's Olympic marathon was won by the host nations' Joan Benoit. Parity for female walkers around the world would take longer. I already knew that Lisa was a very determined individual. Her time would come.

We had dual targets for 1987: The World Cup walks in New York in May and the World Athletic Championships in Rome later in the summer. By helping her with training schedules, I had to take account her study commitments at Leeds University. Prone to injury, she was not without problems. One saving grace was that she was also an excellent swimmer, so when injury did intervene, she was more than prepared to train extra hard in the swimming pool. With all this in mind, I was absolutely astounded by criticisms laid at my door by team management when we both attended a national squad weekend at a hotel in the Midlands that winter.

We were one of about 20 *elite* walkers attending the get-together with four team officials, Peter Marlow, Amos Seddon, David Rosser and Peter Markham. I roomed with Ian McCombie and apart from the actual training there was a lot on the classroom agenda much of which led to heated debate in the conference hall.

Top of the list was the rise in global walking standards and arguments as to why British race walking appeared to be getting left behind. Accusations flew thick and fast, different persons blaming the other. We discussed international and domestic racing fixtures, the need to improve performance standards, and communication between management and individuals. As was often the case, I vocalized the vast differences between our seemingly amateurish set up and the more professional setup where walkers trained together frequently throughout the year with suitable systems of support through top level coaching, medical assistance, appropriate acclimatization and superior facilities. By comparison, *we* met once or twice a year for a day or two of training with minimal time for team discussions; this, I argued, was not enough to turn our squad of walkers into world beaters.

I mooted the idea that perhaps some of us could try living and training together. I said that with the help of contacts made in Plymouth it might be possible for me to organize a large rented flat to be made available at a relatively low cost for up to six walkers. Radical maybe, but the communal flat would provide a base from which we could push each other to a higher level. Detailed logistics like how we may earn part-time money could be worked out if the idea appealed in principle. I said that I already knew of a few men not present who had expressed an interest and wished to be kept informed of any developments. In the room there were a number of nodding heads that suggested I might be onto something.

Peter Markham went someway to bursting my bubble when he argued that if this was an attempt to try and emulate the strict regime of squad training done by

Eastern European athletes, then it was an idea that would probably fail. He argued that they had a different cultural mindset to people like us in Western Europe. Out of courtesy, I listened to opinion that I simply did not agree with. I said that I for one would be prepared to commit and make the sacrifices necessary. One proven way of doing that is to train with others who share that goal. My thoughts were dismissed as fanciful.

If the red mist had not descended after my thump of frustration on the table, I might have been more aware of the audible wave of deep sighing, pursed lips and eye rolling. I was about to go off again on another infamous Maddocks rant:

It serves no purpose to rub our noses in it that Britain once produced walkers that won Olympic and World medals. The likes of Whitlock, Thompson, Matthews and Nihill were great in their day, we know that, but times have moved on. Some of those guys would not come close to even qualifying for the major championships now, let alone win them. I met Don Thompson at the Chippenham race a few weeks ago. He said that he could never walk six miles anywhere near as fast as 40 minutes **and** *be a good 50km walker. The fact is that some of the best 50km walkers in the world now are also the fastest sprint walkers in the world, and the ability to do that takes an awesome amount of training. That cannot realistically be done around full-time work. There are good walkers in this room, but to have a chance of any one of us becoming a great walker it would help if we had the time and resources to train together more often. Some ill-informed people think that we've got it so much better now, that, for example, the athletic tracks are better, and we've now got better quality shoes to wear. Well, 99% of any big race is on the road. As for shoes...I've got quite a few actually, most of them are falling apart! I walk so many miles in training I'd have to chuck them out after a couple of months if I didn't repair them myself with shoe goo. I don't know about the rest of you but I can't afford forty or fifty quid every couple of months. And yes, as some of you do know, Adidas have just started to sponsor me with a few items of kit, including shoes. It will help, but it doesn't mean that I am suddenly going to go faster. It takes a lot more than that. I saw Ken Matthews once. He told me that he had racing shoes made for him. Funny that, because I'd been told that all our best walkers used to wear clogs.*

I drew breath and glanced around the room. The ripple of a few nervous laughs probably did little to compensate for the overwhelming stony silence that ensued once I finally decided to shut up.

I can see how my thoughts would not necessarily have endeared me to the company present. Predictably, my thoughts were met with some derision, and insinuations that I was not being constructive. That was a matter of opinion. I would acknowledge however that for all the critical infighting, the management team was there as volunteers, for the love of a sport that each of them had committed decades as athletes and administrators. Times were definitely changing. Television deals, corporate and private sponsorship meant that there was an

103

increasing amount of money pumped into sports previously considered amateur based, but very little of it was being filtered to our event. For many of us it was galling, but with no significant funding from above there simply was no meaningful budget to work with.

Of course I was not finished. I had also argued that we needed to raise the quality of our race promotions just as my club had attempted the year before when we staged the national 35km championship in Plymouth. I had hoped that it might have set a new benchmark for future national championships. Unfortunately, there had been little sign of it throughout 1986 season. Disappointed yet undeterred, I said that our Dawlish club which we had recently rebranded and renamed, *Plymouth City Walkers*, planned to lay on a 50km race early in the New Year. This would give British walkers a chance of a fast time on a good race circuit in what we hoped might be favourable weather conditions.

For reasons inconceivable to me, my suggestions were rebuffed and in an extraordinary turn of events, a vote of no confidence was made against the proposed race. *A vote of no confidence, were they serious?* I was embarrassed to sit there and listen to counter arguments that suggested it was either the wrong time of year, athletes would not be ready to race, fixture clashes with established races, and so it went on. The event needed a kick up the backside and too many people could not see the urgency for change.

It should have come as no surprise to me when I was later taken to one side by the team management and serious questions were asked of my training methods and whether or not I was the best person to be coaching Lisa. In their eyes I had continually failed to realize my *immense potential*, perhaps, they said, *more than any other Briton, ever!* In spite of all the harsh words spoken, I was covertly flattered by their criticism and moved by it so much that I wrote it verbatim in my training diary as a permanent reminder of that particular verbal assault. My head must have been all over the place, because I also wrote: *My thoughts are now completely mixed up.*

One thing was clear however. I did know how to make life difficult for myself. National squad get-togethers were an opportunity for fact finding and a chance to spend a couple of days training with a number of good walkers. I was mentally exhausted.

Christmas came and went. My Wolseley car, bought from my brother six years earlier, the same one that had seen me through my student days and taken me to and from hundreds of training sessions had failed its final MOT. Until I was ready to release it into the grips of the men at the scrap yard, Mum and Toby allowed me to park it in their driveway. Eighteen months it sat there gathering moss while its replacement, a big, boxy, cheap, dark green Maxi caused me no end of further heartache.

Bill Dawe was forever coming to my rescue when the damn car broke down. Short and rotund with unkempt jet black hair he had a thick moustache that reminded me of many Eastern European men that I had seen on my travels. He was principally a friend of Edmunds', who worked as a mechanic out of a messy garage in a backstreet around the corner from my flat. Bill may have sold me that *pup*, but he was also keen to keep it on the road especially as he thought it might help me get to the next Olympic Games.

A creature of habit, I did not cope well with the last minute change of plans caused by the Maxi not starting in the morning and delaying my preferred training sessions out in the countryside. There would be other times stranded out on the moors after a walk when all I wanted to do was get home, have a bath, and eat something. Instead, there were too many *Basil Fawlty moments* when I had an overwhelming desire to thrash my *dead* car with any available branch, and probably would have done so had I any energy left. On those exasperating occasions, it was more important that I had enough coins with me and find the nearest telephone kiosk and call for help. These problems aside, my 1987 season did at least get off to a good start.

First, there was a course record 15km road win at Steyning in West Sussex. After that, though Ian McCombie did beat me on the Isle of Man late February over 20kms, our race long duel ended with both of us recording fast times of 83.25 and 84.10 respectively. I was satisfied with my race and even more pleased for Lisa when she won the women's 10km event with a British road best of 47.53.

Around this period of time I was also attending various coaching clinics and seminars at Birmingham, at Brighton, Yeovil and closer to home at the college of St Mark and St John in Plymouth. All were interesting but also served as a distraction that was becoming increasingly difficult to justify. I may have got the experience of mixing with men and women who shared my love of athletics and acquired paper qualifications, but I needed to concentrate on my primary goal of achieving the best race results.

I celebrated my 30th birthday by going to Bournemouth and winning the Piers' six miles in 40.27 in spite of feeling truly awful with a bad cold. The symptoms fortunately had subsided by the following Friday when I boarded a plane at Heathrow along with 21 other senior and junior, male and female athletes. I was honoured and a little surprised to have been named team captain by team management for our trip to Bekecscaba in Hungary. I wondered if this was their way of trying to appease me. Whatever the reason, it was a proud moment.

Ten hours it took us to get to our destination, nearly five spent cramped up on a coach driving across country. Tired and hungry on arrival, our hosts at our weekend hostel retreat may have only spoken few words of English, but a smiling face and open gestures can win over many a friend. Basic furnishings, skinny stray dogs, drab clothes, this was not an affluent area, but I thought it had a warmth about it and sensed that this was going to be a good weekend.

It certainly started well. Everyone seemed prepared to walk off the travel fatigue with a quick change of clothes and embark on a short session before our evening buffet meal. Pointed towards a cycle path around the side of the hostel, it proved ideal for a chatty team bonding walk of ten minutes out, ten minutes back.

Less of a highlight was the watery soup, cold meat, bland cheese and stale bread that did little to satisfy ravenous hunger pangs. If there was a time when I may have wished to have been absolved of any responsibility as team captain it was probably the moment when team management gathered us around. They said this was not going to be simply a GB versus Hungary match with perhaps one or two guest walkers toeing the line. Instead we learned that extra race entries had been accepted to the point that it had become a multi-nation contest with 12 different Eastern European countries taking part. The initial silence was deafening. An almighty crossfire of questions ensued: who, what, where, when, why? For a moment, I thought there was going to be a mutiny. It was time to put my captain's hat on.

'Don't let this overwhelm you,' I said. 'See it as an opportunity to produce your best and beat some really good walkers.' A clenched fist was enough. This was my Rocky Balboa moment. If I could have got them to have run up the steps, punched the sky and screamed *we are the champions* I would have done so, only, I think we were all too hungry to be bothered.

Saturday was a designated rest day. The hosts had laid on an escorted visit to the local museum, a treat that held little appeal for me or my team-mate, Les Morton. Instead, we met up with Ed Shillabeer and Richard Pannell. Both were holidaying in a nearby town they had previously discovered two years earlier on a racing trip, and where they knew it was possible to relax and enjoy time wallowing in the most amazing public thermal spa baths.

First impressions walking in, I was unimpressed. It was poorly lit, in places bubbled paint was peeling off the walls, tiles were cracked, and the steamy pool rather than the huge bathing area that I imagined, looked similar in size and as noisy to any regular swimming pool back home. Oh, and the smell? Oh God, the smell was horrible, like being hit by rotten eggs. It was difficult to care if bathing in waters that contained sulphurous acid, salt bromine, carbonate or iodine offered medicinal benefits or not, it still smelt of rotten eggs. It was enough to make novices like me want to turn back.

'It gets better,' Richard said.

The sight and sounds of hundreds of men and women, boys and girls, so obviously having a good time was enticing enough to give it a try. It was cooler than I thought at first.

'Let's move on,' Edmund said.

Les and I were mystified. Move on where? We got out, grabbed our towels and were guided through a marbled archway into an even bigger pool area, more people more heat. It was out of this world, and there would be more to come. We soon discovered that the initial dip was only the first of several pools and would prove to be a brilliant way to spend a couple of hours wafting in the soothing waters until even the tightest muscle relaxed; better than any pre-race massage I could ever remember.

On our arrival back at the hostel it was a lot busier than when we left with lots of unfamiliar faces milling about in tracksuits. Vicky Lawrence, the prettiest junior possibly ever to grace a GB tracksuit unsurprisingly had no end of East European suitors vying for her attention. Sitting in a corner with empty coffee cups, we saw a group of our team-mates. They looked bored. One of them spoke up.

'Peter's not happy. I think you guys might be in trouble.'

Considering it objectively, I guess it was a fair cop. We had not informed team management as to what we were doing and where we were going, *and* we had missed team photographs. Thinking we'd get it over with, we wasted no time in going before the hanging committee. Standing there like naughty school boys we listened to the complaints and duly took the rollicking on the chin.

'What if something had happened?'

'...A bad example to the rest of the team, particularly for the youngsters.'

The air was a bit frosty for a while but I think our apologies were accepted. Certainly everything seemed to be back on an even keel later that evening when all the team reconvened for an entertaining quiz on race walking with Chris Berwick asking the questions. Full of good natured banter, he had an incentive not to make it too late a finish as his race started at 7am.

The 50km men were off first. The junior men and senior ladies started exactly one hour later. By the time I lined up at 9am for the start of the 20km event, the Hungarian folk dancers were in full swing as the musicians played. Race commentary competed with the sounds of horns, claxons, whistles and cheering all from a sizeable crowd that had gathered up and down the one kilometer stretch of flat tarmac.

My spirits were lifted after seeing Lisa win her race in 46.09 for yet another improvement on her British record, and then, amid a stream of other walkers going by I saw Ed continuing to perform well in his race.

Once the gun fired for the 20km men it was immediately evident how much faster we would be walking compared to those already competing by how quickly we caught and sped past. I kept close order with Sandor Urbanik who I knew to be the local hero and the face seen by many on the pre-race advertising banners posted liberally around. One of the fastest indoor walkers in the world, I also knew that if I was bold enough to go at his pace that I might achieve a fast time. It was inspirational to stay close to him throughout the race distance. He crossed the line just 13 seconds ahead of me and my reward for what was a 20km International debut walk was a new personal best time of 83.50. Behind me, Les was the next British finisher in 13th position with Andi Drake a few seconds back in 15th.

Meanwhile Richard was still manning a drinks station and overseeing Edmund splash his way through the rain and the latter stages of his race. He eventually came home in 9th and for a third time achieved a 50km result around 4 hours 28 minutes. He was pleased, as was I. The team had done well, with a number of good individual performances.

There was no room for recriminations afterwards, not least against me as I had ducked below the 84 minute qualifying time for the World Athletic Championships in Rome. After the races, before the evening dinner and disco, the mood was upbeat as most of the competing athletes accepted the invitation to board coaches for the short trip into nearby Gyula for a post-competition sprawl in the glorious spa baths along with the masses.

I am prepared to concede that the quote, *you're your own worst enemy* could sometimes be levelled at me. Mischievous, immature now and then perhaps, but I never meant to deliberately antagonize people. And so it was when I said that I was not available to compete for Great Britain in an important multi-nation walks International match in East Germany. I said so knowing questions would undoubtedly be asked about where my priorities lay, as was the case when I joined the Western College Players.

The Players were a group of local thespians who met every week, and twice a year staged various productions for shows around Plymouth. Richard's wife, Janet, was a local celebrity in the world of musicals. A natural mezzo soprano, she had a beautiful voice and head-lined many shows. The world of theatre really appealed to me, but with no talent at all for singing it was she that initially escorted me one night to the rehearsal hall, not far from my home and left me there like a mother would leave a child on his first day at school.

Relatively young, I was welcomed with opened arms. As wonderful as the group were, they appeared to consist primarily of older, middle-class folk. It seemed that if you were willing and youngish, more often than not, a part was available in the cast list. Within weeks, I had gone from complete novice to playing the part of Jack Worthing – a character known as Ernest to his dandified friend Algernon Moncrieff in an extract from the Oscar Wilde play, the Importance of Being Ernest.

My commitment to the role was sorely tested though when co-directors, husband and wife team Gerald and Jill Nicholas approached me and asked if I might consider having my shoulder-length hair cut for the live performances. It was a heart sink moment. This was big. I rang my Mum and told her that I had reserved her tickets and that scissors were being sharpened.

'Oh no,' she whined. 'You're not having all those lovely curls cut off. Think of what your Nan would say?'

My Mum had spent the best part of 15 years telling me to get my hair cut. It may have been a bit of a shock when the curtain went up, but I think I saw her down there sat amongst the audience next to Toby clapping approvingly. A farcical comedy set in Victorian London, it was a joy to be on stage and hear the laughs as dear old Marion Grinter delivered the famous theatrical line said by her character, Lady Bracknell…*A handbag?*

A variety show entitled, *love and marriage* the series of short plays had proved a success with audiences in our week long run at a variety of venues that started its opening night in a village hall and finished at a beautiful velvet-seated Victorian playhouse. Greeted first on the door by a very prim lady who seemed overly keen to stress how much her WI group and friends were looking forward to the show. Thankfully, numbers were swelled by a collection of farmers and their offspring, some of whom looked as if they had been dragged in off the fields if the mud splattered boots was anything to go by. By contrast, it was the occasional distraction caused by the clatter of cutlery and swing doors that stuck in my mind once we moved on to the Derriford hospital cafeteria. Whilst performing on the temporarily erected stage, it was necessary to ignore the comings and goings of those few nightshift staff who ventured into eat and drink. Some of whom appeared either nonplussed by the intrusion caused by the traveling band of actors, or mildly amused at what for them was a free show. The week at least ended on a high with a standing ovation from an appreciative full house in the sumptuous Globe theatre.

It was different to anything that I had done before and I loved it. I had been bitten by the acting bug. I wanted to learn more and so, one evening a week joined two other younger members of the cast, and drove to the home of former pro-actor Larry Sanders. Larry was a lovely old chap who lived in a remote hamlet with his memories. If only half the stories told were true, he most assuredly had enjoyed a rich acting life before sharing tea and scones and tutoring us in his living room. I think it is safe to say that our level of enthusiasm was probably higher than our wooden, hammy attempts at impressing our host. Larry was too much of a gent' to say so of course.

Acting limitations aside, it was a novel experience that contributed to me being cast in an even more demanding role in the Players' next production of Yellow Sands, a West Country play set in the 1920's and written by Eden Phillpotts and his daughter Adelaide. Unfortunately, I had not foreseen the clash of dates with the International walks in East Germany. I had read through the script and seen that the part of Arthur, a philandering country bumpkin, meant that rehearsals would be particularly challenging. Not least because I would have great chunks of dialogue which included another on-stage marriage proposal and a fight scene with my impassioned idealist stage cousin, Joe.

I even took my script with me to New York in order to read and reread my lines. Travelling out before the weekend of World Cup races and afterwards by staying on for an extra week of sightseeing and training, meant I would miss two weeks of group rehearsals. Either side of the weekend walks, it was a whirlwind of tourist visits to Chinatown, the Empire State Building, Soho, the Statue of Liberty, and a Manhattan boat trip.

The races in Central Park routed over a 2.5km U-shaped course were nothing short of unbelievable. From 7am on Saturday I watched the 50km event with thousands of others and saw East Germans' Ronald Weigel, Hartwig Gauder and Deitmar Meisch complete the first ever 1,2,3 podium finish by walkers from one nation in the history of the competition. Behind them, the east European dominance was there for all to see as the next four places was filled by men from the USSR. A staggering 23 walkers went under four hours.

In women's walking, China was fast becoming the new powerhouse to challenge the USSR. The first race off on Sunday morning was the 10km event. Yan Hong did eventually cross the line in what seemed at first to be a new World Cup record time of 43.03. She was however told by a race official of her disqualification just moments before she was about to answer questions at a post-race news conference. This left two soviet women, Olga Krishtop and Irina Strakhova and another Chinese walker taking the top spots. The men's 20km race was due to start soon after the conclusion of this race.

I had not helped my own cause by dashing up and down the circuit watching the woman's walk unfold and in particular keeping a close eye on how Lisa was doing. I got so wrapped up in the excitement that I had little time to gather my breath before the start of my own race. I was on hand though when she collapsed over the line in exhaustion after finishing 11th in a new British record time of 45.42. The other girls were coming in thick and fast. I was still reeling from what I thought was a brilliant performance when the 20km men were called to starter's orders.

Ian McCombie tapped me on the shoulder and suggested that we might work together. It was a surprise, and if anything I was quite flattered, especially as he had shown the capability of beating me in the majority of our races against each other. I said, okay. We were fairly evenly matched, but neither of us could really foresee what was going to happen.

The gun was fired and as 137 men shot away, I had never ever known anything like it. Like a greyhound out of the traps, I got swept along with the blinding pace, elbowed in the arms in the chest, kicked in the ankles, all accidently returned to anyone near me. I had no idea where Ian was in the melee. There was no time for altruism until things settled down. One lap done I could not hear the time called by the timekeepers such was the noise but believed I was under 10 minutes and in about 50th position. It was ridiculously fast and only about 50th!

At some point over the next two laps, Ian and I came together. We gradually picked our way through the field, passing men who were presumably suffering more than us. Traffic cones separated walkers going in opposite directions. I could see a trio of Mexicans mixing it at the front with more top soviets and two Columbians.

When I detected Ian drifting away from our group, I turned and over my shoulder shouted back 'C'mon, catch up.' I felt an almighty spasm in my ribs as I twisted back. The sickening pain took several minutes to dissipate.

Presumably the call was enough to spur him on towards a fight back. He was back on my shoulder within the time it took to cover another half lap. We stayed locked together somewhere in the top 30 for the next few kilometers, until I started to feel the pace and slipped back. It may well have been my imagination, but at that moment Ian kicked on.

The race was won by Carlos Mercenario. The video footage shown that evening during a lavish prize presentation held at the Sheraton hotel showed the 20 year old birthday boy crossing the line arms aloft in triumphant fashion and immediately draped in a Mexican flag. Just six seconds behind the first of two men from the USSR closed in. Ian pulled 20 seconds and four places clear of me by the finish clocking 84.13 for 23rd position. Of the 38 countries taking part, Britain finished 10th.

The following day as teams departed for home, myself, Andi Drake, Lisa Langford and Irene Bateman all moved uptown to Apartment 320 on 83rd street and the home of Stella Cashman, an Irish immigrant race walker who had agreed prior to our trip to put us up for a week. While our aches and pains settled, we did the tourist bit by visiting more places and training steadily in Central Park along with all the hordes of power walkers, fun runners and roller-bladers while others either went about their business or chose more sedate pleasures like kite flying or picnicking.

Irene and Lisa left a couple of days early, leaving me and Andi to pack in a spot of more intense training and an evening of baseball in the Yankee stadium. In spite of the hosts losing 0 -2 to the Minnesota Twins, the atmosphere under the floodlights that night was magical.

Bags packed, we were ready to go the next morning, but not before one last blast in Central Park. We had heard about the traditional Mother's Day walks where hundreds turned out. Another 20km walk was simply too far, so we opted for the more palatable 5km event. Not knowing what to expect, I shot off at a similar speed to the previous weekend. Amazingly, my legs held up and I coasted to a clear victory in 20.19 – over a minute clear of my team mate in second. We were the toast of the town for the remaining few hours before our departure to JFK airport. It was galling though, turning down all the barbeque and party invitations. We settled for a last bit of sun worshipping on a boating lake and a little bikini-clad bird watching.

Back home, it was like I had never been away. Thrust straight back into group rehearsals, the mood amongst the Players' was distinctly more frenetic. Jill and Gerald did their best to keep some order as individuals paired off and went through their lines in opposite corners. Only half the costumes had turned up, two members were off sick. Agitation levels fluctuated. I was asked how I had got on, but with few sporty types amongst the cast, my response was suitably vague. It was easy to detect that minds were on other things and I thought there was likely to be minimal understanding of what it was I had actually accomplished whilst I was away. More were fascinated by the impression that I was a globetrotting athlete back from his travels and, if the last race was anything to go by, a young man that had conquered America.

There was little time left before the commencement of our four-night run

111

at the Athenaeum theatre. Much as I liked dressing up in period costume and working with people committed to amateur dramatics, I knew that racing had to come first.

I have often heard the phase *it'll be alright on the night*. And so it was. Yellow Sands was performed to audiences that laughed and cried in all the right places, 200 in all at our grand finale. A whimsical tale told in two sets, involving a wealthy dying woman's relatives who gather unaware that they have been cut out of the will. Devonshire cream teas, thick West Country accents, pomposity, there was naïve love, expressions of greed and warm affection, and, according to some, a scene stealing parrot. The play had it all, and was described by one respected local theatre critic as a *cracking good yarn that is still the salt of the earth*.

The after show party held at Marion's home was lovely. Appropriately genteel to start with until the tea, coffee and cakes was set aside for celebratory wine and champagne and episodes of raucous laughter. It was all smiles and great to have played a small part in what had been a successful production. It was also the last time I would ever see the cast together again.

I arrived in Rome feeling very fit. My training had gone well through the summer with a string of good race results. It was important that I did well at these second World Athletics Championships. Like the Olympic Games, after the inaugural championships of 1983, the opportunity to compete on this very different kind of stage arose only once every four years. I missed out last time in disappointing circumstances. This was my chance to make amends. And if I needed a reminder that controversial non-selection was not exclusive to me, I only had to read the papers.

The national press was full of controversies that cited the team exclusion of several athletes like 10km runners Carl Thackery who had beaten the world record holder Fernando Mamede earlier that year, and pre-selected Nick Rose who narrowly failed to reach a time standard. Steve Harris could have been added to the team. His Haringey clubmate Seb Coe was even quoted as saying that he considered Harris to be a good prospect for Rome given that he had beaten the world champion Alberto Cova at the European Clubs Championship earlier in the season. Favouritism was thought to have been shown to a number of athletes on the team, including Steve Ovett who dogged by injury had shown poor form leading up to Rome.

I was one of five walkers on a British team of around 70 athletes. Ian McCombie and I would contest the 20km walk while our only qualified 50km representative was Paul Blagg. Lisa and Paul's fiancée Bev Allan were selected for the women's 10km event.

The entire British team was accommodated in one of several hotels that formed a temporary athletes' village. It was natural that Ian and Paul should choose to room together as they were both close friends and Cambridge Harrier teammates. Until I checked in at reception and was directed to the notice board in the hotel corridor, I wasn't to know who team management had roomed me with. I wasn't short of an elbow nudge or two by nodding athletes when they saw what I saw.

'Blimey, look who you're with mate.'

I was shocked to see that I had been placed with one of our sprinters. For endurance athletes this was an uncommon alliance. The training and mindset of the two disciplines were poles apart. I gathered up my bags, walked to the lifts and pressed the button for the fifth floor.

Allan Wells had a reputation for being undemonstrative, single-minded, and dour to the point of being aloof. The Olympic 100m Champion from Moscow 1980 was also one of the superstars of the British team. When he greeted me with a firm handshake it made me wince, it mattered not one jot that the softness of his Scottish brogue meant I only understood half of what he said. This, I thought, was going to be interesting.

I reminded him that we had previously met at the San Diego training camp prior to the LA Olympics.

'Oh, aye.'

I doubted he had any recollection of it. By his own admission, he said that ordinarily he would not engage in idle chit-chat. While he relaxed back on his bed, I unpacked my bags and laid out my collection of *good luck* cards from well wishers back home. As I did so, I caught his wry smile but he made no mention of it. I did tell him that I liked to talk but would respect his preference.

I was curious enough to want to ask him about all the bottles and silver foil packets on his side of the room but thought better of it. *Vitamins* he later said. He was astonished that I took nothing to complement my diet. I said I struggled even to swallow an aspirin even if I had a headache and knew little about supplements.

By the end of our week rooming together, I would know enough to at least want to return home and start taking a daily multi-vitamin tablet, cod liver oil, and a decent daily dose of vit-C. Much of anything else was way over my head during those times sitting back on our beds burning the midnight oil. To have understood more would have required a degree in pharmacology and a greater appreciation of the peculiarities associated with an Edinburgh dialect.

Preconceptions are one thing, but I found Allan to be very personable. It amused me that he was prepared to concede that his wife was unlikely to recognise his possible change of character should he arrive home and want to share similar levels of convivial conversation.

It was during our third evening when we were about to switch out the lights that there was a knock on the door. At first we considered ignoring it. A second, more aggressive double tap and I said I would get it.

I opened the door. Linford Christie wanted to speak to Allan and what he had to say could not wait. I looked over my shoulder and got the nod to let him in.

The disagreements between members of the British relay squad and team management had been all over the newspapers. Allan had already exchanged a few private thoughts with me, but what had been printed in the British press about the matter had seemingly got blown out of all proportion. Linford had come to clear the air.

As far as I could deduce, at the root of the problem was the actual selection of the four man team and who would run the *glory* last leg when they reached the final. When not if. As one of the fastest teams on paper, the British runners were regarded as medal contenders.

Allan was the established man, though time and injury had taken its toll and his star was fading. Linford on the other hand was the new European Champion, a rising star with faster current times to his name. Some experts thought that the fastest man was best utilized on the second and slightly longer leg of the 4 x 100m relay. It was a moot point that both big men argued back and forth with 10 stone me in the middle doing his best to arbitrate. A clash of egos was a contributory reason as to why the argument appeared to remain largely unresolved once Linford finally decided to walk out around 1am.

The irony is that neither man got to run the relay. Without their services in what should have been a formality run out in heat one, the British quartet was eliminated by way of disqualification.

For as long as I have been a fan of athletics, I always recognised that sprinters were among those who attracted most attention. The Americans have had more than their fair share of superstars through the years, Jesse Owens in the 1930's and Carl Lewis in the 1980's to name just two. The new man on the block was Canadian, however.

I met Ben Johnson the evening before my race. It was at a truly wonderful glitzy black-tie affair, celebrating 75 years of international athletics. The invitations by members of the IAAF had gone out to famous champions of the past and to a host of dignitaries and officials, with a further few limited places extended to a number of current athletes. Neither Helen, a friend and one of the 400m squad or I were on the latter list. Nothing ventured, nothing gained. We thought we might chance it and walk to the hotel and see if we could blag our way in. As it turned out, it was surprisingly easy.

Helen always looked smart. I on the other hand felt distinctly underdressed in slacks and polo shirt. The men on the door checked the athlete accreditation tags hung around our necks and pointed us in. I picked up the complementary glossy book from a pile on a table and thumbed through it as we walked into the ballroom. It was full of photographs of famous athletes, a number of whom I saw in the room as I accepted a glass of orange juice from a waiter: Fanny Blankers-Koen – *the Flying Dutch woman* and winner of four gold medals at the 1948 Olympics; Sergei Bubka, the greatest ever pole vaulter; Edwin Moses, the best 400m hurdler of all-time; it was an autograph hunter's paradise.

Behind the elevated stage, a huge screen replayed footage of great athletic moments like Bob Beamon's legendary long jump at the 1968 Olympic Games, Lasse Viren the Finnish distance runner winning double Olympic Gold, and our own champion decathlete Daley Thompson doing one of his memorable high jump back flips. Helen and I had no intention of staying long, just enough time to experience and enjoy the sense of occasion. We were on our way out when we saw Ben Johnson in the foyer.

I was unaware that Helen knew him. She said hello and the two had a brief chat before she introduced him to me. He was no taller than me, but obviously muscular with a massive chest that made his white shirt seem a size too small. I read nothing into his limp handshake for this was a man that would not have looked out of place in a boxing ring. He was softly spoken, to the point of appearing quite shy. The yellowness of his eyes was something that struck me as we exchanged pleasantries. I thanked him for signing my book. Of course, none of us were to know at the time just how big a global figure this man would become, and not necessarily for all the right reasons.

There must have been at least 50,000 people in the Rome Olympic stadium when the gun fired for the start of the 20km walk. The roar that went up and accompanied our progress around the initial four laps of the track was deafening. A strong Italian presence in the field of 42 starters ensured that support for the walkers was likely to be high throughout. And so it proved.

The temperature and humidity high at 82 degrees and 67% respectively made racing conditions feel oppressive. It was hard, but I was determined to stay with the fast pace of the breakaway pack of 20 exiting the stadium. There was a mile long stretch of tarmac before we connected with the 2.5km road lap. I had moved towards the front accidently clashing elbows first with Victor Mostivik and then Maurizio Damilano. Whether that minor incident instigated a move by them I don't know, but it was followed by an injection of pace that saw the leading pack start to splinter.

By 5kms the Russian and Italian had pulled out a small gap and drawn several men into their slipstream. Though only six seconds behind, I was feeling the strain. I could see the familiar tall figure of Ian McCombie in amongst a large group three seconds ahead. He looked strong, whereas my legs felt heavier than I would have wished.

Over the next few laps he and the other leaders pulled further away as I fought to stay within the top half of the field. I still had more than one lap to go before heading back to the stadium. Given my split time at the 15km mark I estimated that I was on course for a finishing time of around 85 minutes. The crowds had swelled out around the course and were making a lot of noise. Although my view was obscured by a succession of pine trees, the last time I glanced over towards the opposite side of the central road reservation and seen the leading walkers, Damilano appeared to still be forcing the pace.

115

I was feeling below par, but tried to maintain motivation by drawing upon the cracking atmosphere being created by the crowds. I was totally unprepared though for what happened next.

In the space of a few strides my leg started to cramp. I tried pushing on. Then, like an arrow piercing the back of my leg, I leapt into the air clutching my hamstring letting out an almighty scream. I trotted, I hobbled, my head dropped, it was agony, I simply did not know what to do with myself.

In my peripheral vision I saw at least one race judge watching me. In any other circumstance, I would have been disqualified for obvious rule infringements, but of course commonsense prevailed. I was injured and gaining absolutely no advantage as I tried to gather my thoughts. One by one, walker after walker filed passed with more than one sportingly expressing words of encouragement for me to get going again.

I felt sick. There was still the final road lap to complete and in all probability a total of 3kms to the finish line. Muscles had torn for sure. Sprinters would notoriously fold like a pack of cards with the same injury and not even complete the second half of a 100m race. For a brief few moments I thought about the easier option to just step off the circuit and retire from the race. Instead, masochistic belligerent thoughts rose to the surface. I got angry. Deep breaths, I steeled myself for the first few strides of what was likely to be a very long and painful stiff legged march back to the stadium.

I cannot pretend that I did not care that my style of walking looked awkward. In fact it was embarrassing. However, so long as the race judges saw no cause to disqualify me for a bent knee infringement, I resolved to keep going.

The walk back into the magnificent stadium was bittersweet. I heard the last few bars of the Canadian national anthem. The capacity crowd of more than 70,000 was on their feet applauding and cheering wildly, not for me, but I assumed for the three men who I saw accepting accolades from the podium on the infield of the track. It was a reasonable assumption until I saw flashed up on the big screen the image of a certain walker who was still trackside and being interviewed whilst draped in the blue of his national flag. The jubilant scenes that had accompanied Maurizio Damilano's slow lap of honour had by all accounts hardly died down when the 100m men were led out to receive their medals. Ben Johnson had broken the world record.

If there ever was a unique situation when it was possible to feel virtually anonymous when you are the only man performing on a track surrounded by tens of thousands of spectators, then I guess this would be such a time. I walked down the final straight towards the finish receiving a smattering of respectful applause from those who had noticed me. One who probably hadn't until the last moment was a man with silver hung around his neck. Carl Lewis checked his stride as I went past.

Waiting to clap me across the line was Ian McCombie who had finished a brilliant 9th, and the two Australians Andrew Jachno and Simon Baker. Shaking my head in discomfort, I stopped the clock at 92.36. Ian ruffled my sodden hair. Standing a few yards away with his hands and weight resting on the trackside barrier rails was Allan Wells. He shouted over his commiserations. He later told me the ovation that had greeted the leading walkers as they filed into the stadium was nothing like he had heard before.

So sore was my leg in the week that followed that I could only withstand gentle remedial treatment from our team of physiotherapists. The hamstring tear was the worst I had ever experienced. I felt like I'd aged years as I made the daily limp to the stadium to watch the remainder of the championships from the stands.

It was heartwarming to be there to witness Lisa walking well for a commendable 13th position, little more than two minutes behind Irina Strakhova. The Soviet won gold in 44.12 just seconds ahead of Australia's Kerry Saxby and China's Yan Hong.

Six days on from my race, I felt rested enough to join Ian roadside at the official British refreshment table in order to assist with handing out drinks and sponges to our sole 50km representative Paul Blagg. It was hot. It was frenetic. While we intermittently encouraged all 37 walkers and shrugged off the splashes from discarded sponges, Paul stuck gamely to his planned pace schedule as the super fit men at the front powered relentlessly on.

During the final quarter of the race, Ian suggested I should leave him and head on back to the stadium. We both knew my injury would make it almost impossible for any hurried dash back to see the first of the finishers. It was agreed that he would hand out the last of the drinks and catch me up later.

As was the case in New York the East Germans dominated, only this time Hartwig Gauder swopped positions with Ronald Weigel finishing 37 seconds ahead and over three minutes clear of 26 year old bronze medalist Vyacheslav Ivanenko from the Soviet Union.

In spite of the heat, the top seven men walked times under 3 hours 50 minutes. As remarkable as that was, I sat high up in the stands watching with a particularly keen eye, as the remainder of the field appeared out of the tunnel at irregular intervals onto the track and make their way around to the finish line.

Although I had not seen Paul for more than half an hour I was aware that he was on course for a good time, almost certainly a personal best, but would he break Les Morton's British record set in Madrid the previous year? More significantly, was he about to become the first British walker to break the four hour barrier? The answer was imminent. His muscular frame popped out from the shadows of the tunnel. Even from my far-off distance I could see his gritted teeth aggression. With every punchy stride, with every breath, he had the look of a man tearing strips of raw meat from the bone, positively growling towards his destiny.

I looked at him, I looked across to the stadium clock; I looked at him, I looked across to the clock…it was well past 3.59 and counting. My heart was in my mouth. This was the Holy Grail for any 50km walker – a magical moment in any race walker's career. Sure, it had been achieved by other walkers from around the world, but that did not diminish the desire of men to emulate a truly tough athletic landmark. I would go as far as to say, this was harder, much harder than convenient comparisons to the four minute mile.

Was I willing him on as he got ever closer to the line? No! It would be dishonest of me to say otherwise. I wanted this little piece of history for myself. With each passing stride that very personal desire was fading fast. I looked at him, I looked at the clock. His walking action was not pretty. It was functional and solid, so much so that if a brick wall had been positioned in his way, Paul Blagg would have no doubt smashed through it. I held my breath, waited...and saw him have the last word as the book closed on my dream.

His time: 3:59.55. He did it. I was dumbstruck. In spite of my feelings of selfishness, it was important that I applaud a magnificent achievement.

I took a few more moments to gather my thoughts. I stood up and made my way down towards the track and the dispersal area where on the far side competing athletes collected kit after their races and met coaches and waiting medics.

Catching sight of Paul, I approached him with an outstretched hand.

Sweat saturated, he saw me and responded with a clenched fist and shouted through snarled teeth, 'Yeees...'

I offered my hand which he accepted but practically threw it away afterwards whilst turning his back. He was deliriously happy, so whatever his pumped up emotions, this was not a time for me to be churlish. In terms of results, these Championships had not been good for me; yet at that disappointing moment, I felt more determined than ever that better was to come.

'You bastards...you bloody bastards.' The words were spat out with suppressed venom. I stood there in the street, staring at my car, I was so angry, so upset it felt as if at any moment my chest might explode. What a homecoming, I thought.

On reflection, perhaps I really should have let it all out and had a bloody good scream. I did want to lash out but felt constrained by the intrusive stares of people walking by. Just as some faceless moronic thief or thieves had done to my car, my guts felt as if they had been ripped out with an uncaring savagery.

My car had been broken into. Worse things in life happen, indeed, worse things have happened to me, but this hurt. Not only had the morons stolen the radio, but in doing so had ripped out the dashboard and vandalized much of the interior. If that was not enough, the parking ticket stuck to the windscreen was pushing me to the edge of desperation. The Maxi may have let me down a few too many times but it was all I had, it was all I could afford. It was hitched up and towed away to the scrap yard a few weeks later.

I had only just got back from Rome and already I wanted to be anywhere other than in Plymouth. My brother Peter invited me to stay with him and Polly at their home in Yorkshire. A week to recuperate and enjoy some company, he said. As things were, I had to rest and allow my hamstring injury the time to heal. In the meantime, I could help the process by stretching and the occasional swim.

What I had not anticipated was Peter's resolve to see me back on the road and mobile again. My feeble protestations were ignored. Like a dad intent on helping a son with the purchase of his first car, we trawled around dealerships viewing in Huddersfield, Bradford, Leeds, Halifax, we spoke to one or two private sellers until finally, my young brother did a cash deal on a six year old Ford Fiesta. I was embarrassed by his generosity. I drove home in the newest car I'd ever owned.

The arrival of a new flat mate and enthusiastic training partner could not have come at a better time. I was still recovering from my injury and welcomed the change of circumstance. Andi Drake was a 22 year old graduate from Coventry who shared my ambition to compete at the next Olympic Games. He was prepared to put any career aspirations on hold for the foreseeable time. It was hoped that he might be the first of several talented walkers that would commit to the idea of living and training together.

My landlord was the same man who would provide the larger six bed-roomed flat across town that was imminently ready after a complete refurbishment. In exchange for low rent charges, Barry was a successful businessman who seemed happy with the prospect of associated publicity and a vicarious satisfaction in seeing his young tenants aim for the Olympics. Soon after the move, the three of us were photographed by a local newspaper shaking hands where our bold ambitions were reported in an article under the headline, *A New Mecca of Walking*. With the benefit of hindsight, this very public pronouncement proved all too premature.

In spite of a final rallying call to other athlete friends up and down the country, no more were prepared to follow Andi's brave pilgrimage to Plymouth. Even at a national squad weekend early in the New Year, there was a lot of back-tracking on earlier expressed interests. Common concerns ranged from uprooting home life to affordability – all *weak arguments* in my opinion from unmarried men who potentially had a lot to gain as athletes and much less to lose as young independent people.

So there we were, rattling around in a huge property. It was good for us but made little financial sense for our landlord. Finally, the plug was pulled on our grand idea, and in the spring of 1988 we moved again – closer to the city centre, to a double-fronted former Victorian residential home overlooking a busy road.

The self contained one bed-roomed flat above Edmund's converted veterinary surgery was a serious case of downsizing and one that tested our preparedness to compromise. An area was cordoned off in the spacious lounge for Andi's bed and possessions and the walls were decorated with posters and paraphernalia. The big bay windows flooded the room with light, though it also served to highlight the mess that two athletes can quite easily create when living

119

together.   A big bonus for me was that I only had a flight of stairs down to work. Most important of all was that we were knocking out an increasing number of training miles.

There was however an underlying problem that we never really overcame. Once I recovered from my injury I quickly re-established myself as the faster walker.   In our elite squad of just *two*, there were few times when we actually trained side by side. Instead we agreed to spice our sessions up by Andi having a head-start of several minutes on most of our road sessions, with the aim that he stayed in front for as long as possible. It was a method of training that helped both of us achieve fast times, particularly over the longer distances, though I doubted it was always good for Andi's morale.

What it must have been like for him knowing I was somewhere behind in hot pursuit, and at some point any glance over the shoulder would offer up the unwelcome sight of my figure closing him down.   Inevitability, he would be passed at some point during the latter stages of those walks: A case of the hunter against the hunted.   If it had been the other way around, I think I would have found it soul destroying.

I had not mixed running and walking since I was a teenager. Andi, by contrast, liked to run a few of his sessions. I did not think it was helping his development as a top class walker, but to talk about it seemed only to cause friction between us. Our relationship was tested further when he appeared unwilling or unable to offer constructive opinion on my walking technique. However, once we relaxed our attitude again and accepted there was unlikely to be much in the way of give and take with information that might improve the other, the stony silences over the breakfast table faded into memory.

I was undertaking more coaching qualifications at the time and good communication was fundamental in any coach/athlete situation. Of course we were not only friends but competitive rivals who wanted the same thing.

Afflicted by a bout of sickness, Andi could only stand and watch me start the year with a good 20km track walk of 85.35 in Plymouth. A few weeks later, he chose not to travel to Steyning in Sussex, where I would make it two wins from two with a course record time of 63.21 for 15kms. We were both derailed however on the Isle of Man at the end of February.

Without a race result to his name, Andi's season just got worse when he retired after only 3kms complaining of cold symptoms.   No doubt feeling disconsolate, he stood hands in tracksuit pockets, and watched from the sidelines as I battled hard at the front with Ian McCombie.

For more than an hour there was nothing to separate Ian and myself until the moment around 14kms when I made my move to push on. I had barely pulled two yards ahead when I was shown the red baton by a judge for apparent *lifting*. I could not believe it.   It was agonizing to see as I was feeling so good, so technically solid, and confident that a win was possible. Ian went onto win in a time of 83.33.

If I thought my disqualification was unfair, it was galling to see my friend Darrell Stone cross the line in second position, only to be told moments later that he too had been adjudged to have infringed the rules and disqualified just before the finish for *bent knees*. We were all chasing a sub 84 minute Olympic qualifying time. Darrell's *unofficial* time: 83.53.

If sub 84 was plan 'A', then my plan 'B' was an attempt at a sub-4 hour 50km Olympic qualifying time in Majorca three weeks later. The first week of preparation was wasted as my flat mate shared both his dark mood and cold symptoms. By the second week we were both bug free and raring to go again. Andi's spirits were obviously lifted with the visit of his girlfriend Maureen and her friend Anne whose encouraging combined presence out around the windswept moors contributed to his good 35km effort in 2:57.53. We avoided any direct comparison of our respective walks when I opted for a 30km speed endurance session.

The self imposed six minute deficit was pulled back within the first hour of walking and I went on ahead to clock 2:10.02, a fantastic time that excited me so much that I wanted to punch the air and shout *Wow!* Yet, in the company of sweetly smiling guests, I felt strangely uncomfortable and unable to express my true emotions, so paranoid was I that I might be falsely accused of one-upmanship. Pumped with adrenaline, my recovery started with a simple mug of hot tea and a nonchalant chat with Maureen and Anne as we waited for Andi to come back into view on the horizon and make his way back to the car. Alas, great training performances only really count if you turn them into great racing results. So it was incredibly worrying when two weeks later plan 'B' failed so miserably.

I chose to travel separately from the main GB party of walkers and officials departing from London, and instead opt for the more convenient journey from Exeter to Majorca with Edmund and Richard. All perfectly reasonable, I thought, particularly when I explained that my friends and I planned to stay on afterwards, recover from the race and enjoy a short self-catering holiday. Team management was not entirely happy about this, but I guess it might have been all the more palatable had I ultimately raced well.

Alas, I felt tired from the start, and by the 30km mark reached in 2.23 was so jaded that I pulled out of the race even though theoretically a sub four hour time was still possible. I simply had an *off* day when the energy levels were low, when the bio-rhythms were all wrong, call it whatever you like; it was a miserable off day when least wanted. All athletes have the misfortune of these low voltage days and rational explanation invariably sounds futile.

Norway's' Erling Anderson fast 3.49.16 was two minutes ahead of Spanish hero Jose Marin, while Les Morton was not far adrift and reclaiming the British record with his 3.58.25 performance and a certain ticket to Seoul.

I had a week in the sun to contemplate what to do next. Two bad results and but for the intervention and good sense of two friends, I may have begun to panic. Richard cooked, and we ate like kings. I relaxed and listened to wise words. All was not lost. By the second day I was again invigorated as I chased down my friends along the Porto Polensa coastal road around the bay towards Alcudia. It was hot and beautiful. We did no more than 15kms at a time though my pace got quicker by the day. We hired a car and toured the Island. I felt inspired by our treks across the rugged mountainous region though there was little Richard or I could do about Edmund's unbelievable ability to surge over the hilliest climbs at twice our rate.

'Where the hell is Ed now? I haven't seen him for ages.'

Richard pointed to a peak in the far distance. 'There,' he said. 'To the left of that group of ponies, follow the line of rocks to the top. The silly old sod is waving at us.'

I looked over an expanse of landscape towards a hill back lit by the brightness of a setting sun and squinted until sure enough I saw a silhouette of a man waving. 'How did he get over there so quick? He's like a mountain goat.'

'Yeah, only he's got a bigger nose. Hey, have you thought more about us helping you when we get back home to find another 20km race somewhere in Europe over the next few weeks?'

'Yes.'

I had been reluctant at first to even contemplate another race so soon, but the training in Majorca was going well and it made sense to capitilise on my fitness. We already knew of an important six nation International match in Czechoslovakia in May, but reasoned that there was no guarantee I would get selected for it. Aware that my maverick tendencies were irritating some in the British walking hierarchy, I felt it necessary to try to retain some control over my major championship destiny by choosing where I raced.

Our original thoughts had been to go home and see if there were any suitable races in France or Spain, two countries where we were sure to find a high quality national championship that might accept a foreign guest walker. We did not know it then, but in little over two weeks I would be back boarding a plane and making my first ever solo trip abroad to…Hungary.

Back home, conspicuous by his absence was Andi, who had left me a note to say that he had gone skiing with friends and would be back in two weeks – just about the time I would be away again and touching down in Eastern Europe.

On my arrival at Budapest airport I was met by two men, one of whom had held up a placard with my name spelt incorrectly. Through a mix of animated gestures and finger pointing they had made it known that it was necessary to wait a further two hours in order to meet a Polish contingent before moving on to Bekescsaba. It was exasperating but I was determined that nothing untoward would faze me. I sat down, alone with my thoughts in a bustling lobby paying little attention to a stream of incomprehensible tannoy announcements. I reasoned that so long as we eventually got safely to our destination, any short delay was a small price to pay.

I felt ready to race. My confidence had been boosted with training sessions during the past week that included a fast 20km mid-week walk and an inspired 1 hour 48 minute 25km walk around the Burrator reservoir. Those great back to back walks followed by two rest days meant that Sunday morning could not come soon enough. Not least because my friends had also done so much organization at short notice to make the trip possible, I felt the extra motivation to do my absolute best and return home with the right race result.

Sat on a packed mini-bus for four hours was one thing, another was responding to two attractive Polish teenagers who appeared to relish the opportunity to practice their English on a captive participant, willing or not. The girls' engaging, somewhat giggly personalities did at least help pass the time in spite of being scrunched next to a burly man who I later deduced was their team coach and chaperone. As pleasant as their attention was, I would not let it affect my focus. Nor would I let it slip whilst rooming with a mad, live-wired athlete from Yugoslavia. The fact was that Milan Balek's zest for life and gift of making those around him laugh probably helped keep my spirits high even though I seldom understood what exactly it was that excited him.

Less exciting for me were the organised bus trips on Saturday with other visiting nationals to the museum, Folklore House, library, and a civic reception with the town Mayor. Flatteringly, both Monika and Beata made valiant attempts at language interpretations on my behalf during what might have been a potentially mind numbing cultural tour.

Come Sunday morning, it was heartening to know that the format of races was exactly the same as the previous year. No unwanted surprises. The 9am start suited me fine, as did the presence of Sandor Urbanik, the man who narrowly beat me the previous year. His welcoming smile whilst shaking my hand on the start line was appreciated all the more this time around. I can only presume that he sportingly wished me luck, though it was conceivable that he may well have been making any kind of blasphemous comment.

We were called under starter's orders. I muscled my way to the head of the large group of assembled 20km competitors and waited for the digital race clock to tick up to the hour. As we did so, the men in the 50km event continued to walk on by, whilst the last of the junior 10km women on the opposite side of the road were being cheered through the finish gantry.

On the crackled blast of a fired pistol I started my aggressive surge. Shrugging off an accidental lung sapping elbow to the ribs, I pulled alongside Urbanik with clear road ahead and at least three or four walkers snapping at our heels.

The European indoor bronze medalist was a class act. Superfast with sound technique, I knew that so long as I walked to his high standards and stayed close for as long as possible as I did the previous year, then a good result was achievable. Also staying close were Swede's Stefan Johansson and Jan Staff, two young men who must have had similar thoughts until their eventual disqualifications at 14 and 18kms respectfully.

As hard as it was, I gritted my teeth and never allowed the gap between Urbanik and myself to widen beyond 50 metres, a distance that would prove close enough for me to witness his one arm victory salute. Trailing just 12 seconds behind, it was the most amazing feeling approaching the finish gantry and seeing the clock merge into focus, realizing that I only had to keep forging ahead and my Olympic dream could become a reality.

Recollections of trailing around the travel agents with Richard on those damp, dingy days back in Plymouth and the anguish of uncertainty, all the phone calls, all the reasons for not risking this solo trip, all the doubts, all of it began to fade away as I readied myself to cross that line and thrust my arms aloft and scream...*Yes.*

It was one of the most beautiful moments of my racing career. A photograph taken at the precise moment and given to me later is still one of my most treasured.

Post-race, all walkers were invited to Gyula where I for one enjoyed savouring the whole experience whilst wallowing in spa baths that felt even more intoxicating than the previous year. The disco in the evening seemed louder and more fun; and perhaps funniest sight of all, Milan Balek hanging like a trapeze artist upside down from a beam above mine and Beata's head and those of other wary smoochers on the dance floor.

I returned home so appreciative of the kindness of so many that helped make the occasion so priceless. I had traveled across Europe in order to walk up and down a stretch of tarmac, supported by people who hardly knew me, and all for 15 crucial seconds.

Walking up the stairs to my flat I saw an A4 sheet of paper pinned to the door. On it was a skillfully hand sketched scroll with a written message that read: Chris MAD MAX Maddocks, *Sly Fox of the Year Award.* Congratulations on your 83.45.

Andi was inside and ready to shake my hand. He had a small bottle of champagne he had been saving for a special occasion. We shared it the next morning with our bowl of cornflakes. Our training resumed in earnest a couple of days later leading to an uncharacteristic yet sensible agreement to walk side by side at Plymouth City Walkers' inaugural series of races at Burrator Reservoir. It was sensible because both of us had been selected to walk in Trinova in Czechoslovakia the following weekend. The 42.49 that it took us to walk the 10kms around the picturesque reservoir was just about the perfect result before another big race. That is, it would have been had I genuinely felt like doing it. I was confident of my fitness, but would have preferred to have waited a few more weeks before racing again.

When Andi and I met up with the dozen or so members of the British team for an overnight stay Heathrow, it simply felt too soon after my race in Hungary. I could not say as much for fear of recriminations. I suspect that by the time we had made the early morning flight to Vienna and mini-bussed it on to the Czech border I might not have been alone in wishing that I was somewhere else.

Armed military guards gestured for us to get out of our vehicle while passports were checked. The leg stretch was welcomed, what wasn't, was the lengthy time hanging around in the middle of a dust bowl wondering what was going on. Other vehicles pulled up, similar checks seemed to be made before they were waved through. In the heat of the day, agitation levels were raised, but with no guards seemingly able to speak English we appeared to be stuck there at the mercy of men with rifles. A scene from a cold war movie was joked about until that exchange of whimsy wore thin with the passage of time. Then, for no apparent reason, after nearly two hours the shout went up for us to board the bus and pass through the rising barrier. The sense of relief was palpable once we were moving again.

Nine hours after leaving Heathrow we arrived at our hotel. Salubrious, no, but by eight in the evening all we wanted was something to eat and drink and go to bed; nothing fussy either about the cold buffet which was perhaps just as well given that the 20km race was at nine the following morning. Breakfast for all was at 6.15, one sitting only.

The course was a 1km loop around the Baroque style town square with its imposing 16th Century tower at its heart. From the gun, the Czech walker Roman Mrazek looked fluent as he shot to the front. Andi, Ian McCombie and I formed part of a group of ten that followed until it splintered beyond five laps. Such was the ferocious pace, Andi was first of several to drift off the back, leaving myself and Ian to fight it out for second with another Czech and a Pole. We went through the tenth lap in 41 minutes at which point I moved steadily ahead in pursuit of Mrazek. He was in my sights on the 14th lap when one of the British judges stepped forward and showed me a baton for apparent *lifting*. I was astounded, first by the fact that he was British and secondly by the possible adverse message that this action sent out to the other foreign judges adjudicating. I made what concentrated efforts I could to heed the warning by trying to ensure that my walking technique was fair. Alas, my worst fears were realised. Before the end of the next lap a judge stepped forward and showed me the red disqualification baton. *Agh*! I slowed to a stop, knowing that I had just been denied the chance of a great race result.

I stepped off the circuit and unpinned my number. Feeling more exhausted than I would have done had I continued to the end, I stood on the sidelines amongst cheering spectators and watched the remainder of race in contemplative silence. The Czech extended his lead eventually winning in 81.53. Ian came fourth with a time of 84.33, whilst Andi Drake disappointingly finished 11th with 89.49, a result that was several minutes slower than he had hoped for.

The morning races were completed with the women's 10km event. There

125

were four hours until the start of the men's 30km race during which time lunch was served. I was hungry and so fed up and tired that I did little more than pick at my food. I also had a multitude of things weighing heavily on my mind. After lunch I decided to knock on our team manager's door.

'Come in. It's open.'

Met with my tired, surly face it was hardly surprising that neither Peter Marlow nor David Rosser seemed pleased to see me.

The air was distinctly frosty as I sat down and discussed what had happened. I stopped short of making unwise accusations over the objectivity shown to me during the race, but did express how disappointed I was and if possible that I wanted to do the 30km race, a second chance if only to redeem myself.

Reminded that I had already lost the team valuable team points, they argued there was little purpose in me racing a second time that day – a glance at the time showed that the afternoon race was only about an hour and a half away. They may as well have waved a red rag at me; consumed by bullish arrogance, I said that I wanted to race, and insisted they do what they could to get me on the start line even if it meant me walking as a non-scoring guest competitor.

Of course, on reflection I was being an idiot. I was in no fit state to race again. There was no question that my stupid impulsive behavior should have been overruled. Ordinarily most walkers would need at least a few days, in fact anything up to a week to recover from the level of effort that I had expended that morning. After a few moments of deliberation they agreed to do what they could.

An hour and a half later I was stood alongside 30 other men bracing myself for the sound of the starter's pistol. Wry smiles, and what I thought might be acerbic banter from the East Europeans had to be ignored. Paul Blagg possibly spoke for the majority when he shook his head and muttered, *twat*. Even before the gun fired I knew I was making a mistake. My legs felt leaden, I was light headed, undernourished and the sun was beating down. It was too late to back down. I was committed.

I tracked the pace of the leaders up until 10kms by which point I was walking on empty. My head dropped. An inextricable slide back down through the field of competitors was all so predictable, with no hope of sympathetic eye contact with British team officials looking on from the sidelines. I finally ground to a halt around the 21km mark.

I had raced a total of 35kms that day without a finish to my name. Exhausted, fed up and all I probably gained was a few more dissenters.

Why I bothered going to Hoddesdon in Hertfordshire for the national 20km championships two weeks later, I do not know. Held around another soulless and near deserted industrial estate, it was the wrong place to be if I was hoping for any sort of redemption.

Ian McCombie took the lead once Andi Drake had been caught after his rush of blood to the head that initially had seen him blitz to the front at the start. It was a naïve race strategy that saw him accumulate enough warnings to be disqualified before halfway. I was only a short distance behind when it happened and saw him throw his arms up in disgust. Instinctively I was thinking about how disillusioned he would be, and certain that he would not want to return to Plymouth afterwards with Edmund and myself. So distracted was I that I was unprepared to see the same man stand firm and show me the red baton as well. For the third time in two weeks I was prematurely out of a race. I was dumbfounded. So, it was with some surprise and relief that very good news came my way during the following week.

After a few days away, Andi surprised me by turning up at the flat. He was just in time to see me open a letter from Mary Tupholme, the Deputy General Secretary of the British Amateur Athletic Board (BAAB) informing that I had been selected for the Olympic Games. Inwardly I was ecstatic, but felt unable to let rip and jump for joy – not just because I was in the presence of a friend who wanted the same, but because the past few weeks had largely been so disappointing. Just how much my news adversely affected Andi I am unsure, but it was possibly the catalyst for him telling me there and then that he was leaving and going back home to Coventry. His parents collected his belongings two weeks later.

I could not afford to dwell on the consequences of Andi's departure. Dating Zillah, one of the veterinary nurses, certainly helped fill any void left by my training partner. More pertinently, as one of four British walkers selected for Seoul, I was in desperate need of some good race results. Olympic selection helped reinvigorate my appetite for training, so much so that just three weeks on from that dismal day at Hoddesdon, I was winning the national 35km road championships at Leicester by a clear six minute margin. It was the confidence booster I needed. Edmund racing well was a bonus that ensured our journey home was one full of renewed optimism. A succession of good race wins over the next couple of months helped keep my spirits high.

Winning the South West track 10kms at Basingstoke in a fast time of 41.14 was particularly encouraging as it was done against tough combating gusting winds during the 25 laps. At the National inter-counties track & field championships at Corby I tested my fitness by competing in two races within the space of three hours. I won both – the 10kms in 41.16 and the 3kms in 12.01. A few weeks later I was unfazed by *only* winning the South West track 3kms in slower time of 12.33 as I was feeling below par at the time after a second series of mandatory pre-Olympic typhoid and cholera vaccinations.

I was really looking forward to my final competition before flying to the pre-Olympic training camp in Japan in four weeks time. The AAA's track & field championships at the Alexander Stadium in Birmingham was an opportunity for me to renew my rivalry with Ian McCombie, whilst for others it doubled as the British Olympic trials and last chance saloon for those still hoping for team selection.

127

Basking in summer sunshine, a crowd of around 15,000 was in good supportive voice for both the early laps of the 10km walk and for the athletes simultaneously competing in the pole vault, men's hammer, and the long jump. It was obvious from the outset that Ian was on a mission to beat me, so much so that I had to work particularly hard just to stay close to him. The possibility of losing touch imminently became the least of my problems when the sounds of clapping and shouts of encouragement rapidly changed to ones of horrified screaming.

'Oh God, get out of the way.'

'Chris, look out!'

Out of the corner of my eye I was shocked to see a hammer swirling through the air towards me. In a split second of sheer terror I ducked as the 16 pound ball and four foot chain whizzed across the infield and plummeted to the ground to within a whisker of me before crashing against advertising hoardings as I was scampering across the track. Weakened by heart palpitations and legs of jelly, I was uncertain whether I should stop or continue. A walk judge stepped forward and asked if I was alright. A coherent reply was beyond me. The sight of Paul Blagg going past stirred my competitive juices. Other walkers were closing in fast. I started to walk again, though it was all in vain. Ian was away in the distance and it was all I could do to hang onto third position.

Afterwards I was still sweating when I was asked if I wanted to lodge an official protest. I was too tired to be bothered, though I would have appreciated it had the culprit for the wayward hammer approached me and apologized. Whoever it was unfortunately did not have the decency to do so. I was assured that the matter would be discussed at the next AAA's committee meeting, though I heard no more about it. I had a wry smile when I read how it was mentioned in Athletics Weekly. In an extraordinarily dry paragraph, AW reported it as *an incident that could have marred the whole championships*.

In response to being asked about it by the local press back home, I said, *imagine if it had happened during the 800m or 1500m to Coe or Cram – it would have been splashed all over the tabloids*. Fortunately, the local media were equally interested in my Olympic prospects.

Walter Gammie was one particular journalist who took the time to ask intelligent questions about my hopes and about challenging the high standards set by the opposition highlighting some of the targets that loomed ahead. A sense of perspective was noted with Ernesto Canto of Mexico holding the Olympic record with his 83.13 win in Los Angeles; and, a measure of how much the event had developed was underlined by Ian McCombie's British record being faster at 82.37. Though at Commonwealth level, Dave Smith of Australia had walked 79.22, whilst the European and World records stood to East Germany's Axel Noack with his 79.12 mark. I told Walter I was frequently improving my training times and averaging around 163kms per week or a little over 100 miles. I said that getting close to the British record would at least give me a chance of a great result in Seoul.

Both television stations took turns to interview me and show good footage of training on the roads around Plymouth and in the gym lifting weights. Combining work with training, it was unsurprising that I felt constantly tired. I was however alarmed when my doctor took a precautionary blood sample and diagnosed a liver disorder, possibly caused by the series of required vaccinations administered over recent weeks. I was flattered by his determination to help me. I even had a hair analysis done aimed at offering ideas about how I might improve my diet. Until then, I was unaware that such procedures were possible. Given the belief that Seoul was to be my Olympic swansong, this kind of long term strategy, though frustrating, did at least make me feel that there were some people beyond my circle of family and friends who cared. Alas, mentioning this particular gripe to other journalists probably backfired on me.

Immediately prior to my overseas departure I allowed myself to be cajoled by a newspaper into a photograph opportunity on a near deserted Plymouth railway platform. Standing next to a stationary train attired in new Olympic kit with suitcase and holdal bag in hand, I struck a forlorn and lonely figure about to board. True; I had minimal finances in which to prepare more professionally for the Games, true; I had tried in vain to raise local corporate sponsorships funds, and true; I had been declined by British Rail one of the free tickets to Heathrow available to some Olympic athletes. I was grateful therefore, to The Sunday Independent who paid the £59 return rail fare but was less enamoured when their reporter wrote a thought provoking article under the big headlines, *FORGOTTEN HERO Chris sets off for the Olympics – but does anybody care?*

What should have been a proud moment was tarnished in some way by harping back to suggestions of an Olympic athlete on the breadline. I was very fit and needed only to stay positive for a little bit longer. I was after all used to a Jekyll and Hyde existence, where I scraped by at home yet by contrast occasionally got to taste the highlife when I was away on international duty.

The training camp in Japan was fabulous. Situated in Chiba, a suburb of Tokyo city, the Nihon Aerobics Centre was luxurious – the perfect antidote to any lingering disappointments back home. Surrounded by mountains and greenery, the expansive resort provided lodging accommodation in amongst wooded grounds, and had the best indoor and outdoor high-tech training facilities imaginable. Membership fees to the attached golf course alone, was reportedly $250,000 per year! Though many of the visiting athletes accessed the free facility, I felt my limited pitch 'n' putt skills honed with the lads at Exeter probably unsuitable for these immaculate fairways.

Adjacent to the huge five-star glass fronted restaurant was a *green* all-weather track, the like of which I had never seen before. It was possible to eat and observe athletes going about their training outside, where the hot topic of conversation over many meals was the alleged prevalence of drug taking in athletics; who was taking steroids, who wasn't. Chinese whispers and covert

129

finger pointing was fast becoming the new Olympic sport. Ironically, I was quite flattered and amused when I heard through the grapevine that, particularly for an endurance athlete, my unusually muscular 10 stone frame had put me on the list of suspects.

During the two weeks at the training camp I frequently used the indoor gym, swimming pool and opulent sauna rooms. When it came to table tennis, I took on all-comers and reigned supreme. Opponents were routinely flummoxed by my game style. Essentially, a game based on defense, combined with net cord flukes and luck with clipping table edges. Exasperated, they came back for more, and still lost. The food was exquisite and plentiful which was appreciated, given the mile upon mile of tough high humidity affected training that my roommate Les Morton and I did before and after breakfast. Ian McCombie and Paul Blagg arrived several days after us.

The entire British athletics team shared the complex with the American track and field team, a number of whom made an entrance straight off a Hollywood movie set. I had been at the camp for a few days when rumour spread that as part of a publicity stunt *stars* of the US team were arriving by helicopter. Sure enough, when it happened, it was all very dramatic. While the sprinters were whisked away for interviews, I got caught up in the crush caused by the entourage surrounding sprint sensation Florence Griffith-Joyner and the baying photographers who pursued their hurried dash through reception. Manicured and bejeweled with designer clothes and shades, looking every inch the movie star. Protected amongst the skirmish, black and beautiful, she glided past with the accompanying stampede forcing me to stand aside as if no more than a bit player in a sideshow. Did I resent it? Of course not, it was pure theatre. It was great!

The wonderful thing about an extended period spent at a training camp is that everyone is much more relaxed about sharing their time, especially when in such convivial surroundings. Here was a unique opportunity to enjoy sociable chats over a drink with the likes of Carl Lewis, Edwin Moses, Calvin Smith, Butch Reynolds, and of course with Flo-Jo. After many a glorious evening sat trackside watching these same great athletes go through their training practices, it was a pleasure and privilege to go on to Seoul and see each win medals and further cement their respective places in athletics history.

The contrast between the Nihon Aerobics Centre and the Olympic village was marked. On our arrival we were speedily taken through accreditation before moving on into the village. Presumably looking beyond the flags and banners and all the other Olympic paraphernalia, I heard one athlete rather crudely describing the village as resembling a large London council estate, albeit a new one that would be put to similar use after the Games. With athletes from 160 nations taking part, it was crowded. Surprising then, that not long after we had set bags down in our nine-man apartment and ventured out, Les and I bumped into two East German walkers who like us were finding their bearings and ended up browsing in the shops. Their command of English though limited was sufficient for us to understand that they had just arrived from a six week high-altitude camp where they had averaged around 300kms of walking per week. Les and I walked out of there asking each other a succession of rhetorical questions:

'Did you hear that? Three hundred kilometres…that's nearly 200 miles a week.'

'I know. If I do much more than 100 I start getting injured. They're doing nearly 30 miles a day, that's incredible. Don't *they* get injured?'

'I'm sure that they said sometimes they do three training walks a day? I sometimes do two.'

'And me. They must walk, eat, sleep and walk again, I guess.'

In spite of the cafeteria being open 24 hours a day, queues for food at conventional times were enormous. Catering for all tastes, the meals were so wonderful they were worth waiting for; at least that's what I thought until my second evening in the village. Ian McCombie and I were sharing a table with Judy Simpson, our top heptathlete, and marathoner Angie Pain, when suddenly, part-way through my seafood pasta meal, I felt queasy. I got up and lurched towards the exit. In a state of desperation I found the nearest bush outside and buried my head within.

It seemed that no matter what the British team doctors did for me, I could not stop being sick. My pulse was racing and I had become severely dehydrated. For that reason, I stayed in medical quarters under overnight supervision. The following day it was all I could do lift my head and put one foot in front of the other. To look and feel so pathetically ill when surrounded by many of the world's fittest athletes was an embarrassment difficult to disguise. I retreated to my room and remained in isolation until the afternoon when I joined a coach party of competing walkers in order to view the competition circuit. With less than 48 hours to the first of two events that would start and finish in the stadium, it was too hot to stay out long. I was feeling so tired I only made token responses to the banter flying amongst the nervous smiles. It was enough that I knew the flat, multi-lap road course was less than a mile from the arena. At the time, I was unsure if I would regain sufficient strength to warrant my position on the start line.

The following morning, whilst my friends walked on the training track, I attempted to inject some energy into my listless body by doing stretching exercises and a few sets of press ups. During the afternoon I whiled away the hours by writing around 50 postcards to family and friends back home. I made light of my predicament, if only to stay positive about the impending race. It had only been two days, but I felt like a holidaymaker sitting there in my t-shirt, shorts and sandals. I didn't know it at the time, but my choice of footwear was I believe partly responsible for the terrible time I would have during the race.

It was fast of course. This was the Seoul Olympics. All the fastest walkers in the world were present. Unlike the two previous Olympic Games, no American or East European boycott this time to detract from the quality of

131

competitors.

I tried to follow the aggressive charge of the leading pack. Of the 53 starters in the 20km event, I estimate that until the quarter distance mark I was still in contention and not far behind the leaders where I was timed at 20.22. The problem was my feet almost certainly had swelled inside my shoes and felt as if they were on fire. Blisters bubbled up within shoes that felt so tight compared to the loose fitting aerated sandals I had worn until 30 minutes before the starter's gun.

I did my best to ignore the increasing pain by instead concentrating on retaining as smooth a technique as I could manage. As the race progressed, it was galling to see the leading men pulling out an ever lengthening gap. The leading group had whittled down to seven by half distance, with a succession of pursuers including Ian between them and me. In spite of my problems, my 10km split of 41.39 meant that I was still only one minute behind the men at the front. The pain in my feet however was almost unbearable, and while men ahead of me moved up a gear in speed, mine suffered.

It was an incredible relief to make it back to the stadium and walk on the track and hear the roar of 50,000. On the opposite side, Ian had just finished. I still had a lap to go and there were other walkers immediately ahead and behind me. Rounding the final bend I was able to focus on the clock in the far distance. Given that my mind was befuddled with pain, I was surprised to see that the digital display had not gone far beyond the 1 hour 23 minute mark meaning, that if I raised my pace over the last 100m I still had a chance to salvage something respectable out of a tough horrible day. With one eye on the clock I finally crossed the line and punched the air so sure was I that I had, in spite of the food poisoning and sore feet, remarkably achieved a personal best time albeit by a mere one second.

Barely able to stand, I was exhausted and wandered aimlessly around for a few moments with my hands on my hips gasping for breath. In my peripheral vision I saw and heard a cameraman being directed to move closer to me with the frantic message, *Get his feet; make sure you get his feet. Zoom in on his feet...* I looked down and saw the focus of their attention. Blood-soaked, my white Adidas striped racing shoes had turned crimson red.

The scene inside the athlete's room deep in the stadium afterwards was extraordinary. An hour and half after 53 superbly fit men had stood tall awaiting their orders, many lay strewn over the floor with team managers and doctors bending over them. It looked as if someone had just thrown a bomb in and carnage ensued. I was obviously not the only one in discomfort, though some had more reason than others to smile through it all.

Josef Pribilinec had won with a new Olympic record, just strides ahead of Ronald Weigel who in turn held off the reigning world champion, Maurizio Damilano. Moments later, and on the back of a succession of other fast finishing walkers, Ian McCombie re-entered the stadium to be rewarded with a new British

132

record time of 82.03.

It's a moot point, but such was the high standard of this race, that had I recorded the same time four years earlier in Los Angeles, it would have been good enough for fourth position, missing a medal only by a matter of a few seconds. Instead, on this occasion I was twenty-fourth with an *official time of 83.46* – a time that meant I actually missed my personal best by one second! In more ways than one, times had obviously moved on.

The Olympic Games still had a week of action to go. I wanted to get out there and enjoy as much of it as I could but, with the predictable physical ravages caused by the race, magnified by the affects of food poisoning and shredded feet, I felt limited for a few days and shuffled about like an old man. I did see Ben Johnson win the 100m sprint in a world record 9.79 seconds, ahead of Carl Lewis and Linford Christie. The merits of the bronze medal won by Christie was for a short time in some doubt when it emerged that traces of a stimulant had been detected in a drug test; it was being explained away by claims that he had erroneously drunk ginseng tea. The rights and wrongs of it were still uncertain when news broke that would shake the entire Olympic movement and completely overwhelm any other indiscretion.

I was having my feet re-dressed in a busy medic's room when a British athlete came strutting in and gleefully said, 'Hey, guess what? Ben Johnson's been done for steroids.' It was startling news and the talk of the village for the remainder of the Games. While he was sent home in disgrace, every other sprinter in the final was elevated by one position. In the women's sprints Flo-Jo was untouchable, streaking away in both the 100m and 200m races. The latter event was won in an almost unbelievable world record time of 21.34 seconds, cause for even more wild, unsubstantiated speculation.

The 50km walk at the end of the week was for me no less exciting if a tad slower. Vyacheslav Ivanenko was technically brilliant in winning gold by the length of the track from Ronald Weigel, who in the space of a few days achieved an amazing *double* by winning another silver medal for East Germany. Ian and I assisted Les and Paul with drinks and sponges and saw both perform well and respectively record times fractionally either side of four hours.

Apart from athletics, I saw medals won in the weight lifting arena including one by the USSR's Yury Zacharevich who astounded everyone with a world record snatch and clean & jerk combined total lift of 455kgs. I was also one of a group of athletes from my apartment that went to the boxing and saw light, middle, and super-heavyweights in action, including seeing Lennox Lewis fight. British born, Lennox acquired dual citizenship after he moved to Canada when he was a young boy. Wearing the colours of the Maple Leaf, he was possibly responsible for helping to put a smile back on the face of most Canadians by going on to eventually win a gold medal with his final amateur bout.

A taxi ride away from the Olympic centre was the local market in Itaewon, a bustling downtown area packed with trading stalls where haggling over goods was the norm. In spite of all the money changing hands, it reeked of poverty, and for that reason alone, I am almost ashamed to say it was a novelty to visit. It at least offered a chance to experience a small taste of what real life was like for many in South Korea, one that was in complete contrast to the relative riches surrounding the Games back down the road in Japan.

The British team received a small daily spending allowance and combined with the little bit of money that I scrimped together, I went shopping. Over the course of a few trips, I spent every penny I had on fake designer wear and an assortment of goods. I knew nothing about bartering before this trip. Alex Kruger, a gentle giant and successful Decathlete was my mentor. He seemed to know everything there was to know about fashion, prices and tactics when buying. At first I felt uncomfortable about trying to buy as cheaply as possible from people who looked like they had so little. Good or bad, competitive instincts took over and by the time I left for home with my *Rolex* watches, *Armani* leather jacket, cuddly toys, *Yves Saint Laurent* silk scarves, and landscape oil paintings, I was a master of the knockdown bargain; but then again, I guess that's what all the athletes and tourists think when they go home. This would be the one and only time that I would have all my Christmas shopping done by October.

I was at a bit of a loss when I arrived home. Slipping back into a routine of working and light training – my feet were sore for weeks, I did not know what to do next. I always said I would retire after Seoul and get on with the rest of my life. Problem was, I had no plans in place and possibly, because of that, I think few people believed I was ready to quit anyway.

Though the local press reported my race, I did manage to avoid any requested post-games interviews for nearly three weeks, by which time I had enough time to consider what it was that I really wanted. The first person I shared my thoughts with was Richard Pannell.

We were meeting his two children, Katie and Greg from school. This was a special occasion as Katie was doing an afterschool run with other kids from her year. While seven year old Greg was gathered up and carried on his dad's shoulders, we all watched as one by one the girls and boys filed past on the first of two laps around the school grounds. Once the back-markers had gone by and the noise had died down, I chose my moment to speak.

'Huh, Richard,' I said rather hesitantly. 'Hmm, I've been thinking that I might like to go on racing, maybe one more year. I might even try for one more Commonwealths. They're in New Zealand, less than a year and half away.'

No immediate response was forthcoming. I wanted to hear what my trusted friend had to say and he wasn't saying anything. I looked at him, almost willing him to utter something. Greg wriggled on his shoulders and asked for another sweet. He was hoisted down, given a sweet and sent on his way to play with another friend.

'Well, what do you think,' I asked.

Richard smiled. 'I'm not surprised. Of course, you've got to do it. I've spoken to Edmund. We'll all help you in any way that we can.'

He could not have put it more perfectly or succinctly. I was afraid of what I was letting myself in for. I needed my friends.

Though I hated the thought of living on housing benefit, I did appreciate a system that helped those on low part-time incomes, even where mine was one of choice because of the commitment and energy required to train like a full-time endurance athlete. The price I paid for this was the occasional call from the job centre for an interview to review my situation. When the call did come, I would have cold sweats worrying about it. I may have stopped short of pulling my collar up, wearing a hat and false beard, but each time I entered that building, my head would be down, and I prayed that no one, absolutely no one would recognise me. Answering questions as to why I had been unable to find full time work was sheer purgatory. On those days, it was impossible for me to even think about training. I was more likely to crawl into a hole and hide.

Only Richard and Edmund, and perhaps my brother Peter really had any idea how I felt about this. Housing benefit was one thing, but stubborn pride would not allow me to even entertain the thought of taking advantage of income support, even though I apparently qualified for such assistance. It may be hypocritical to say it now, but I was once again probably my own worst enemy. I hated the mere thought of choosing a life that included more time with financial worries and having so little to live on. I simply had to rationalize that if I had my close friends supporting me, more athletics success was possible.

We all knew that Seoul had not seen the best of me. It would have been a shame to have stopped when I had not fulfilled my true potential. I said as much when Walter Gammie interviewed me for the Herald. *Fire still burns bright in Chris*, he wrote in his headline. In public I was always conservative with saying how I really felt, but did add that the extra time spent in the heat and humidity of Japan had helped with preparation for the stifling climate of Seoul. I took the opportunity to mention that sponsorship might help finance future major championship preparations. Whatever the future held, from that point on I privately vowed to take one year at a time. And from this point on, I will summarize each year that led up to one final momentous period that was an unimaginable ten years hence.

PART FIVE

Part 5. Beyond Seoul, one year at a time: 1989 - 1999

1989

Though I was committed to training long and hard, I also wanted to add to my coaching experience. I did this by studying more and accepting invitations to help other athletes on regional weekend coaching courses. Throughout the year I was happy to involve myself with both runners and walkers and be a part of practical assessments, lectures and tutorials. We would discuss technique, biomechanics, training and racing schedules, fault correction, conditioning, alternative forms of training, rule interpretation, race tactics, diet, and modifications necessary when helping female athletes. Exchanging views on the latter went someway to helping me understand the difficulties in trying to help Lisa with her walking, particularly when I visited her at Leeds Polytechnic.

Though her race results were consistently good, our relationship was becoming increasingly fractious. The geographical distance between us did not help. I was a hard task master when it came to advice. There were a number of times when I oversaw track sessions at Becket's Park and endured stony silences. Her attitude to training was fantastic, but I failed to appreciate that her fluctuating weight from light to too light affected her propensity to injury. Partway through the year we agreed on an amicable split.

I could not have foreseen that this would turn out to be one of my best racing years. It was all the more surprising because it seemed that before and after virtually every good race I had to contend with a new injury strain, whether it was another damaged hamstring, bad back, sore abdominal muscles, aching knees, more blisters, and even a prolonged and unexplained neck and shoulder stiffness. It was Richard that introduced me to Kevin Kelly, a friend and local chiropractor who would become a constant ally for the remainder of my racing career. In return for occasional associated publicity, he could not do enough to help me stay on the road to fitness.

This time around, I got my visa organised for what turned out to be a much more confident solo trip to Bekescsaba in April. A time of 85.17 was enough to win by a margin of 24 seconds over young Hungarian, Karoly Kirszt. I was also awarded an additional trophy for best foreign stylist. This unexpected recognition was particularly gratifying, as I had been experimenting in training by concentrating hard on trying to replicate the smooth form of fast walking reminiscent of the world's best.

During the four hour return bus journey back to Budapest, a youngish man, probably in his late twenties congratulated me on my win and asked if it was alright if he sat next to me. I had no objection. Unaware that he was a

Czechoslovakian team coach in charge of a group of junior walkers, I was completely unprepared for his offer to make suggestions on how I might improve further. His command of English though limited, was sufficient enough for me to understand that he had an association with all the top Czech walkers including the Olympic 20km champion. I was fascinated when he produced files and pointed at aspects of their training schedules. I only understood a fraction of what he was saying, but felt so inspired by his preparedness to help me that I got home feeling even more determined.

My next big target would be in May and another 20km race, this time in Barcelona for Great Britain at the bi-annual team World Cup. Before that, and by comparison our club's annual bank holiday promotion at Burrator Reservoir was relatively unimportant, but I thought a short blast over the 10km distance would be a good warm-up race and an accurate test of my fitness.

As usual, there were only a handful of us available to muck in and help Richard and his kids with final race day preparations. Edmund's dad, Eric, who so often in the past had done so much to help keep the club operating was by now confined to a wheelchair and too frail to be actively involved. It was he who originally persuaded the local Water Board to allow us to use the large grassy spot for the erection of the hired marquee for race headquarters and for setting up refreshment barbeque facilities. Mercifully the job was done under warm sunshine amid smiles and plenty of laughs.

Burrator is a beautiful, peaceful area with scenic views in all directions particularly when standing on the century old granite stone dam and looking across the wide expanse of water. The sight and sounds of free roaming ponies and grazing sheep dust the area with a sprinkling of magic. It has long been a popular draw for rucksack laden hikers, pram pushers and dog strollers. Particularly on a clear day, Burrator is picnic heaven.

Come race day however, a blanket of mist had descended from surrounding moors. The murky early morning gloom may have struggled to lift, but for most spectators, spirits positively soared watching two historic British record breaking walks.

Certainly, the festive atmosphere accompanying Les Morton winning the 50km event and me blitzing the 10kms made for a truly memorable day.

At a speed close to 13kms per hour, Les covered the eight and a half laps of the tree-lined reservoir in a time of 3:57.48. Meanwhile I was operating at a virtual sprint, walking speeds closer to 15kms per hour when I completed the 10km walk in 40 minutes 16.57 seconds. Afterwards, under cover of the marquee, there were a few touching moments when a giant poster signed by more than 100 present on the day was given to Eric Shillabeer in appreciation of all the work he had done over the decades.

I had seldom gone into a major race so excited by what I might achieve. So fired up was I that it possibly contributed towards me having a less than perfect

137

race – in truth, that in itself is an improbable dream for anyone.

I started super fast in Barcelona, so keen was I to banish memories of the last World Cup 20km race in New York where two years earlier I was swallowed up in the initial mad frantic sprint and knocked off balance by flaying elbows and kicked ankles.

By the end of the first undulating 2km lap I was joint-leading with Ireland's Jim McDonald. Timed at 7 minutes 48 seconds, we were on world record pace. It was both frightening and exhilarating. Packed tightly behind us were all the fastest walkers in the world. Poised ready to strike, the red vests of the USSR, the best Mexicans, a blue blur of Italians and East Germans. I told myself not to panic.

I had no idea what McDonald's plans were; I guessed he was out to win. I was told that shortly before this competition he had caused quite a stir by walking an un-ratified sub 11 minute world record for 3kms. True or not, the inevitable happened on the next lap. We were caught and passed. An army of British supporters had traveled over to watch the weekend of races. I felt under immediate extra pressure, so sure was I that the knives were probably already out for my act of impetuosity. Indeed, I later saw and heard a home movie version of the race recorded by members of the Sheffield club.

Watching from the sidelines and sparing me nothing during that first lap, Yorkshire voices can quite clearly be heard extolling their condemnation of my race tactics, 'Oh my God, what's he doing? The daft beggar's only leading…'

I was determined not to fall apart. A halfway split of 40.45 was good and meant I was still in contention and on British record pace at the very least. But of course I had only reached that point by overzealous pace judgement contributing towards my slight slowing during the second half.

Franz Kostiukevitch was supreme and the first of four Soviets in the top five winning in 80.21. After them, walkers continued to finish in quick succession. I was *rewarded* with a personal best time of 82.35, good enough for 15th and, if only for British bragging rights, three places ahead of Ian McCombie who recorded 82.58. Jim McDonald meanwhile had slipped back to 29th recording a respectable 84.50. Our teammates walked well, but were several more minutes adrift.

Travelling home, alone with my thoughts on the last leg of my journey, I replayed the race over and over again in my head. Thinking of what might have been: a top ten place for sure was possible, something that by itself seemed almost ridiculous. It was late at night, and the other coach travellers were unlikely to be able to see me or even if they could, be concerned by the tears running down my cheeks. I had started to over-analyse the hopelessness of my situation back home. Two minutes I thought, separated me from the best walkers in the world. I was sure I could make that difference up, but I was in a rank amateur situation. Helped by great friends was never going to be enough. It needed more than I had to bridge the gap. Negative thoughts did not help. I simply had to put them to the back of my mind.

I had regrouped by the time Richard and I were joined by his son Greg and set sail on the Roscoff ferry towards France. It was June. After a peaceful sea crossing, we made our way by transit van and caravan on to Laval, a town in north-west central France around the Loire Valley, meeting up with the 20 strong British walks team two days later.

I may have beaten Maurizio Damilano in Barcelona, but the Italian was back to his imperious best when I raced him next over 35kms. His European record win in 2:31.52 put him well clear of an International field of walkers from seven nations. My 6th place result of 2:37.20, though good enough for another British record left me feeling pleased *and* frustrated. As good as it might have appeared, I was sure that but for a shoulder and neck stiffness that had bothered me for weeks, I could have at least challenged Spain's Jorge Llopart for second position and with it an even better record.

Like so many injuries, this would be another discomfort that would take time to treat and clear. Bless Kevin Kelly for his perseverance. The big Geordie was photographed by the local press working on my problem in his clinic and clearly flattered by their description of him as the man with magic fingers. As good as Kevin was, nearly two months passed and we were still trying to make light of the fact that I was training hard as he continued to stretch, pull and generally pummel that same problem whilst dealing with other new and exasperating niggling strains. My next important competition in Leeds was more than a month away, so it was a surprise to some when I showed up with Edmund at Hendon's Metropolitan Police training centre and mixed with other walkers preparing on the track for the start of their national 100 mile race.

Generally, but not exclusively, it was the more mature walker that usually contested these type of *ultra*-distance events. I think it is fair to say that with runners too, any distance run beyond the marathon is considered by many as utter madness and often done by men and women affectionately thought of as a little eccentric. In truth, these walkers and runners are athletes to be admired, and that was the real reason why I was there, but, not before I had a laugh.

Wandering around, I was asked more than once, 'Hey Chris, what are you doing here? You're not racing are you?'

With my best enigmatic grin, answers were deliberately vague. 'Why not? I've often thought about giving it a go. It can't be that hard.'

I wasn't offended at all by the variety of dismissive guffaws aimed at me, particularly when I stripped off my tracksuit and revealed race numbers pinned to my kit. The banter flew thick and fast. I was either going to smash the world record or be dead on my feet some distance after halfway.

Perhaps for posterity, several grouped around with their cameras as Edmund and I smiled and posed for pre-race photographs with our helpers, Richard Pannell and Barbara Shillabeer. The eagle-eyed observer should have noticed that Ed and I wore the same 43 bib number. It was approaching 5pm. Competing athletes were called to starter's orders. This was my cue to end the ruse and ask Richard to unpin the spare numbers I had borrowed off our forever youthful, 49 year old friend. Cue a barrage of more deserved light-hearted verbal abuse.

Edmund of course did not disappoint us. He set off with walkers from eight European nations on the first of 100 laps of the road and track circuit. In spite of some tough times during the early hours of the morning when we practically had to *drag* him out of the toilets and kick start his resumption in the race, he rallied in fine fettle to win in a time of 18 hours 11 minutes, well clear of a young, thirtysomething Gordon Beattie.

Things got serious again for me in September. The English Commonwealth trial walks at Roundhay Park in Leeds proved to be a severe test of speed and stamina. First two past the post in each of the men's 30km and women's 10km races would mean guaranteed selection for the Games in Auckland. A third team selection was a discretionary decision, based on fitness and racing form.

Perhaps the leading men could have taken a leaf out of the women's book and contrived a joint 1-2 finish by agreeing like they did to come in together and thus avoid a potentially damaging defeat. Both Lisa Langford and Betty Sworowski had hard races the preceding week; Lisa finishing a credible 10th at the World Student Games, and Betty setting a new British best for 5kms at Gateshead. Their equal first position in 47.15 assured both of a team ticket to New Zealand in February.

Neither Ian McCombie nor I were prepared to make a similar pre-race truce. Without exception *all* the best walkers in Britain toed the line, and together with a number of guest Commonwealth athletes, battle over the hilly parkland circuit was brutal.

Fast and furious from the start, walkers quite quickly got strung out with many paying the price later, either by not finishing or walking themselves to a near standstill. Top Australian, Andrew Jachno was one that chose to step off the road by complaining halfway that the course was *ridiculously too tough for a fast race*. Meanwhile Ian led the way. As much as I gritted my teeth, I could not contain him and by 20kms he had built up a lead of over one minute. I was suffering, but spectators from the sidelines shouted that he looked as if he was feeling the pain even more.

Gradually I ate into his lead. With less than a half mile to go I could see him in the distance, probably 20 seconds ahead. As tired as I felt, I tried to remain strong whilst I saw in him a brief sign of weakness. His legs had momentarily buckled. It was a blood thirsty, eye-popping invitation to go for the kill. Bit by bit I hauled him back until we were both directed off the circuit onto the final straight towards the centre of the park and a finish line that was about 200m away surrounded by supporters. People stood along the tiered grassy embankments shouting for both of us as the end drew closer. In my peripheral vision I saw a man a distance away running on the grass attempting to keep up while repeatedly shouting at me.

Above all the noise, Richard Pannell's booming voice was unmistakable. 'C'mon Chris, you can do it. C'mon, c'mon. Oggy, oggy, oggy!'

With just 80 metres left I pulled up alongside and injected as much extra pace as I could muster. Fearful that he would counter attack, I lunged at the line, and with my arms aloft I let out an almighty yell probably unheard by most such was the din all around.

I had won in a time of 2:11.38. Five seconds adrift, Ian had almost folded in the last few strides. A brief congratulatory hug precipitated our collapse to the grass.

With the benefit of hindsight it might have been better for both of us had we agreed on that arranged joint finish. Had we done so, and in spite of the hills, I don't think our race would have been any slower. Mark Easton was too close behind to have allowed that to happen. For the neutral spectator, the race could not have been more dramatic.

I was in the England team and suddenly in demand. I was invited along to the new East Devon athletics club at Ottery St Mary in Devon. The opening night attracted 80 youngsters who made me feel like a star as they crowded around for my autograph. I was happy to talk to them and the press, sure to make no mention of my appearance fee. Which was nothing actually, a big fat zero. I did receive £20 to cover my fuel costs. I was a little more circumspect when negotiating an appropriate appearance fee, after owners of a local trophy shop had gone through a major refurbishment and asked me to cut the ribbon in front of the press at their grand new opening day.

Friends nudged me in the ribs and sheepishly asked, 'Go on then Chris, tell us how much that was worth.'

For pride and self preservation alone, the response was met with another of my non-committal enigmatic smiles. In fact, the shop owner was surprised when I asked for any payment. After some embarrassing negotiation, we agreed on £50. The fact that I only had to walk across the road to perform my duties did not seem relevant to me. Of course others may beg to differ. It depends upon your point of view.

I was reasonably certain that I would not be competing at the next Olympic Games in 1992, but hoped I might be involved in a coaching capacity if I was suitably qualified *and*, so I rather naively thought, if I spoke Spanish. With that intention in mind, I embarked on a course of adult evening classes at a nearby college.

I had all but mastered...Buenos dias, Buenas tardes, Buenas noches and how to say my name and ask someone how they were, when I was off to New York to compete in the marathon. No sooner than I'd arrived at the Sheraton Hotel I was being introduced to a party of Mexican walkers and their Polish coach, the legendary Jerzy Hausleber, a man considered the best in the world and solely responsible for that nation's worldwide success. They were all sat in conversation with Andrey Perlov, a man who had finished a *disappointing* second for the USSR over 50kms at the World Cup in Barcelona yet more recently had set a new world record time for that distance.

I was in awe. I doubted they knew very much about me, but for the short time that I was there were prepared to engage in a little chat. I say *little* advisedly because we talked in Spanish. I was rescued by Ian Brookes, my old friend from Bristol who by then was living in New York and working for the road runners club. It was he who was responsible for my all expenses paid trip to the Big Apple. He convinced me that I was invited on merit. Power walking, or fitness walking as some Americans preferred to call it, was becoming increasingly popular in the States, and I knew that Ian had an idea that a good Englishman taking part would be welcomed.

The principal organisers had established a reputation for not only inviting the best runners in the world to their annual event but also extending it to a handful of the most successful walkers in the world. In addition to Perlov and the Mexicans, I was told that also starting was Olympic silver medalist Bo Gustaffson, no doubt hoping to add to his previous seven wins here, and a trio of top Italians including the best of the lot, Maurizio Damilano. I had enjoyed a good year of racing, but questioned whether I genuinely fell into that category. Ian's natural ebullience helped me overcome my natural tendency towards self doubt.

Starting on Staten Island, and in order to avoid the crush, the elite walkers were lined up alongside the elite women runners on one side of the highway, whilst the elite men lined up on the other side all looking across the Verrazano suspension bridge towards Brooklyn. The 25000 masses were primed a short distance behind. A Cannon fired and after an initial surge of thousands of runners sprinting past, I soon found myself amongst a cluster of six leading walkers torpedoing its way through the masses. That group whittled down to three by halfway.

I could hardly believe that I was rubbing shoulders with Andrey Perlov and Carlos Mercenario and starting the gradual ascent over the long Pulaski Bridge. Had I not been alert to Perlov's ferocious kick and obvious intent to get away, it would not have been for long either. I was eye-balls out and hanging on. We had probably gone from 13kph pace to 15kph, and we were going uphill. My lungs were on fire and I was unsure if I was going to be able to stick with it for much longer when amazingly it was the Soviet walker that cracked first, slipping back off the pace leaving myself and the Mexican superstar at the front, albeit surrounded by hundreds of good standard runners. We were being cheered all the way by thousands. Estimates put the crowds at close to two million throughout the route.

Three miles from the finish, desperate for a drink, I accepted a plastic cup from one of the assistants at a refreshment station. I had no idea what I was about to slurp down my throat but it did have the effect of making me retch uncontrollably. It was revolting. I later found out the green fluid was a cabbage based concoction, one that brought back distant childhood memories of Mum force feeding me my *greens* at Sunday lunch. I was sick then, and only avoided being sick again by spitting out the remnants left in my mouth. Capitalising on my predicament, Mercenario pulled away, lost amongst the runners forging ahead towards the finish in Central Park.

I eventually crossed the line second, over two minutes behind. My time of 3:14.37 was another British record, and one that also proved good enough to beat nearly 23000 runners. As important was the joy of taking to the stage later that evening in a glitzy affair and joining the top six runners and being one of the top three walkers accepting our respective awards.

I was more than happy to take home an unexpected trophy. I do not know if any of the other truly world class walkers received more than me, but I did read afterwards that Juma Ikangaa and Ingrid Kristiansen respective winners of the men and women's run also earned $26,385 each plus a Mercedes Benz sedan worth $32,500. The diminutive Tanzanian attributed his great performance to his training at high altitudes in Alamosa, Colorado. Meanwhile, I looked forward to a tasteless boiled sweet on the plane home and more training miles notched up on the busy A38 dual-carriageway bypassing Plymouth.

New Years Eve would not ordinarily be celebrated with another race, not even by the odd ensemble of members at our club in Plymouth. It was decided however, to move our annual opening race of the year forward one weekend in order to accommodate my preparations for the Commonwealth Games in New Zealand early next year.

Traditionally, our event was a 20km club race – 50 laps of the track. For training purposes only, I opted to start early and walk an additional 25 laps in order to cover 30kms by the end of the morning. Covering these in 43.35 I was joined by the rest of the field who were mindful to leave space for me to shoot through as I was moving at a pace none would be able to manage. Two more 10km splits of 44.23 and 43.56 saw me complete the 75 laps in 2:11.54, an unofficial Commonwealth track record. We had plenty of judges and officials present but not enough for record purposes. I was not unduly bothered by this as the performance had set me up in the best frame of mind ahead of a Major championship, one that I not only believed I could medal in, but, actually have a chance of winning.

1990

I thought it fantastic that the English team organisers had presented many of us with the opportunity to spend a number of weeks abroad training and acclimatizing before a major event. I was in great form and considered this my big chance to raise my game further and peak at just the right time, five weeks hence. If only things were so simple.

The New South Wales Academy of Sport did provide good training

143

facilities. The cramped chalet accommodation block meant, however, I did not sleep properly for all of the three weeks there. Apart from our marathon runner, Geoff Wightman, who became a good friend during the trip, all the other men in our chalet seemed to work off a different time clock, going to bed late, rising late; in fact, the complete opposite of what I was used to.

It also seemed ironic that I should travel to the other side of the world with the majority of the England athletics team and end up walking on my own. Both Ian and Mark Easton chose to travel out much later and go straight to New Zealand. It sounds like lame excuses, but by the time I saw them I was seriously sleep deprived. We did one session together, a 20km road walk that Mark aborted early, leaving Ian and me to complete it in 89.08. The following morning Ian flatly refused to join me for a similar walk, claiming that it was crazy to even think about it. I felt at a bit of a loose end; the only way I could motivate myself to walk again on my own was to push it hard, which I did. I completed the same undulating circuit in 85.48. It would be the last time I found the energy to walk fast again before boarding the plane and heading home. It was a classic case of an endurance athlete leaving his best miles on the training roads prior to a race.

Race day I finished 6th. I was so disappointed and so desperately tired even before the starter's gun fired. French Canadian Guilluime Leblanc won with 2:08.28, half a minute ahead of Andrew Jachno with Ian seconds behind claiming bronze. No disrespect intended, but even Mark slipped past me in the closing stages.

Both Edmund and Barbara were there to support me; he wearing a typical mish-mash of the most patriotic items of clothing he could cope with on such a hot day, she looking elegant in wide brimmed hat and colonial whites. They had such high hopes for me, and I just know it would have pained Ed when he put a comforting arm around me while both offered up consolatory words and said that *I had done by best*. They of course were being very kind. I had messed up, again.

Out of principle, I could not end my racing career on those terms. Half-hearted thoughts on retirement were put on the back-burner again. Trouble was my confidence and motivation had taken another hit by my failure in Auckland. Money, as always was tight. A lifeline came at the gym. Offered work on an ad hoc basis covering holiday time, meant I had a bit of extra cash now and again. It was ideal really as it allowed time for weights and mobility work and use of all the other facilities. I trained, and I trained hard, but lacked the real impetus to move up to another level. I won races and did achieve a European athletics championship qualifying time later that year, but was unsurprised and not unduly disappointed when I did not get selected for the British team.

I was, however, part of a large British walks team that travelled to Munich in Germany. Alas, my heart was not really in it. An 88 minute 20km meant that my race result and points contribution to the overall team score was modest. I was being beaten by walkers that ordinarily would not have done so. Aside from competing, I was in bullish mood.

Taking advantage of most of the best British walkers being present, including a number of top officials, I spoke with fire in my belly about the need for a quality end-of-season 50km race in England where *we* might prepare accordingly and race against each other with the ultimate aim of new best times for all and more qualifying for major championships. Some of the younger men might consider stepping up and trying their hand at the longer distance, I said. We needed to do something different if we were going to have any reasonable chance of closing the gap on the rest of the world. I even suggested that if there were enough of us interested, that we might agree on walking the early miles together and attacking final positions in the latter stages.

Everyone was aware of the Burrator venue, and knew that my club had developed a solid reputation for staging a successful series of races. I may have been accused of a preoccupation with drumming up support for our idea, but if nodding heads and positive verbal responses were anything to go by, it was worthwhile.

The prospect of this race coming to fruition served to galvanize my attitude to training at least. If anyone was going to beat me they would need to be in top form. I got aggressive again, sometimes too aggressive.

Walking on the relatively new stretch of A38 dual-carriageway, more commonly known as the *Parkway*, had its advantages. It had a good smooth surface, and was close to home; meaning that it was quick to get to and I saved on fuel costs. The disadvantages however could not be ignored, and the fact that we continued to train on it for several years was another matter.

The cycle lane Edmund and I walked along was about one metre wide. It was all there was between us and the inside lane of a wacky race circuit that saw hundreds of cars rush by during each and every session, sometimes even in the dark when we opted to start early. On those occasions we did at least take extra precautions. We wore reflective bibs over our kit in order to protect us against being struck by any half-asleep car driver, or by a monstrous articulated lorry. In spite of these distractions, I did some superfast walks on the Parkway, even if it meant being a tad reckless.

Negotiating the stream of cars exiting the dual-carriageway via the various slip roads was hazardous. Invariably my belligerent attitude saw me tearing along the road and resisting all the honking warning signs of irate drivers. To have slowed up would have cost me precious seconds on the stopwatch. Then there was the time when I nearly had my head crushed by a rock thrown as I was about to walk under a bridge.

I realize now that I should have ignored it, but I was not going to let those school kids get away with it too easily. I was after all on another blitz that had just been ruined by an act that had threatened serious injury. Anyone watching me scrambling up the steep embankment on my hands and knees frothing at the mouth will have seen the funny side. It was the shortest route to the group of children responsible for the assault, and I was ready to commit murder.

'Oh God, he's coming after us,' one squealed.

'Run,' said another.

'C'mon here you little, shits,' I shouted.

They scampered away before I could get really close. Their cackles of laughter however were clearly heard as I stopped, put my hands on my hips and cursed their very existence. Thankfully, there were lighter moments during this period.

I was requested to return to my hometown and don my Commonwealth Games blazer again as guest starter of Tiverton's half-marathon and charity two mile fancy dress fun run. In spite of the rain, around 300 took part with many more lining the streets.

I chose less formal wear for the invitation to attend Plymouth's St Dunstan's Abby school for girls. Around 250 took part in a very excitable sponsored fun walk of 20 laps around two netball courts. I am not sure what the greater attraction was, me turning up and agreeing to pose for photographs with each individual, or the fact that they were allowed to wear pyjamas for the occasion and carry their favourite cuddly toy. Whatever it was, it all made for some good images in the local press. The event raised a total of £1000 half of which was later offered to me in a school assembly presentation, on the premise that the money would go towards funding my preparations for the Barcelona Olympics. In truth, I didn't know what I was going to do. For sure I needed the money, but continuing to train for more major championships? I felt closer to retirement.

By late October it was becoming clear that more and more walkers were withdrawing their interest in the Burrator 50km race. All the excuses were coming out: *It's been a long season, I need a rest; I've got something else on that weekend; I'm going on holiday; There's another race that I want to do.* I was so angry.

The race went ahead anyway. Thankfully, most of the officials stayed committed, and together with a well supported 10km race and a junior 2.5km event, plenty of people turned up and, not only enjoyed themselves, but witnessed an historic day in British race walking.

In what evolved into a solo effort against the clock, I put together five 10km splits of 45.04, 46.06, 45.30, 46.15, and 48.12. The timekeepers recorded a final time of 3:51.37. I had broken the British record by more than six minutes. Hugged by my Mum at the finish, it was a great day. Edmund was more than a lap of the reservoir behind in second place. He eventually came home in 4:43.28.

High on adrenalin, I was enthusiastic to get back to hard training as soon as possible. I reasoned that whilst I was fit I wanted to improve the training times that had got me to this level. My belief was even marginal incremental improvements would see me in a position to start recording 50km times in the 3:40's. Both Richard and Edmund tried to dissuade me, saying that I should rest for a few weeks. A fast 41km walk two weeks later was, I thought, a great start. No! In the days that followed, I realised I had strained my left knee.

1991

If I trawled through my training diary carefully, I could tot up the number of different physicians that I saw throughout most of this year. Suffice to say it was a lot. All kinds of manipulations and anti-inflammatory tablets were tried whilst I attempted to stay fit and ready for a new season of races. Unfortunately, a number of the tablets caused the unwanted side affect of intestinal bleeding every time I pushed myself hard.

There was little chance of me feeling too sorry for myself, particularly after visiting Eric Shillabeer in hospital. Diabetes had led to a spread of gangrene. It was pitiful seeing him in agony asking anyone, simply anyone, to cut his leg off. When the decision was made to do just that, he made what seemed like a good recovery, only to relapse. His death at the age of 79 left a void in many people's lives, not least my own. He was a remarkable man who got things done where others would have given up. He was very proud of Edmund, his only child, and such a shame that he did not live long enough to see him become British athletics oldest debutant at the age of 50.

This was no ordinary International debut. This was the Bazancourt 200kms, an annual 125 mile ultra-distance road race that would this year include an official international match between France and Great Britain. I had long been used to seeing Ed wearing international kit that I had given to him; now it was great to see him with a puffed chest walking tall in his own red, white and blue combo.

Edmund was not the most senior man named in the British squad. Don Thompson, a small man, only 5'5" tall, won gold at the 1960 Rome Olympic Games. Thirty-one years on, and at the age of 51, *Il Topolino*, as he was famously nicknamed by the Italians (translated, *little mouse*), became Britain's oldest International athlete. Although the four man team would not be short on helpers, Ed of course wanted his personal entourage, and no wonder, he has always been high maintenance when it comes to feeding, sponging, fetching and carrying. Neither, Richard, young Greg or I were under any illusions that we were travelling to the lovely Champagne-Ardenne region of northern France for a mini-holiday. And, so it proved.

While Richard and Greg oversaw the first couple of hours handing out drinks and anything else our man requested, I set about walking five of the 4km laps in order to bank some meaningful training of my own. Once that was done, the long day and night of relentlessly supportive work truly began.

We had to be on our toes as not a lap would go by when Edmund was not wanting something, either a drink, something to eat, grease to stop the chaffing, more grease.

Other than those competing for France and Britain, guest walkers from a total of 10 European countries meant that 52 had started. Just how Ed found himself isolated for such long periods is difficult to fathom. During the early dark hours where street lamps lit only parts of the course, Greg cycled merrily alongside offering continual encouragement, whilst I was back at base-camp preparing the next refreshment. Porridge was a staple part of his race diet, though on successive occasions he had complained that it was not sweet enough. *Not sweet enough*? I had originally added enough sugar and syrup to make an ordinary man's eyes turn inside out.

'Right that's it,' I moaned. We were all tired. It was three in the morning, Richard was lying in the back of the motorhome having a nap, and Greg was somewhere out there on his bike. 'You're getting the bloody lot.' I spooned in copious amounts of extra syrup until the jar was empty. As Ed appeared out of the darkness I readied myself to handover the sugar bomb.

'There you go,' I said.

Ed grabbed the bowl and spooned up a mouthful. 'Perfect,' he said.

The locals had much to cheer about as Nicholas Dufay was a clear winner in 21 hours 3 minutes, more than a lap ahead of Britain's Richard Brown. Over the remaining hours, the principal aim for many of the walkers was to try and complete the 50 laps within 24 hours. In dribs and drabs they came across the finish line, their personal milestone achieved.

With around three hours to go, it was looking tight as to whether or not Edmund would make it within the cut off time. Reduced to a plod, his head was down. I walked alongside him for his final five laps, cajoling him all the way in an effort to get him back on target. He finally made it with nine minutes to spare. Thirteenth, and ahead of the great *Il Topolino*, he was ecstatic. I needed a drink for my dry throat.

Back home, at city civic centre, I attended a Plymouth Advisory Sports Council, sub-committee meeting for travel and coaching. I was able to make a case for Edmund to receive a retrospective grant of £120 towards the Bazancourt trip. I already knew that I could not make any similar claim because I had received a few hundred pounds from the Sports Aid Foundation and from the Devon Sports Supporters Association, therefore effectively disqualifying myself from any further assistance. How ironic.

I got back into the routine of more intense walking, coping with my aching knee and sore stomach as best as I could. Daily training sessions varied from very good, to none at all. I thought about pulling out of the World Cup team, but hoped I might simply hit one of my better days come race time in San Jose.

We stayed at the State University campus along with a number of other competing teams. I was flattered and mildly bemused when team manager Peter Markham told me members of the Chinese delegation wanted to chat with me. I sat down with them in the foyer and over soft drinks and through an interpreter I was questioned about my training and approach to racing. It transpired that they were impressed by news of my British 50km record and they simply wanted to know more. By all accounts the same people probed other nationals for similar information. In the years to come, China would become one of the super powers of the race walking world. Just how much I contributed to that is open to conjecture. I seriously doubt my performance in the race will have impressed them though.

I started fast, got to halfway in a little under two hours, and slowly but surely slipped back down through the field eventually finishing 45th. For much of the second half of the race I suffered stomach cramps, vomiting on several occasions. After the race, my troubles were far from over. I was assisted to the medical tents and helped onto a stretcher. I was in a bad way, feeling nauseous to the point that I could not hold down the sips of fluid offered to me. I was put on an intravenous drip and comforted for a while. All around me other athletes lay prone on other stretchers. It had been incredibly hot during the race, a fact that probably contributed to 41 walkers not finishing – around a quarter of the starters.

Whilst I was lying there, I heard that Carlos Mercenario had won the race in a championship record time of 3:42.03, simply amazing considering the sultry conditions. Apparently, Andrei Perlov had looked set to win but was disqualified just yards from the line for a final red card rule infringement. I had more questions to ask, but the doctors overseeing me were more concerned about my pulse and fluctuating state of consciousness. The decision was made that I had to be taken to hospital. Suddenly, I was scared.

Whoever made the call, made a mistake. Minutes later, crews from all three emergency services turned up, each with their own sirens sounding. Had I not felt so ill, it would have been funny.

I was bundled into the back of an ambulance and taken, presumably, to the nearest hospital where I was put on another IV drip. Ian McCombie accompanied me, and there we stayed for several hours until my condition stabilized, and it was deemed safe for me to be released.

Ian and I got back to evening awards banquet just in time for desert. By the end of the night, and with a little encouragement, I managed a few slow steps on the dance floor with a pretty American girl. I was already on the road to recovery.

Before we went our separate ways at Gatwick airport, I was asked if I still wanted to be considered for team selection for the next important seven nation international match at Ornskoldsvik in Sweden. Though I said yes, I was not at all sure if I would be fit enough to actually compete.

I had four weeks to get over the nightmare that had just gone before, and be ready to go again. Meanwhile, I had been billed by the hospital for nearly £900. I was worried sick, until people at British athletics headquarters agreed to cover it. So relieved and grateful was I, that during those next few weeks I pushed extra hard in training.

In complete contrast to the stifling heat of San Jose, rain and buffeting winds greeted us come race day in a coastal town bordered by densely wooded hills. If I ever needed a result for some form of redemption, I found it here in a highly competitive 35kms. Allowing the result to speak for itself, here is a list of the top 10 finishers:

1.	Martial Fesselier	France	2:34.45
2.	Hartwig Gauder	Germany	2:35.36
3.	Tio Trampelli	Germany	2:35.45
4.	Bo Gustafsson	Sweden	2:36.11
5.	Chris Maddocks	Great Britain	2:36.19 * British Record
6.	Jo Brosseau	France	2:36.22
7.	Les Morton	Great Britain	2:37.27
8.	Sandro Bellucci	Italy	2:37.57
9.	Marco Quiriconi	Italy	2:37.57
10.	Andres Preusche	Germany	2.38.02

I simply had a great race in conditions that suited me perfectly. Of course I could speculate as to what I might have achieved had I not experienced all the problems leading up to the race, but there seems little point. In all the circumstances, I was more than satisfied. It was pleasing too, that from a British perspective, in each of the other races, including the men's 20km event, the women's 10kms, the junior men's 10kms, and the junior women's 5km race, most of the team walked well, particularly young Vicky Lupton who won the latter event in a time of 22.43.

The result would ultimately be enough to confirm my selection for the World Athletic Championships in Tokyo. It was a false dawn. The problems with my knee and stomach reoccurred, and throughout the summer training was a continuum of stop, start and treatment. I agonized over whether or not I should go, until finally deciding, *yes*. I would just do my absolute best.

If I thought the race in San Jose was tough, then there are few words to describe the agonies that I put myself through in Japan. The average humidity throughout the 50km event was 97%. The placard on the roadside used to inform competitors and spectators of the current weather conditions was adjusted at one point to read 100%, by which time it started to drizzle with rain. It felt as if we were walking in a sauna. Some athletes coped with it better than others. I saw great walkers like Ronald Weigel, Simon Baker, Bo Gustafsson and Martial Fesselier who at one time were all ahead of me, weaving from side to side trying to maintain some sort of momentum. Some collapsed, while others were just dragged off the circuit.

Andrey Perlov linked arms with his compatriot Aleksandr Potashov and shared a unique joint win. Les Morton was inspired; he finished a magnificent 10th. The top Japanese walker acquitted himself well with a 7th position. The pressure on all the home nation athletes must have been immense. It was evident that each one was individually filmed by TV, and that included the poor soul who appeared to be suffering as much as me in the second half of the race. Never far apart, we seemed to take it in turns to vomit. I know this was captured in all its glory on screen as my roommates back at the hotel said that they had watched much of it whilst lying back on their beds squirming.

Of the 38 starters, I finished 24th. It was all rather academic. In truth, I was not fit enough to race. I am pleased I went though. The chance to go back one more time to the Nihon Aerobics Centre and train in the most wonderful location. I saw great action and mixed with the best again. The experience would be a motivating force that I could feed off during the hard winter months that lay ahead.

I had an arthroscopy on my knee, where floating bits of debris were finally flushed out. Solving that problem helped resolve my stomach issues caused by the side effects of taking different anti-inflammatory tablets. This of course all took time.

During the enforced period of rest I had more time for family and friends, including going back home to Tiverton to see everyone, helping Richard with home renovation work, going to rehearsals with his wife Janet and her lead up to a starring role in the Merry Widow at the Theatre Royal. Long strolls with Zillah gave us both the necessary time to realize that we were not suited. She had always struggled to understand what she thought was my *obsession*. I was genuinely happy for her when she met someone else.

Provisionally, I agreed with the owner of the gym that I would take on part-time managerial responsibilities when the current incumbent left for pastures new. I did more coaching at Yeovil in Somerset, and with the club at Dawlish, watched several races, and attended a national squad weekend in Birmingham where at last it felt good to be part of more positive discussions about the future.

On the downside, I had taken my car off the road as I could no longer afford to pay the running costs. The extra cash earned at the gym could not come soon enough. Both Edmund and Richard offered to help by lending me their vehicles when possible. Ed had several cars connected to his veterinary practice and Richard was using his transit van less since he had embarked on a full-time three year podiatry course at the local Polytechnic. Undoubtedly, and most worrying of all, was Mum's health. She had collapsed at the shop where she worked and been taken to hospital with a suspected heart attack. Her recovery afterwards was an absolute blessing. She said that if I made it to another Olympic Games, she wanted to be there. It was all the motivation that I needed.

Qualifying times for the three walks were:

Men	50kms:	4:00.00
Men	20kms:	84.00
Women	10kms:	48.00

1992

Early season results were good.   But, at the first important race of the year on the Isle of Man, I was not quite good enough. The top 5 read:

1=	Andy Penn and Martin Rush	83.34
3	Steve Partington	84.53
4	Chris Maddocks	85.10
5	Ian McCombie	85.32

Neither Ian nor I had achieved the required time. Two young walkers had come to the fore and stolen a march on all of us; *a changing of the guard*, some called it. Our backs were already to the wall. I travelled home with Edmund. He was very happy, and I was happy for him. His 98.26 time equated to a new British veteran's 50-55 age-group record. We talked about that and about my situation, and what to do next.

Bekescsaba it was, only this time my fourth consecutive top two finish did not give me what I wanted: 85.47 would not do. There was only one thing for it. I was going to have to try and get a 50km qualifying time.   The national championships at Droitwich also doubled as the British Olympic trials and were only two weeks away. It would be my sixth race of the year and it was only mid-April. Desperate times call for desperate measures. Maybe that's why, after all my years at, or near the top, I still did questionable things in training.

My friend, Darrell Stone, himself a good young walker and Olympic contender, telephoned and said he was holidaying in Devon with his girlfriend, and did I want to do a training session with him? I was unprepared to deviate from my plans to walk a fast 25kms at Burrator the next morning. I said that he was welcome to join me if he got out there, but, if he was late, I'd start without him.

Darrell was late. I was already on the third of four laps of the reservoir when a car drew up alongside and a face hung out of the passenger window.

'Bloody hell, Max,' he said. 'You're not hanging about.' Darrell usually referred to me as *Mad Max*. I usually referred to him as *Rocky*. 'We'll park up, and I'll join in with you, okay?'

'Okay.' It was time for few words; I was on a mission.

Rocky did walk with me – for about a half mile. 'Shit, I'm going to have to run,' he said. And so he did, for the remaining lap and a bit.

I was pleased with that 1:46.19 effort.   World class was mentioned. Rocky liked his superlatives.

That 25km session was a great boost to my confidence and should have set me up fine for the 50km race on Saturday. It was alas, the last thing on my mind when I found myself lying on the grassy verge staring up at the sky puffing like a train, more out of frustration than exhaustion.

I had covered around 30kms and still held a lengthy lead of several minutes. Several faces were leaning over trying to encourage me to get up and start again. My feet had been killing me for at least 10 miles, and the pain from it had worn me down. My shoes and socks lay scattered by my side.

No one could afford to touch me or I would automatically be disqualified. Richard Pannell threw me some adhesive pads to stick to my feet. My Mum and my brothers Peter and Pat implored me to hurry up.

Begrudgingly, I rose to my feet, dusted myself down and started up again. It was hot and I was fed up. Though I held onto my lead, those next 20kms were a grind. I had won but was way outside the required time and felt knackered. As I was helped away, I heard several dissenting voices predicting there was no way I was going to be fit for the Olympic 20km trial at Lancaster in three weeks time. At that moment, I was hardly in any fit state to disagree.

When we got home, Richard examined my feet. With his apprentice podiatry hat on, he diagnosed that the simple irritating cause of my demise at Droitwich had been *seed corns* – hard congealed skin that, unless removed with a scalpel or a sharp fingernail, would leave anyone feeling like they were walking with little stones in their shoes.

I trusted Richard to do the deed. I was back into training within two days. It was a risk, but I decided to bring my plans forward by one week and not to wait until Lancaster to race again.

Saturday midnight was the start time of the Burrator 100km race. *Yes*, that does say midnight! Whilst I was not prepared to venture out to the moors at that time of night and witness a bunch or hardy souls set off on their long 17 lap trek around the reservoir, I was ready to give it another go over 20kms at 0800 hours. As things went, it turned out rather well, and probably raised quite a few eyebrows.

I recall Richard saying to me afterwards, that in an ironic way, he was relieved that I did not walk 10 seconds quicker; had I done so, I would have broken Ian McCombie's British record, and he doubted anyone would believe it.

My time of 82.12 was done as a virtual time trial. Ireland's Michael Lane was a distant second, recording 90.25. The only other walkers I saw on the course were those loosening up for the 10km event, and those *nutcases* who had been out since the witching hour and viewed as useful intermittent targets in the distance before zipping past at twice the speed. The mere presence of these tough, resilient men inspired me. My thoughts turned to Lancaster. I had six days to think about it.

The morning of the race, after a leisurely stroll around Lancaster town centre, I returned to my B&B room. While Edmund and Mum chatted, I commenced my pre-competition exercise stretch routine. It was a ritual that had served me well for years. We had walked the course the night before when few people were about. The road lap around the university campus was, I thought, surprisingly hilly, one where fast times might be difficult to achieve. It went through my mind that this was all right. Given that I had already walked a good time at Burrator, it was not in my best interest for this race to be fast.

Like all athletic events, a maximum of three men could be picked for the 20kms; three of us had already done the necessary qualifying time of 84 minutes or less, anymore, then things could get complicated with selections. Paranoia or not, I did not rate my chances of being chosen if *four* or more men achieved the time, particularly if Ian McCombie was amongst them. It was worth remembering that the winner in either of the men's race or the women's 10km race would automatically be selected if they recorded a qualifying time. Winning without a qualifying time to your name would not get a ticket to Barcelona.

It was a deliberate ploy to arrive at the race venue later than usual. Already in my tracksuit, I needed only time to collect my race numbers and do a last minute warm-up. Needing to stay focused, I did not want to engage in too much pre-race chat. This proved easier as attention was on the women's race already in progress. Vicky Lupton had a decisive lead after the surprising and disappointing withdrawal of Lisa Langford around half distance through injury.

My attempts at remaining anonymous lasted only so long.

'Hiya Chris, hey, well done on last week. You're not racing today are you?'

'Hey, Mad Max, you'd be crazy to risk it today. What if you bomb?'

The comments came thick and fast. It was exactly what I wanted to avoid. Now I was confused. Tracksuits were being stripped off. Suddenly I was unsure whether to risk starting. If I failed because of fatigue, few people would have any sympathy. The starter's call came. I took a deep breath, peeled off my top and handed it to Mum.

The pressure was immense. All the best British walkers were there. Initially I stayed at the back, locked on the heels of the six or seven men that had quickly formed a leading cluster. I had no interest in helping to make the race fast, so was happy to sit back and cover any tactical move. My intentions were just to win, time was not important.

During those early laps, I felt comfortable with a pace I believed was too slow to trouble the eventual qualifying time. So, it was a shock when I heard the 5km quarter distance split called out by the timekeepers...20.19. It meant that a sizeable group of men were all on schedule. Negative thoughts entered my head. Before they had time to ferment, one by one, walkers slipped back, unable to sustain the pace. I was feeling strong. It was left to me and Ian McCombie at the front to battle it out. I heard him speak.

'Well,' he said breathlessly, 'it looks like it's down to you and me again.'

I had no intention of responding. This was no time for mind games. We went through 10kms in 41.03. To my utter surprise, Ian started to slip back behind me. I could only assume that he was hurting. I pushed on. Minutes later, I rounded a corner, glanced back and saw that he had just been shown a red card. Disqualified, he was out of the race. Suddenly, I was isolated. Andy Penn was second but a good distance behind. All I had to do was finish in front and a third Olympic place would be mine. No heroics, just cruise to the end, I thought.

That final stretch of road to the line, university blocks on one side, trees on the other, the digital clock in view, masses of people shouting encouragement, it was all wonderful. Crossing the line in 83.38 was one of the highlights of my career.

Andy Penn and I were called for a post-competition drug test, a routine and sometimes lengthy procedure after a big race. The resulting delay in getting away afterwards caused both of us to miss the prize presentation. It didn't really concern me. I'd got what I wanted. My position on the Olympic team was secure.

Ian McCombie made a valiant effort to get a qualifying mark when he raced in Europe a few weeks later and fell short by just eight seconds. He would retire before the year was out. A persistent ankle injury had finally got the better of him. In British walking terms, if I was black, he was white, if I was *Steve Ovett*, he was *Sebastian Coe*, if I was brash, he, was measured. Our race rivalry that effectively began in 1985 was now over.

A few weeks later, I lost something even more important. My Grandad passed away.

Mum did get to see me compete in Barcelona. Radiating a proud smile, wearing oversized shades, red, white and blue summer blouse, she was there, standing in amongst thousands of others lining the streets along the Paseo Zona Franca where most of the walks took place at the foot of Montjuic. With her was Edmund, Barbara, their youngest daughter Helen, and a whole crowd of familiar supporters from the Isle of Man.

Loosening up, I was bemused and slightly disappointed that I had not spotted Richard, Janet, their kids and all the friends supposedly travelling with them in the transit and caravan. It was only much later that I discovered that too many complained about the heat and humidity so the decision was made to turn back and return home. The irony would not be lost on me.

So often, it was extreme weather conditions that proved my toughest enemy at summertime major championships. Even hot British summers seldom compared to the oppressiveness experienced when oversees. However, it should be said, that *we* had enjoyed an unusually prolonged period of warm sunshine prior to my departure for Spain. In fact, it had been hot enough for one well meaning person at the gym to suggest that it was probably ideal in terms of acclimatization for my imminent race in Barcelona. I reminded him that in order for me to be able to fulfill my day long managerial responsibilities, I was out on the roads at 7am when it was significantly cooler. My prickly retort was balanced with a conscious effort to say again how proud I was to be representing my country at a third Olympic Games. No matter what the circumstances, I would be doing my best, and thanked him for his support.

Of the fans that did make it, most took advantage of the 20km race starting outside the stadium for the first time. Walkers started on a straight back and forth nine lap 2km circuit before turning away towards a finish beyond the summit of Calle Del Foch, a long tortuous hill that would test even the best.

The race was characteristically fast. Spain had long developed a reputation for producing top walkers, support for their stars ensured it was noisy throughout. Occasionally I heard my name above the hullaballoo, which was particularly encouraging as I did not feel great. My stomach was churning up.

I knew that Andy Penn and Martin Rush were some distance behind me, and I could see at the turns that at the front, Damilano and his Italian teammates were forcing the pace with the Spaniards, the Canadian Le Blanc and Chinese walker, Chen Shaoguo. The sight of Hungarian, Sandor Urbanik and Ireland's Jim McDonald not far behind the leaders made me think that was where I should and could be, but for an irritating gut problem affecting my concentration.

Distracted by the discomfort, I was determined to hold it together for a final push when directed off the circuit towards the uninviting hill. Halfway up the long assent, I passed three walkers in quick succession, a Czech, a German and an Italian. Still well outside the top 10 place that I had genuinely believed was achievable, I aimed to at least claim a good scalp or two before the finish. Pavel Blazek had held the 20km world road record for about a year. Passing the blonde haired Czech along the plateau of Calle Del Foch was very satisfying. Entering the stadium, I had Stefan Johansson within my range, but the world track record holder saw me coming and managed to hold off my advances. So, 16th in 88.45 was what I had to settle for.

Daniel Plaza delighted home supporters with his 81.45 win. Guillaume LeBlanc won silver with a time of 82.25, with bronze going to a fast finishing Giovanni De Benedictis in 83.11. Great performances yes, but ones that with the right preparation and better luck, were perhaps within my capabilities.

As if to try and prove the point, after the Olympics I went in search of the proverbial end-of-season fast time and landed on the beaches of Dunkirk. Unfortunately, my ambitions were blown out of reach by a howling wind coming in off the English Channel. The presence of strong East European opposition, men with significantly faster times than me, should have ensured that it was the very fast race I wanted. Unfortunately, the adverse weather conditions meant it was more a case of, right place, wrong time. Winning in 85.15 was frustrating as it proved nothing other than I had beaten a lot of good athletes. If there was to be a consolation, it came in the evening at the awards presentation. Along with my trophy I was handed an envelope with 3000 francs inside. On the ferry home, Edmund and I sat down in the restaurant and had a fantastic slap up meal. The rest of the money I blew on a new Sony stereo system. CD's were all the rage, and until then I had nothing to play mine on. It was a frivolous treat that was hard to reconcile with my conscience, but one that at least offered several years of enjoyment. I never regretted it.

Roundhay Park: Ian McCombie and I during one of many race duels.

Exhausted, after the completion of the English Commonwealth 30km trial in Leeds where I narrowly beat Ian McCombie

In conversation with the Queen in New Zealand 1990

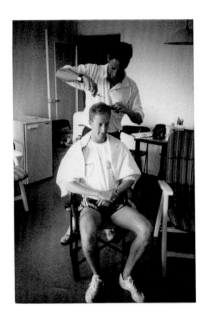

ood haircut: England teammate, Stewart aulkner, long jumper and part-time stylist gets snippy before my race at the 1990 Commonwealth Games

Bad haircut: I've started, so I'll finish. British teammate Andy Penn gets what was probably his worst ever crop, and all before the most important race of his life – the Barcelona Olympic 20kms.

A hotly contested 20km race on the Isle of Man in 1992

Pictured with a bevy of Spanish beauties at the
Barcelona Olympic closing ceremony.

8-Pack: Pictured in 1993 with GB teammates in
Monterrey, Mexico. Probably the last time I felt 100% fit.

I'm praying the Princess Royal won't remember the umbrella incident from the previous occasion we met.

With Linford Christie at the Commonwealth Games in Victoria, Canada 1994.

Posing with Rocky Stone during the Queen's Commonwealth Games walkabout in Victoria, Canada 1994.

L-r, flanked by race rivals Les Morton, Andy Penn and Steve Hollier, shortly after I had won the 1995 national 10 mile title in Sutton Park, Birmingham.

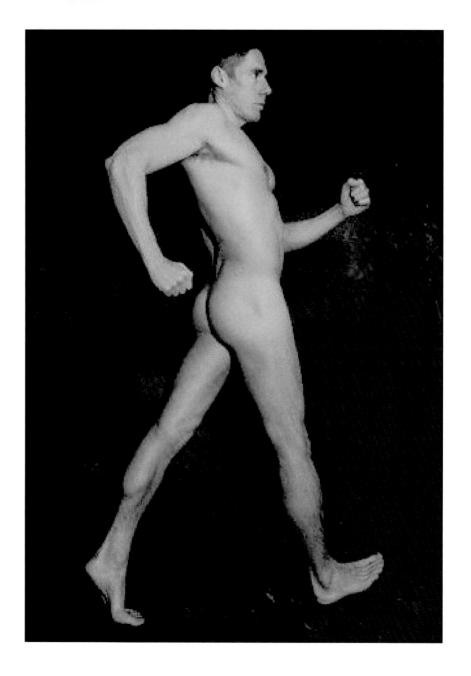

Surprisingly this photograph by Alistair Morrison did not scare the punters away when it was exhibited in the National Portrait Gallery in London.

Meeting my sporting hero – Muhammad Ali at the Atlanta Olympics.

Former world champion boxer Marvellous Marvin Hagler makes my day with a photo and autograph.

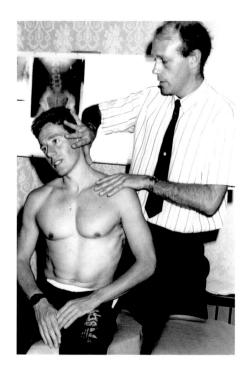

Chiropractor Kevin Kelly promises it won't hurt.

Elated to share Steve Hollier's fantastic 4th place in the 50kms at the '98 Commonwealth Games in Kuala Lumpur.

1993

Could I justify this? Could I justify yet another year of sacrifices, where I muddled along, brushing under the carpet any constructive thought about doing anything meaningful towards trying to secure a future for myself? One man who I only saw occasionally but whose friendship and advice I valued immensely was Murray Lambden. Once a very good international walker himself, he now ran for fun, though with a best marathon time of around two hours 40 minutes I was sure his training still took up much of his free time. A family man, I usually stayed with him and his wife Marie and their two energetic young boys at their home anytime I raced on the Isle of Man. Things in life can usually be put into perspective when you hear of someone else's problems.

I had heard about Robbie's learning difficulties and seen for myself the change in him through the years. When a form of autism was finally diagnosed my heart went out to all the family. I won the Isle of Man 20km race in February. Murray convinced me that I still had a lot to look forward to, and lest we should forget, no one really knows just what is around the corner. It was important that I made the most of what talent I had while there was still a chance. The carrot of competing at a World Cup in a country where top race walkers were revered like any international footballer was one such chance.

On the face of it, meeting up with the British walks squad at Gatwick airport a full four days before the weekend of races in Monterrey, Mexico appeared to be perfectly acceptable. Via a flight into Dallas and a reverse seven hour zone change, we flew on towards Monterrey. After touch-down and baggage collection we boarded a bus and moved on to a small suburb of Monterrey, a town seemingly in the middle of nowhere. We attempted to book into Hotel 88. I say attempted, because the chap on reception certainly did not appear to be expecting us. It was dark, it was hot and sultry, wearily tired, agitation levels were rising within the camp.

I for one did not want anything to go wrong. My training had never gone better; I knew that I was in the form of my life. Four months in, I had already recorded a series of good race wins. At the gym I was lifting great weights; never mind a six-pack stomach mine was looking more like a freakish eight-pack.

As manager, I had devised a test of strength and strength endurance for all members where they could plot their progress on the bench press with a choice of light to heavy weights. My hand-sketched charts hung on the wall for over a year and proved both a popular test and talking point. Leading by example, my first serious attempt at the heaviest 200lb weight scored 21 repetitions. Over the months I steadily upped my best by increments of one to an eventual best of 26 reps. Strength endurance was aptly tested by repeated attempts with the lighter 50lb weight. My first attempt saw me push out 150 reps. It took a while but I eventually managed 210 eye-popping reps; my chest may have been tender to the touch for days afterwards, but I felt great. Whether these exercises helped me walk

157

faster was a matter of opinion.

I was so looking forward to the 20km race on Saturday that I thought it would be disastrous if my plans were to begin to unravel in the final days. Ray Hall, our team manager wiped his sweaty brow, held up a bit of paper and, after a prolonged verbal jousting match with Mexico's version of Basil Fawlty, declared that everything was all right. We were in.

Stepping outside the following morning, in the cold light of day, it looked as if we were in a one horse town; a dust bowl where even John Wayne might have thought twice about pulling up and unsaddling. The good news was that the food was okay. The bad news was that we were staying another night. Surprisingly, that evening, we were joined by walkers from three other national teams, Russia, USA, and Norway.

One of the Norwegians asked me where our team had been training. *Training*? I told him that we had all met up at Gatwick the day before, or was it the day before that, I was unsure by then. He laughed. He didn't believe me at first, until I reiterated the point. He thought it inconceivable that our team were contemplating racing in the heat and humidity of Mexico without at least some level of acclimatization. His team had been at a training camp for the previous three weeks, other teams he knew had spent several weeks longer. I tried to put the knowledge of our compromised position to the back of my mind.

Comparing Hotel 88 to the Fiesta Americana found in the heart of Monterrey could not have been more stark. Five star luxury. I roomed with Andy Penn. We put our bags down and marveled at a room so big that our two king sized beds appeared the only obstacles preventing us from doing an indoor training session there and then. The balcony at the far end looked particularly inviting. Inside it was cool and air-conditioned whereas outside it was a baking hot.

I was coaching Julie Drake by this time; a young, ditzy blonde with potential to be a top walker. Low level training to unwind the legs was all that was required. We joined the throng of other nationals going up and down the barren, traffic-free stretch of road just outside the hotel. She expressed all the typical pre-race anxieties about not feeling good, this hurts, that hurts, look how fit the others look. Whilst I tried to reassure her that everything would be all right, I think sub-consciously I was also trying to convince myself. Thirty minutes was enough the first night, less on Friday morning. In the end, you just say, stay hydrated, drink a lot, and relax.

The organisers had laid on wonderful outdoor shaded eateries for us to frequent. If only we were on holiday, it would have been perfect. I did not sleep well that night, first worrying about the bouts of dizziness that I had experienced during the day and then thinking about the race. I was so fit, and yet I was beginning to doubt what I might do.

Mid-afternoon, it was time to board the bus to take us downtown to the race venue, fifteen minutes away. On our arrival, the automated doors whooshed open and out we stepped from a luxurious air-con vehicle to a blast of heat, the like of which you only feel when opening an oven door during preparations for Sunday lunch.

Against the backdrop of the Sierra Madre mountains the views beyond were breathtaking. However, with the thermometer nudging towards 100 degrees, I suspected that the surrounding scenery was the last thing on the minds of the women taking part in the 10kms – the first of three races all covered by live TV. Journalists swarmed everywhere. I spotted Carlos Mercenario sat beneath a canopy surrounded by men and women thrusting microphones towards his face, presumably wanting comments prior to his 50km race the next morning.

The crowds were incredible. Flag waving, whistle blowing, 50,000 it was estimated were spread around the 2km circuit. I had the speed at the beginning, but no strength. After starting in white searing light, I was already feeling faint when we dipped sharply down into an underpass and semi-darkness that would last for about 30 or 40 seconds before rising up again into the light and another blast of heat on cobbled ground.

I felt as if someone had taken a sledgehammer to my legs. Whilst local star Daniel Garcia was heading a lead pack with teammate Cruz and whipping the crowds into frenzy, I was already ruing the day as I pushed hard but was slipping further back. It felt truly awful.

It was all I could do near the end to claw back, catch and pass Andy Penn for the consolation of being first Briton to finish. He and Rocky Stone found me later in the hotel corridor behind an ice-cream cabinet cowering on my hands and knees, retching. They said they had been drawn towards the area of my predicament by a noise reminiscent of a cow giving birth. I said I wanted to be alone, but would they go away?

Whilst the Mexicans danced the salsa with an overall team victory, Spanish eyes were filled with tears of joy in second, and taking top honours as always for looking catwalk sharp, it was the Italians who stepped up to the stage to collect their bronze medals. Meanwhile, the entire 12 strong British team could only lick their war wounds. Finishing as high as 13th overall team actually flattered us. Collectively, *we* gutted out finishes, where other arguably stronger teams had competitors who aborted the united cause.

Julie was first female Briton and though outside 50 minutes she acquitted herself well in the oppressive conditions, and yet, like the other three, spent time in the medical tent on stretchers; for poor Sylvia Black, matters got off even worse after a table collapsed on her resulting in a back injury that needed attention and an overnight stay in hospital. She was later assisted by wheelchair to the steps of the plane taking us home; a seat in first class was at least of some consolation to her.

My economy class seat was comfortable enough, but I was far from happy. I sat there and stewed for a while. Super confident that I was ready to walk a time below 82 minutes, it was galling to record an actual finishing time that was over 90. The adverse weather *slowed* even the great walkers like Garcia in the 20kms and Mercenario in the 50kms, as illustrated by their respective winning times of 84.26 and 3:50.28. But, I could at least have been closer, I thought; *we* could have all been faster.

Heated views had already been exchanged between the team about the apparent hopelessness of us having a genuine chance of performing at our best when so woefully unprepared for extreme climatic conditions. It was a tired complaint, but one that was just not getting addressed, or if it was, not with any suitable answers. Someone with more scientific knowledge even argued that, had anyone cruelly wanted to maximize our team's chances of performing at its worst, travelling four to five days before racing in Mexico was the optimum time! True or not, whispered moans between the walkers never changed anything.

I did not care if I was perceived as the ringleader, I was determined to gather support around me and speak out. We move down the aisle and approached Ray Hall with our gripes.

To be fair, he understood our concerns, but his hands were tied by a lack of financial resources. The budget for the Monterrey venture was around £7500, a sum meant to cover all expenses for the entire British party. As measly as it was, the funding for the British walks team was the best to-date. Unlike Finland, who sent their walkers away for seven weeks, Slovakia and Hungary for four weeks, there was no money in the coffers to send our team for pre-race acclimatization. The irony, he quite rightly argued, was that almost all of Brits had unsympathetic employers who were unlikely to allow the time away even if the money suddenly became available. We were not like Spain, Italy, Germany and Mexico, countries that supported full time athlete status for their walkers.

Without a higher profile and the input of outside corporate sponsorship, the situation was unlikely to change in the foreseeable future. It seemed almost frivolous to say it, but someone did; more success usually equals more funding. It was a chicken and egg situation, a situation not helped by an unavoidable home truth. *Football* attracted approximately 95% of available corporate sponsorship. Of the remaining 5%, as much as 4% was swallowed up by the other big and popular sports in Britain, sports like rugby and cricket. This meant that only a paltry 1% of the sponsorship pie was left to be fought over by all other sports trying to grab a piece of the action. What chance did race walking really have? It was a rhetorical question that left me returning to my seat feeling quite deflated.

A few days later, it was simply nice to be back amongst friends again at Burrator. No razzmatazz, no glitz, no funding here, just honest hard-working people putting on a race for enthusiast traveling at their own expense. I may have been jet-lagged and sore with a hamstring that had tightened on the long journey home, but I still managed to coast to a winning time of 86.02, more than six minutes clear of Ireland's Michael Lane.

I did not know it then, but that latest niggling hamstring problem would ultimately bother me for the rest of the year, and seriously curtail my racing. It would also lead to a further injury problem that would not be diagnosed properly until seen by medics in Stuttgart shortly before my 20km race at the World Athletic Championships.

I really should not have gone to Germany, but, like the Olympic Games, these particular championships, back then, only came around every four years. However, if you cannot be inspired by the sight and sounds of 70,000 spectators in a stadium with many more out on the road, there is something seriously wrong. My heart simply was not in it. Matters were not helped by only being about 80-90% fit.

Frustrated by irregular training caused by my persistent sore hamstring, I had also a developed a small inguinal hernia as well. The fact I finished first Briton had more to do with the fact that both Andy Penn and Rocky Stone were ill before the race started. Both were around 10 years younger than me and our 50km teammate, Les Morton. They had undoubted potential to record top class times. Without the kind of support I had talked so much about in the past, actually achieving that potential was always likely to be difficult.

The four of us roomed with British athletes who could boast about their contracts with various companies, a fact that allowed many to train full time. As interesting as it was to hear, it was equally a bitter pill to swallow. Our roommates meant no harm by what they were telling us, but it highlighted once again that *us walkers* were undoubtedly the paupers of the team. The British athletic federation knew this and it rankled that they were not doing enough to help more with some financial support that could make a difference. It got under my skin so much that I encouraged my friends to join me when it was arranged at short notice for us to discuss the matter with head coach, Frank Dick.

Frank was a straight talking Scot, a respected leader of athletes whose motivational *climb mountain* team talks were legendary. He listened to what we had to say, and suggested we formalize our requests into a document and present it later for proper assessment at committee level. Our female walkers were upset I had not included them in the discussions. Angry that they dared to have a *pop* at me, I counter argued they could have been involved had they not gone shopping. I invited additional input from members of other clubs from back home. Once everything was collated, a professionally presented dossier was sent to British HQ outlining a range of issues from much discussed top coaching to warm weather training. We waited and waited for a response. I heard no more about it. The cynic in me thinks that the document probably took a scenic route to the bin.

On reflection, I look back to that time and wonder whether I should have announced my retirement there and then. Indeed, but for a twist of fate I might have done so.

Andy and Rocky both declined the opportunity to travel with a young England athletics team to compete in a two-sided international match against the Ukraine. Second choice or not, I jumped at the chance to say *yes* to what would be a five day trip away to Kiev. All I had to do was walk the comparatively short distance of 10kms.

I loved going to Eastern Europe. Since the fall of the Berlin wall in 1989, evolutionary changes were happening. Borders may have been easier to cross, but

161

I rationalized that it would as likely be a long time before I went back unless I had this kind of extra incentive.

As I discovered in my travels, football often shared their facilities with athletics. The home of Dynamo Kiev was magnificent. The crowds may have been sparse, but it was a wonderful arena in which to compete. Only two races were televised live in their entirety. The men's 100m sprint and the whole of the 10km walk: four men on a track for 25 laps in the pouring rain. Those England athletes watching it on screen whilst receiving a pre-event massage could not understand it. Extensive TV coverage such as this was unheard of back home in Britain. I finished a very close third to Kozlov and Popovich – the star athletes of the Ukrainian team. It may have been mine and Mark Easton's misfortune to have come up against two of the world's fastest walkers, but it gifted us the higher moral ground when chatting to our young impressionable teammates. It also helped me feel good about walking again, so much so that I decided against stepping off the revolving carousel and instead stay on the ride and see what else I might achieve.

1994

Though the hernia operation at the end of December had been a success, the recuperation period of six weeks did mean that in terms of training my year got off to a slow start, literally. Burrator is a beautiful place at anytime. Accompanied by Katie Pannell, it was all I could do to gingerly put one foot in front of the other and inch forward whilst she gleefully talked about school and boyfriends, and her dad race walked one lap of the reservoir.

The big carrot for the year was to compete at the Commonwealth Games in Canada. First, I had to qualify. I guaranteed selection by winning the English 30km trials on a multi-lapped circuit around the leafy grounds of Christ's Hospital, a posh *bluecoat* school at Horsham in rural Sussex. Though I was pleased, it was far from a vintage display of walking.

My hernia problems may have dissipated, but the grumbling hamstring simply would not heal. I was advised that without a reasonable period of treatment *and* rest, I was going to be continually hampered. The thought of a third Commonwealth Games representation however, was too much of an inducement not to keep going. Sadly and reluctantly, I had to accept that there appeared to be a maximum controlled speed I could manage before I risked creating a muscle spasm in the back of my left leg.

The fact that I did put together three fairly even 10km splits of around 46 minutes in Victoria was an accomplishment in itself. Others might not see it that way. Australian, Nick A'Hern won, walking at a pace closer to 43 minutes. Good for only twelfth position, my time of 2:18.14 was really the best I was ever likely to do.

Far from being disillusioned, I took solace from the belief that I had more to come. I enjoyed the sun-blessed Games, saw lots of great action, said *hello* to the Queen and Prince Philip during their walkabout in the athlete's village, took time to smell the roses at the glorious Butchard Gardens, and, after seeing the conclusion of the women's marathon, went whale watching for three jaw-dropping hours.

It would be nice to say that I returned home and with the passage of time and the right sort of help, all my various injuries resolved. The facts were, I was 37 and I had covered tens of thousands of miles over the years. I did improve. I also went go-carting with my brothers; saw other family, including my dear old Nan who was ill; bought a second-hand Ford Capri for a bargain knockdown price, helped not least by the continued efforts of big hearted Bill Lawrence, a stoical member of my club who saw it as his personal mission to approach anyone who would listen and raise funds to aid my walking ambitions. Bill wanted to see me compete at a fourth Olympic Games with the only proviso that if I succeeded, I might send him a signed postcard. We're not talking huge sums of money, perhaps, £25 here, £100 there, but it all added up, and for that, I would be eternally grateful.

It was a proud day when I collected the pre-ordered adhesive car stickers from Mamba Sign Makers. The set of two Union Jack flags and Olympic rings stuck on either side of my Capri looked fantastic, the colours especially vibrant against the newly polished black paintwork. Metaphorically, I guessed I had publicly pinned my colours to the mast: I was aiming for Atlanta '96 and hoped no one would get in my way.

1995

Jeff Ford was his name. A respected athletics coach and mentor to many a fine walker in Yorkshire. If there was ever a man who called a spade *a bloody shovel*, it was Jeff. I had just finished a disappointing fourth in the national 20kms at Christ's Hospital behind Rocky Stone, Chris Cheeseman, and Andy Penn. It was a below par performance, but on the strength of a faster 20km walk earlier in the season, I was still ranked 3rd on paper for the year. So, when the posse of walk officials retreated to the *smoke filled room* in order to deliberate over their final four-men per event team selections for the World Cup in Beijing, I ate my sandwiches and drank tea believing that things would be all right. I was wrong.

First the prize presentations were made. I had no medal to collect but did want to wait to hear the team announcements. We all did. It seemed to be an inordinate amount of time until at last they all filed back into the room. The crowded room fell silent as the names were called. My name was not amongst them; I was dumbfounded. There was a lot of handshaking, backslapping and a few consolatory words directed at me.

I was still feeling bemused and undecided about whether or not I should just up and leave with Edmund and my Mum when Jeff Ford approached.

163

Jeff had a lisp and because of it, an unfortunate habit of spitting when he spoke. He seemed to glorify in telling me he had argued long and hard that I did not warrant a place on the team. Apparently, not everyone agreed with him, but he was satisfied that when it went to a vote he got his way.

'You're finished,' he said. 'You're too old. It's time for the younger ones to be given their chance.'

My argument that it was a speed contest and not an age contest fell on deaf ears. Jeff was not interested in anything I had to say.

'You're finished,' he reiterated.

I wiped my face and walked away.

There were no last minute changes or U-turn by the selectors. I was not part of the eight man team that went to Beijing. I did, however, have a number of very good races throughout the rest of Spring and the Summer months. Meeting Sally at an International walks match in France was just the start of a long, on-off distant relationship that remarkably never once descended into anything bitter. Her sweet and understanding nature, the most probable reason for our amicable *off* periods.

It was decided I would have another crack at a 50km race in September. The plan was that after many weeks of heavy mileage, I would do a 20km *sharpener* in Dublin's Phoenix Park two weeks prior to travelling out with Richard and Edmund for the big one in Holland.

Rocky Stone may have beaten me with his 85.21 to my 86.34, but I was nevertheless still very pleased. I had done so much hard training in the lead up to the race and knew that my priorities lay ahead. Now, I should have been wary, but when Jeff Ford finished congratulating me, he suggested that when I raced in Holland I would do well if I chose to walk alongside his protégé Les Morton. I knew that Les was an excellent walker, so considered Jeff's advice to be sound, and so I thanked him.

We had heard that various groups of British walkers were heading for Barendrecht, near Rotterdam.

Come Saturday, the day before the race, we were strolling around the parkland course taking stock of all its nuances. More and more familiar faces were turning up, among them, Rocky and his girlfriend, a large party of walkers from Sheffield and York with supportive friends in tow each with glasses in hand enjoying the banter.

Things appeared less rosy by mid-morning the next day. Les was one of several walkers that had dropped out of the race. Suffering from a pre-race injury, he called it a day by the 22km mark. I had deliberately allowed Andrzej Chylinski, a naturalised American to slip further ahead, thinking it wiser to walk alongside the normally reliable Sheffield walker. Our pace turned out to be too slow for a sub four hour time. Left isolated in second position, I panicked and rashly set off too fast in pursuit of the man ahead. I caught him, but the erratic pace proved to be my

164

undoing. I faded during the final 10kms and fell once again outside my schedule ending with a time of 4:02.47. Disappointed, I did my best to appear magnanimous when a jubilant Chylinski offered me a high-five at the finish, so sure was he that his 3:58.39 would secure him Olympic selection.

My head was still down when I squeezed in amongst the excess bags on the back seat of Richard's Vauxhall Cavalier. For a while at least, my friends left me to my brooding thoughts. There was a long car journey ahead; there would be plenty of time to talk.

Sitting in the front passenger seat, I was aware that Edmund had been thumbing through his papers for some time. We had already passed through Antwerp in Belgium and heading for the docks at Calais when he spoke up.

'I see here, that there's a 50km race in Romania in November.'

'Is there?' I heard Richard query.

'Yes, in Constanta at the end of November. That's seven weeks time. You could do that Chris.'

My knees were wrapped around my ears; I was stiff, fed up and Mr Shillabeer was casually suggesting that I might like to do another 50km race. I was unsure whether I wanted to dignify his question with an answer. I liked him too much to say exactly what was on my mind. Instead, I took a few moments before I said, 'No!'

It killed the conversation dead. Eventually I heard the two of them in front resume talking about other things. Meanwhile, I was in the back, thinking. Edmund had sowed the seeds of a ridiculous idea. It was good enough for me. The only condition was that I would do the Chippenham to Calne six mile race in six days time. If I felt okay afterwards, I would train for that *damn* 50km race in Constanta.

The following weekend I won the Chippenham. The die had been cast. I set about training like my life depended on it. The aim was to improve any similar session that I had done in the lead up to Holland. My attitude was resolute. If I was going to it, it would have to be worthwhile. Contacts were made, paperwork completed, the race appropriately sanctioned by necessary personal at home and abroad. At times it was completely exasperating until finally, was given the *go-ahead* by Malcolm Arnold at British athletics and by Peter Marlow on behalf of the walking commission.

Travelling solo, I flew to Bucharest. After a night spent alone at Hotel Olympia, I was met by Triain Badea, the Romanian General Secretarial and two colleagues, a young man and a young woman, who I deduced by their tactile behavior to be boyfriend and girlfriend. None of my travelling companions spoke English.

Kristie drove the entire 280kms east to the Black Sea coast. For much of the time, I sat mute in the back of the Mercedes Benz transit. It worried me that our driver's attention was not always on the road ahead. Gabrielle was admittedly very attractive, but as we hurtled through the rural countryside, I was more concerned by the on-coming train about to cut across *our* tracks than how lovely she looked. While I stared out of the window and watched that train get ever nearer, it crossed my mind that if we all died, few people back home would have any notion as to where I was. I was sure by then that Kristie saw an irresistible challenge of *chicken*. I held my breath.

We made it across the open railway tracks with moments to spare. I hardly dared look over my shoulder; there was no need, for the great roar of carriages trundling pass made my spine shiver, whilst the gust of wind blowing my way might well have been the Grim Reaper teasingly brushing my neck. I shut the side window as Kristie whooped with delight. I settled back and prayed that the rest of the journey would be uneventful.

We had gone from brilliant sunshine in the west to nightfall and icy wintery conditions in the east. My heart sank. I had travelled so far and I was beginning to doubt that the race could take place.

Fortunately, by daybreak, it was evident that no more snow had fallen overnight. The army had been out and tirelessly cut a path through the flat, out and back, 3km road circuit. The temperature throughout the morning only rose to a maximum of four degrees. Crisp and bright, trees on one side, the beach on the other, it was perfect.

I had a great race. Finally breaking clear of local star Costan Balan around the 38km mark, I went onto win in 3.53.14, well inside the Olympic qualifying time. Unable to contain myself, I needed a hug. Mr Badea, a great big bear of a man, was the only man I recognised; he seemed happy to oblige, punching the air in unison.

I could sympathize with Balan when he eventually crossed the line in 4.00.04, for I too had once similarly walked a 50kms tantalizingly close to four hours, only I was two seconds quicker. Here, when it mattered, I walked two 25km halves of 1.57.25 and 1.55.49, thus recording a very satisfying negative split.

1996

I did not have to wait too long for that all important telephone call. It was mid-January. Jack Thomas, chairman of the international walks selection committee said that, following a meeting earlier that day at British athletics HQ in Birmingham, it was decided I should be pre-selected for the Atlanta Olympics. I thought it fitting for Jack to be the one to have broken the news. Where others chose any opportunity to criticize, the kindly Welshman had always remained a staunch supporter of mine. Contentment, probably best describes the overwhelming feeling I experienced at that time.

Media interest was incredible. Much was written about the significance of me becoming a four time Olympian; only two British men before me had achieved the same: Decathlete, Daley Thompson and walker, Paul Nihill. Perhaps one of the most amusing things I read in the press was after Giles Smith from the Daily Telegraph visited the gym and interviewed me in the office. He was moved to write, *traditionally, the walker's physique tends towards the twiggy, whereas Chris, who is of medium height, has some of the largest pectorals I have ever sat opposite.* This particular physical attribute I can only assume was of interest to the man who I encountered next.

Alistair Morrison was unknown to me till we met in Plymouth. I had never previously been a paid up subscriber of the Esquire magazine, so I wasn't to know he could claim world renown for his many celebrity photographs. He was on a quest to photograph a number of Olympians in unique poses and I was on his list!

Firstly, we drove to Plymbridge Woods where he and his female assistant, had me walking up and down the old cycle path beneath old disused railway bridges and over mammoth viaducts. Flakes of snow fell, conveniently, so I thought, to add a wintery touch to his pictures. It was bitterly cold, but I hoped he had what he wanted. No!

Back at the gym, we discussed things in the privacy of the solarium room. Take off my kit? *Okay*, I said, but only if his assistant left the room. It was agreed. The full page print chosen to grace the pages of the magazine caused quite a stir, not least by my Mum. I believed she bought more than one copy. Completely naked, my modesty was preserved by a strategic shot showing me in an imaginary full-length stride. My brother Pat framed his copy and hung it on his wall at home. Another similar copy hung at the National Portrait Gallery in London for quite a while.

This obsession with my *newly discovered* physique knew no bounds. The local press, rather than photograph me in the usual guise, either walking, lifting weights, or holding a trophy, suddenly appeared eager to see me in the buff, well, topless at least. I agreed only once. Janet Pannell and her friends at the theatre were keen to promote their production of, *A Night with the Stars* – a benefit night on my behalf to raise funds for my final Olympic push. Rehearsals had already started and publicity was needed to encourage ticket sales.

Attired in showy Arabian clothes, Janet draped her arms around her bare-chested slave, smiled, and struck a pose. Whether it helped the sell of tickets is another matter?

Training had been going fantastically well, until…my dreaded hamstring pulled again. I carried on walking. Both Richard and Kevin Kelly worked tirelessly on helping to keep me going. Richard had learned the art of deep friction massage. Oh God, did it hurt. Some days I could train, others I couldn't. By the time I was set to walk 50kms at Podebrady in the Czech Republic, my doubts were such, that I felt compelled to tell team manager Bob Dobson at the airport that I perhaps should not start the race. He acknowledged my predicament but considered it worth trying. I did, and pulled up injured after 12kms.

I was distraught. A repeat round of training and treatment ensued. A brief enjoyable respite came when I was invited to guest on Radio Devon and speak about my career whilst choosing six of my favourite records: Simply the Best, by Tina Turner; Don't You forget about me, by Simple Minds; Back for good, by Take That; Don't look back in Anger, by Oasis; These are the days of our lives, by Queen; and, What a wonderful world, by Louis Armstrong.

There was nothing wonderful about my next race. I had wanted to withdraw from the British team traveling to Moscow for the eight nations match, but was under pressure to prove my fitness. I failed miserably to do so. It was supposed to have been 35kms. I lasted about 500m, or about three minutes of walking. My hamstring went into a virtual spasm from the moment I started. I pressed on, just hoping that it would resolve itself. It didn't.

There were a number of good British performances, but none that would trouble the minds of the Olympic walks selectors later in the year. Only myself and Vicky Lupton held provisional tickets in our hands. This sad fact was touched upon back at the hotel during our post-competition team de-brief. At the conclusion of the discussions, I was asked by Peter Markham to hang back for a private chat. I was anticipating something being said, but totally unprepared for the tirade of abuse that followed.

Jeff Ford was positively venomous in his criticism of me. Incandescent with rage, he opinioned, that I was *a disgrace*, and, *not fit to wear the British vest*. Though I was astounded by what he had to say, it was how he said it that caused me to smile. I wiped the spit from my face and calmly turned to Peter and asked if he had anything to say. Peter, bless him, suggested that emotions were running high and it might be best if we spoke about this another time. I nodded, Jeff snorted a half-hearted agreement.

I later retracted my threat to report Jeff. There was an insistence that I should prove my fitness at a later date. Reluctantly, I agreed.

I won the next 20km race in London. Jeff Ford watched from the sidelines. I hated every moment of it.

The Olympic 50km race was not exactly a low point for me. How could it be? It was what I had trained so hard for. My hamstring held up; but, all the weeks of painful treatment and stop-start training had taken its toll. In the final analysis, I was not fit enough, as the hard fought yet ultimately disappointing walk of four hours 18 minutes in Atlanta demonstrated.

Though nothing could excuse Jeff Ford's comments, it could be argued that he was partially vindicated. Cold statistics however do not tell the full story. Because I had managed several top quality walks since that London race, I still believed I might have pulled off a worthy performance, befitting of a four-time Olympian. Alas, too often I was on the treatment table and squirming in pain. If I had withdrawn from the team, what purpose would it have achieved? With no other British man qualified, there was no other walker to replace me and represent our country.

No such problem for Poland. Robert Korzeniouski had begun to cement his place in history with a gold medal walk. I was pleased for him, especially as I remembered four years earlier in Barcelona, trying to lend a supporting hand as he sat in tears, crestfallen shortly after being disqualified for a rule infringement when in sight of the stadium and a *certain* silver medal. I was standing alongside his teammate and my girlfriend Beata Kasmarska, the Polish woman I first met in Bekescsaba all those years ago. If proof were ever needed that even the very best have setbacks and bounce back better and stronger, then Robert is a prime example.

The disappointment of my own race was balanced by other more memorable moments to take home. The undoubted highlight was meeting my all-time sporting hero, Muhammad Ali. Afflicted by Parkinson's disease, Ali was seen by billions shakily lighting the Olympic flame at the opening ceremony. I had my own brief encounter with the great man one morning mid-way through the Games when I was walking through the athletes' village. I came across him and a small entourage that included his old trainer Angelo Dundee as they were all exiting a building. I spluttered some gobbledygook whilst Ali shook my hand and one of his minders agreed to take our picture. They walked on while I clicked away with my camera until we were all enveloped by a mass of other captivated onlookers.

Ali was not the only boxer that I met. The great Evander Holyfield was a delight to meet. I would have liked to have shown photographic evidence of that occasion, but my roommate, 1500m runner John Mayock used his girlfriend's camera to capture the moment and I never saw her again. Edmund and Barbara were there to support me; as was another friend, Dave Fox a marathoner from the gym. It was Ed's birthday on the day of my race.

Afterwards, and after a shower and a miniscule bite to eat, I dragged my aching body around to meet the three of them in the British hospitality lodge. It was particularly gratifying to see the look on Ed's face when I presented him with an Olympic poster that 40 members of our athletics team signed for me. By the following day, I was feeling a little more recovered and able to smile in wonderment at the gloriously over-the-top closing ceremony, at least that was, until a moment near the end, when songstress Sheila E threw her drum sticks into the crowd.

Surrounded by 100,000 spectators in the stadium, I had already made a hobbled dash from my seat towards the centre of the grassy infield, chasing hundreds of other swifter athletes in order to stand close and gaze up to the raised platform where Stevie Wonder, Little Richard, Gloria Estefan, Al Green, the Pointer Sisters and Sheila E were all jamming on stage. Things were rocking until that fateful moment when the sticks were launched high into the night sky and I was just one of many who reached up in a vain attempt to grab a memento. Next thing I knew, a man mountain – a shot putter, a basketball player, a heavyweight boxer, I'm not sure; but, whoever he was, whatever sport he did, he was huge, and when he toppled backwards bowling others over in the process, it was me that was flattened to the ground. Assisted to my feet, a forced grimace disguised the true agony.

I was still coping with a severely bruised coccyx two weeks later when I saw Lisa Langford become Mrs Kehler. Her church wedding to Martin, a fellow doctor, was delightfully traditional. There was nothing conventional however, about the evening reception held a short distance away at Eyam youth hostel on the edge of the Derbyshire Dales, where every guest was encouraged to dress in character from Peter Pan.

I borrowed Edmund's stripy pyjamas, tucked a teddy bear under my arm and played safe as one of the children. Whilst I made a pig of myself with the delicious barbecued food, I did my best to oblige the various Captain Hooks, Tinker Bells, even a horizontal standing crocodile all of whom appeared to have an insatiable appetite for any anecdote that I may have about the Olympics. Quite surreal, especially when a man on stilts, a juggler, and a fire-blower were never far away, and all this before retiring to a bunk bed dormitory. It was like being in the cubs all over again, only with wacky dreams virtually guaranteed. In the morning, all guests were asked to reconvene for a group hike on the moors with a bride and groom, whose lateness when arriving in an open-top convertible was met with a barrage of innuendo and smutty mockery.

It was with considerable apprehension that I attended a school reunion held at the Elmore football club in Tiverton. I have since learnt that misgivings similar to my own are quite common. Did I really want to meet friends not seen for more than 20 years? How would I compare? Who would I recognise? What would they think of me? All valid questions perhaps, but in the end, ones that simply did not matter.

It was a boozy affair. Well, that's how I remember it. Teaming up with Richard Jarman and a bunch of other old football friends for an earlier pub crawl ensured that our entrance was noticed. Sure, I did not recognise a lot of faces from my senior year; we were after all, close to 40. Name tags on lapels helped, but slightly embarrassing when trying to sneak a quick look before engaging conversation.

Some men were bald and so rotund I was unsure whether they were old classmates or teachers? Some of the women were unrecognisable, apart from Clare who was probably still the prettiest. I thought I had a chance until my so-called mates unceremoniously dragged me away from the smoochy dances near the end. It didn't really matter. I had a great time, and would encourage anyone to attend their own reunion. What's the worst that can happen? And that's where I guess it is impossible to generalise.

You will undoubtedly hear something about kids, marriages and divorce. I think that I heard that Jimmy was on his fourth marriage. It was just as well that he had apparently made a lot of money in scrap metal, but as it wasn't directly substantiated by him, we quickly moved on to who fancied who and how our respective football teams were doing.

I did get asked about my racing career. Unsurprising, as it was what defined me. One or two expressed some surprise that I was not retiring.

'How much longer can you keep going?'

'Surely, you must be getting too old by now.'

'You know all that muscle will turn to fat when you do stop.'

My final race of the year in December was as memorable for the prize presentation as it was for another seven mile Pewsey cup win. There was something very poignant about accepting the special award made by Wally Emery and the Mayor of Calne. Wally was a proud man, a chief judge and race organizer in the South West region, and a man who had been another staunch supporter of mine over the years. Speaking to a large gathering in the sports centre, he spoke movingly of his recollections of my racing career before leading the applause and handing me a specially engraved tankard to commemorate my four Olympic appearances.

1997

My part-time work at the veterinary surgery was interesting on so many levels. Dispensing prescribed tablets, responding to the reception bell, or answering the telephone may have all been routine duties. But I also watched in amazement at the birth of puppies and kittens. Helped where I could with a whelping, occasionally stepped in to hold forceps during assisted operations, watched grown men cry at the demise of a much loved pet, and shared tears of gratitude when an animal was brought back from the brink by the skills of my friend, Edmund Shillabeer.

I had long become used to working with Edmund. When he was unavailable, all staff appeared to adapt reasonably well to working with a locum vet. None of us were prepared however for his enforced absence following a near fatal road accident in January.

Whilst being driven on the M5 motorway, Ed sat busying himself with paperwork in the back of the mobile surgery when suddenly a heavy lorry's slipstream caused their vehicle to swerve violently. Before he could grab hold of anything he shot through a side window landing on the road and sliding along scraping skin off his body in the process. The fact that no vehicle hit him was a miracle in itself. He was airlifted by helicopter to the burns unit of Frenchay hospital in Bristol where he underwent a series of skin grafts.

Richard Pannell and I visited him as soon as we were allowed. In spite of head wounds that required many stitches, severe skin abrasions and tendon damage to his right arm, plus painful back and leg scrapes, Ed was incredibly positive about his future aims. The most immediate of which was to doggedly go ahead with plans to compete in the London marathon in April.

171

The same weekend that he achieved that aim, I took part in what I thought would be my seventh and final World Cup appearance for Great Britain at Podebrady. Each of the three races, the men's 20km and 50km races plus the women's 10kms was awesomely quick. No amount of superlatives could do the 20km event justice. I watched reigning Olympic champion Jefferson Perez win in majestic style and first of 11 men to dip below 80 minutes. That equates to a walking speed of around 10mph for over 12 miles! Though five of those 11 were Russians and two Belarusians, a fact that highlighted the might of East European walking, none could contain the power of an Ecuadorian who enjoys superstar status in his homeland.

The next day, the 50km walk was equally competitive, a race ultimately won by Spain's Jesus Garcia. Inspired from afar by Edmund, I was determined to go out fast. A halfway split of 1.56.08 was good and enough to keep me close to the leaders. Alas, repeated bouts of sickness beyond the 30km mark resulted in my pace dropping like a stone. I was relieved to rally and find strength within the closing stages to eventually record a respectable 4.05.42 finishing time. The vomiting cost me at least 20 places, so the fact that I was easily the leading Brit' was of little compensation. Overall, the cup was won by Russia, just a few points ahead of Mexico. Great Britain was 18th, one position behind Guatemala, but, and as if to emphasize that even the strongest nations can also get it wrong, *we* finished one position ahead of China.

Globally, race walking had become so strong. Evidently, Great Britain as a team was no longer a force. I felt that I had done my best. Speaking up for the common cause was akin to climbing a greasy pole. I was probably ready for a change; I just wasn't expecting it to start during this particular weekend.

From the time of our arrival in Podebrady, we were assisted by Erika, a stunningly attractive Czech student who turned the heads of all red-blooded males from the moment she stepped up onto the bus, smiled, and announced that she would be our interpreter for the duration of the British team's stay. The clamour to find any excuse to converse with her was excruciating, and I include myself in the queue of those prepared to risk potential ridicule by any witness to such a scene. She seemed genuinely pleased to accept my few British lapel pins – a tactical ploy that generally held little water when chatting up the girls back home.

No one was more surprised than me when she asked me to join her for a drink. Before the team's departure, addresses were exchanged and an agreement was made to stay in touch. I returned home and prepared for best man duties at the wedding of my brother Peter to Sarah. I might have spoken more about this encounter but for our eldest brother Pat being so besotted with tales of a new girlfriend called Ruth who was unable to attend that blissful weekend.

My family never really got to know Erika, in spite of the fact that she moved to Plymouth and came to live with me. She immediately set about changing the décor within the flat. Posters came down, replaced by walls painted in various shades of pastel. Potted plants were introduced, and out went the piles of magazines. Grubby trainers were either tucked away or thrown out. I learnt ice skating. She was very good, I was hopeless. We went to Prague where I met her parents. I did some training but with no plans to race, it seemed natural to think about future possibilities. She got a job waitressing. I applied for the role of national event coach.

Interviewed in Birmingham, I waited to hear the outcome, knowing if it was positive then it was even less likely that I would return to racing. During the summer I had helped with some regional-area weekend coaching, and agreed to personally coach Steve Hollier, a 19 year old walker from the Midlands who I had first met in 1995 when the tall gangly teenager roomed with me and Andy Penn during the International weekend in France. I also met up with Andi Drake at his bequest, so as I might offer technical advice on his return to walking after five years away on the running circuit. We were both aware of the difficulties that had risen on the national scene.

The British Athletic Federation had gone bankrupt with alleged debts of half a million pounds. A new governing body sprung up called Performance Athletics Services. *PAS* would prove to be short lived, until UK Athletics was formed. In the meantime the sweeping changes to the structure of British athletics saw the appointment of new event coaches, with the exception of one discipline – walks! It was left to PAS Endurance Technical Director, Norman Brook to tell me and two others that we were to be offered a joint role, in effect a task force of three to lead and co-ordinate British race walking over the next three years.

The official public announcement of all event coach appointments was made at a National Endurance Conference held at Cardiff where attendances numbered around 200. Although the weekend conference on the whole was a triumph with informative lectures and outdoor practical sessions, things were distinctly less convivial when the names of the walks appointees were made public. Quite a few of the forty or so representatives from the walks community were quick to express their scepticism during episodes of heated debate over lunch and mid-afternoon coffee. It was impossible not to overhear some of the things being said.

'It's a cop out,' some argued.

'A bloody disgrace, more like,' another said. 'Why, have we been treated differently again? The other athletic events get what was advertised, a leader who has a remit on how best to move forward. And, I've heard that our men will be limited by a shoestring budget anyway.'

Others mooted, 'We're not even sure they even like each other.'

A pacifying opinion was made, 'It may work. One has the scientific background and the enthusiasm. Another has shown that he is great at coaching club athletes up to international level, particularly as we know, with his group up in the North. And Maddocks has coaching experience, and perhaps more importantly, the knowledge gained from a long career racing against the best walkers in the world.'

173

The arguments raged on. It was obvious that few people, including myself, were happy about this proposed *task force* arrangement. With reluctance, this diluted, poorly paid role was accepted by the three main protagonists and plans were made for a first squad get-together early the following year.

Working with Andi Drake *and* Jeff Ford was not going to be easy. Exactly what Jeff thought about it, I never established. He was absent for reasons of ill health. Initial surgical operations had apparently helped his plight, though many months later cancer would ultimately claim his life.

Meanwhile back home, and it may appear trivial to mention it here, I was less than enamored with all the attention that Erika was attracting. Richard Pannell once told me, *if you choose to go out with someone who looks like that, you'd better get used to it; for the next twenty years at least.* Attractiveness aside, she was also a very good tennis player, and by joining a local club and playing tournaments we both developed a new circle of friends. By Christmas the cracks in our relationship were widening. We got through it, but questioned whether it would last. It did, but only for a year-long cycle of emotionally draining break-ups and make-ups.

1998

My private life may have been a mess, but salvation as ever was found away from home. *Mad Max holds the whip* someone wrote following the successful coaching weekend held in Birmingham. Well, it's true to say that when 25 male and female senior and junior walkers gathered at the Great Barr Hotel and heard me extol the benefits of a more professional approach to training, few, would have been left in any doubt about how important it was.

I was in bullish mood. 'Motivation can be learned and developed,' I said. 'Raise the standard of your own motivation. The decision has to come from within.' Resorting to air punching, I emphasized through gritted teeth, 'Tell yourself, I can, I will, I am going to.' I said it like I meant it, though looking around the room I doubted some of those staring back at me would soak up the advice. In truth, the depth of young talent coming through was decreasing. As with anything, you work with what you have.

Roadside or trackside, I was by reputation a hard taskmaster, always demanding maximum effort. When the athletes took to the track and put through their paces with a series of interval repetitions, they were right to fear that it might be tough. Video analysis of technique was constructive and enlightening. Blood tests were taken and analyzed. In the classroom, Andi applied his scientific knowledge with graphics and paper handouts. Lectures on sport psychology and strength training gave those assembled much more to ponder on. An evening quiz lightened the mood, before the hard physical work started over again the next morning.

I insisted that all walkers along with their coaches had a clear agenda

174

when it came to planning their racing year. Because qualification standards were high, not all could realistically aspire to competing at the year's two Major championships, the Commonwealth Games or the European Athletic Championships. Most could however, target the eight nations' walks international in Italy at the end of May.

For me, it would be my first venture oversees as a team coach rather than as an athlete. It proved to be a bittersweet experience that helped me make an important decision.

Meeting old friends at the airport was a perfect tonic for the miserable time that I was having back home. Erika had moved out. Though it was a doomed relationship, we persevered anyway, not least because she had only moved around the corner into a terraced house where Edmund's widowed mother lived. It was a bleak time that needed the likes of a sunny beachside location alongside the Adriatic Riviera to help begin lifting my deflated spirit.

I had *ballooned* to over 11stone in weight. Some of the more senior walkers joked that they had never seen me with cheeks before. Their ribbing was merciless. Prods in the stomach were dismissed with a shrug of the shoulders and a wry smile. It's a man thing. I was retired, what did they expect?

It was while sitting at a shared long table eating a meal in the hotel that I thought I recognised another ex-athlete across the dining hall. Excited, I stared long and hard before uttering a conclusion to the deliberations bouncing around in my head.

'That guy over there,' I said. I nodded towards a table of four black men who were chatting, oblivious I hoped to my open-jawed gawping. 'That bald headed guy in the white polo shirt...I think that's Marvin Hagler.

'Who,' someone asked.

I was astounded. 'What do you mean, who? Look, I'm sure that is *Marvellous* Marvin Hagler. He's one of the greatest boxers that ever lived. He was middleweight world champion in the 80's.

'What that fat bloke?'

I ignored the fact that my friends did not share my enthusiasm. That *fat bloke* still looked fit and muscular. I downed my knife and fork, dashed over to the lobby and requested some notepaper and pen.

Minutes later, Marvin not only signed the paper but invited me to sit down and chat for a while. His friends politely smiled as I regaled memories of the time when he beat fellow American, Thomas *The Hit Man* Hearns within three brutal rounds – a fight of truly epic proportions that I recalled watching with Mike Judd in a TV room at St Lukes. I remembered slumping back in a chair after I had stood and thrown every quick fire simulation punch that ultimately sent Hearns sprawling across the canvass.

The following day, Marvin true to his word, appeared by the beach, sat on a wall near a café with a friend and watched the races. I so wanted to speak to him again but was preoccupied darting up and down the road shouting encouragement to our walkers.

British results were a mixed bag. From a team of 20, six recorded personal best performances, whereas on the downside, three saw red and were disqualified, whilst three others failed to finish their race. Andi Drake in 10th position was our leading 20km finisher, with Steve Hollier the next Brit in 12th. I felt sure that had I been fit, I could have done better. My competitive juices had been stirred. It was a tantalizing thought, but rather than just being on the sidelines willing others on, I realised I still wanted to be out there in the thick of the action. Shortly after arriving home, I tendered my resignation from the so-called *task force* and plotted a return to championship racing.

I had only trained sporadically over the previous 14 months and never further than 10kms and only then with Edmund for company at his steadier pace. If I was going to make a comeback, it had to be for a good reason. The English Commonwealth trials in London were only seven weeks away. Top three and a qualifying time of sub 90 minutes for 20kms was required, a time that ordinarily would not have been a problem for me. But that was then, and this was now.

The first few days of serious training were hell. I was overweight, felt stiff, and ached everywhere afterwards. There was no time to waste. I forced myself to push on. It was two weeks before I could contemplate a full 20km walk.

Starting early in the morning, I very deliberately used Plymbridge Woods and an out and back cycle path route where I deduced few people other than the odd dog walker might see me huffing and puffing to any manic conclusion. It was pointless being too downbeat afterwards about the 105 minutes that it took me to walk the distance. Instead, I made it my goal to chop chunks of time off in most subsequent training sessions. There were few days when I did not require some form of remedial treatment either for a sore back, a grumbling hamstring, even a strained gluteus muscle. Richard Pannell, Kevin Kelly, and Mike Elliot, the new man on Maddocks' free treatment team, each took turns to alternate their time and skills in order to help keep me going.

Three weeks before my deadline, I gathered extra inspiration when I saw my protégé Steve Hollier race at Stockport and qualify for the 50km team. He finished fourth, but counted as third English qualifier as one of the men ahead of him was Scotsman, Graham White.

The 20km race at Imber Court in East Molesey, London was held over a 13 lap circuit, much of it around a quiet residential estate. I knew if I pulled off the best performance possible that day, I would be only able to sneak under the 90 minute barrier by a small margin. If a group of men were fit enough to go significantly faster, there was little I could do about it.

Andi Drake was not going to be denied. He won in a time of 88.44 and drew compliments on his improved style of walking. In second place, my battle was one with the clock. Going through the bell for the 13th and final time I was in danger of slipping outside the necessary schedule. Up until that point I had walked 5km splits of 22.23, 22.13, and 22.42. Responding to the cries of encouragement around the circuit I dug deep and raised my pace sufficiently for a fourth 5km split time of 22.22. It was tight but at the end enough to see me across the finish line in 89.40. Slow by previous standards, but it felt great and easily the best thing to have happened all year.

Rocky Stone came in third, albeit outside the 90 minute time, but later named in the England team by virtue of already having walked the qualifying mark during the previous 12 months. I was so pleased for him, because he had extra pressures associated with his dad's serious illness. A month or so later I visited him at his home in Sussex and trained together when he wasn't working. It was during this period of time I was drug tested on several occasions.

One morning, I had just returned to Rocky's home after a particularly hard solo walk and feeling especially light headed with dehydration. Wiping the sweat out of my eyes, I was confronted by a man who apparently had been waiting for sometime outside in his car. *Norman* introduced himself and said that he was from the English Sports Council and that I was required to provide a random out-of-competition urine drug test. My whereabouts, he explained had been established by telephoning and speaking to someone at the veterinary surgery.

Considering he had to wait nearly two hours before I was sufficiently hydrated to pee into his plastic bottle, it was surprising to see Norman again so soon, when I was back in Plymouth five days later busy managing the gym. Though I had completed a super-fast 20km session in Central Park that morning, and was partway through a customer induction when he arrived, we were both relieved that he only had to wait a matter of minutes this time for me to do the necessary deed.

Generally, my fitness and form was improving by the week. That said, after talking things over with Richard and Edmund, we decided I should decline the opportunity to fly out early to Kuala Lumpur and instead leave it until the last minute. We reasoned that I was more likely to be at my best if I continued training on familiar roads and receiving regular supportive massage from Richard. The Church – Church 19.4 mile road walk in Guernsey was a race I had always fancied doing but somehow never got around to it.

Edmund on the other hand had competed in the Channel Island event several times before, even winning it a couple of times. He felt the tough undulating road race could be ideal preparation before I flew out to meet up with teammates. The prospect of targeting Mark Easton's 2 hour 24 minute course record was an extra inducement particularly as I knew it was done in 1992, the same year he walked his best 20km time of 84.04 narrowly missing out on an Olympic team place.

A crazy, action packed day started quietly enough in Devon with Edmund still sipping his tea when he walked out to his car that morning.

Waiting outside, my patience had been tested. 'Hurray up Ed,' I said. 'We can't afford to miss that plane. Give me your bag. I'll chuck it in the back with mine.'

We had gone no more than 50 yards when he braked to a standstill. Ed leapt out while I counted to 10.

'Sorry, I left my mug on the roof of the car.'

There was no time to lose. We had to be at Exeter airport by ten. Our flight to Guernsey departed 55 minutes later.

We touched down at 1140 and met in the foyer by the wife of one of the local competitors who reminded us that the race started prompt at 1pm. It was suggested that if I wished there was just enough time for her to point out parts of the course that did not deviate too far away from the direct route from the airport to the promenade, where the race started and finished. Edmund knew the race circuit like the back of his hand. If we were going to have a whistle-stop tour of the various Church landmarks on the island, the decision was up to me.

Losing a few minutes on our arrival time was a price worth paying if I were to have a visual image of the circuit, albeit a fleeting one. 'Yeah, okay, let's do it,' I said.

Walking towards her car she handed me a sheet of paper with a map of the course. 'Okay. No doubt Ed will have told you that the first mile is quite hard. The climb up Cornet Street and Hauteville is steep. I think you might know Carl Thompson. He will be your lead cyclist, so you won't get lost. If you look at the map, you'll see highlighted some of the churches that you pass en route. We have race marshals at most check points. Around the seven mile mark there's quite a drop down at Les Sages in St Peter's. You've gone just beyond halfway when you reach Les Vauxbelets. I'll point out as much as I can. Ed might have already told you this, but, the ladies start half an hour before the men. You're obviously going to be so much faster than everybody else, so that will at least give you some other walkers to chase.'

'Thanks.'

We reached the promenade with little more than 20 minutes to spare. My head was pulsating with recollections of the route. I remember smiling at the craziness of it all as we rushed to officially register our names, collected our race numbers and think about stripping off our tracksuits to begin loosening up. The adrenaline was still pumping when, minutes later, the gun fired.

My eyes were fixed on the lead cyclist. I followed him towards the end of the prom where we were to turn sharply up into the hills. Eight and a half minutes later I was at the summit and on a quest to better Easton's time.

It was exhilarating fun. In spite of the skies clouding over and the wind gusting up, one by one, I caught and passed women who appeared to be giving it their all through the country lanes and hamlets. Marshals offered hearty words of encouragement as I shot past, as did a cheerful band of hikers who at the same time as me were striding through Les Sages at St Peter's.

I felt so fit and so strong, I resolutely would not allow my pace to drop for one moment, and I didn't until the moment after I had dropped back down from the hills onto the prom, where an almighty headwind threatened to stop me in my tracks. I pushed and pushed. I was determined that the *damn* elements would not blow me off course in the final mile.

Nearing the finish line I saw the digital clock, smiled and thrust my arms in the air. Recording 2.22.35 was a two minute six seconds improvement on the old record. Once I gathered my breath, I was told that the next three men were battling it out more than half an hour behind me. I waited for the first of them to come into view. Spotting Edmund made it all perfect.

A fog delayed flight home allowed us time to slip out of the airport and dash to the nearest pub for a celebratory drink and quick snack. Even then, we were home and parking the car by ten in the evening. It had been a fantastically enjoyable whirlwind of a day.

I was in Kuala Lumpur four days later. News of my Guernsey win had already reached my teammates by the time I met with them in the athlete's village. Apparently, speculation was rife about my race prospects, causing many to believe that I was suddenly another medal contender. Though I was flattered, reality soon to set in. Most athletes had been acclimatizing for up to 10 days prior to my arrival. If I needed further evidence of how crucial this factor was, I received it the next day when I went out for a training walk with the lads.

It was so hot, so humid, my legs felt like jelly. I had six days until race day to get accustomed to it. The problem was that my legs never really stopped feeling like jelly.

In the end, I was relieved to finish as high as 10th in 90.21. The gamble to travel out late however, had backfired. There was little point in dwelling on the frustration of knowing I was capable of walking several minutes quicker, but once again beaten by the effects of the weather. I had made my choice and I was going to have to live with it. Nick A'Hern meanwhile had controlled the race from the front eventually winning in 84.59.

The Welsh born Australian was a known world class walker. Not far behind, Rocky Stone finished a magnificent fourth, a result beyond reasonable expectations given the turmoil caused by the recent death of his father. Andi Drake appeared to be so disappointed with his 12th position, that few of us in our crowded apartment saw much of him to speak to for days afterwards.

I may have dreamt of greater things, but because of my rapid progress in the space of a few months it was important that I remained more philosophical about my result. Watching Lisa win a bronze medal in the women's 10kms was a pleasure, as was witnessing Steve Hollier punch the air and scream ecstatically after achieving a result beyond realistic hopes with a quite brilliant fourth position in the 50km walk.

He said afterwards that however tough the race, what nearly killed him was the bear hug I gave him just after he'd crossed the line. First of the Brits, I was so proud that he pulled through where others almost died.

The results will show that Govindasamy Saravanan famously won the host nation's only athletics gold medal of the Games. For so long, that outcome had looked impossible. With less than two miles to go, Craig Barratt appeared to have an insurmountable lead of around six minutes, until the moment his metronomic pace suddenly faltered. I watched the man in the black vest of New Zealand walk through to start his final lap. Though the life blood appeared to have drained from his face, it was difficult to imagine that he would not hang on for a few more minutes and reemerge at the finish area and claim a much deserved victory. Amazingly, it was not to be.

Part way around the final road lap, thousands saw him zigzag to the point of collapse. He had led for over 49kms and yet failed to finish. Stretchered away to the medical tents, I later saw him and several other walkers screaming in distress. It was truly horrific. I was preoccupied with Steve who was also lying down and recovering with the aid of fluids and ice packs, when we saw Barratt on an adjacent stretcher grab a man by the throat and try to throttle him. He was so delusional that when he was placed in the back of an ambulance, he raised his arms and released a triumphant cry in the apparent belief that he had won.

By the time of the Games closing ceremony, I was heartened by news that Barratt's astonishing non-finish and loss of a certain gold medal had so touched the hearts of his countrymen that, as a result of a poll conducted back home he was awarded a new car for his valiant efforts.

I felt energized by the whole Commonwealth Games experience. I resumed training and three weeks later lined up for the start of the Chippenham to Calne six mile walk. It was amusing when, beneath a warm glow from an Autumnal sun, I appeared to cause a bit of a stir amongst the other competing walkers when I stripped off my tracksuit and handed it to Erika.

'Hey, guys, look at Mad Max.'

'Wow, does this mean you're going to try for another Olympic Games?'

'It looks a bit scabby.'

'Yeah, bit like his face. By the way, how'd you pull a bird like that?'

'Five rings, five Olympics, well?'

Revealing the new, and still slightly tender Olympic ring tattoo on my right bicep was one thing, saying whether or not it meant I was thinking of aiming for a fifth Olympics was another matter all together. The crackle of the starter's pistol brought about the immediate cessation of banter and the commencement of a race long duel, with Rocky Stone at the head of the field I eventually edged with a quick time of 40.32.

It was my first big win in a while and one that was made all the more enjoyable for the mass splash around in the sports centre pool with so many good friends prior to the prize presentations upstairs.

At home I discussed with Edmund and Richard what I was going to do next. Between us we agreed that if competing at another Olympics was to be an option, a final two year plan was required. This was significant. During the previous five or six years I had not wanted to look beyond one season of racing at a time. Richard in particular was at pains to suggest that I should concentrate only on short races and nothing longer than 20kms throughout the 1999 season, with the principal aim of achieving a 50km qualifying mark in time for the Sydney Olympics the following year.

Nothing was said directly, but between us we knew that my moods fluctuated to the extent that sometimes I was reasonably upbeat whilst other times I was downright miserable. These kinds of mood swings were not conducive to the mental strength necessary for long training sessions of 20 miles or more. The mere thought of stepping out for three, even two hour long walks was almost too daunting to even contemplate. Richard recognised this and quite wisely suggested that I did not burden myself further with the necessity to do these longer walks and instead said that I might try a late season 50km race, but only if I had rediscovered the physical and emotional energy to train sufficiently beforehand.

In advising me, both friends needed to take account of discussions I was having with a local business woman who I had originally met at the temporary England HQ press offices whilst in Kuala Lumpur. There was a possibility of me working part-time with her sports and media public relations company, based a few miles across the county border into Cornwall. None of us knew if I could successfully juggle my desire to pursue a potential new career with training and work at the vets and the gym.

Following an interview in December with co-directors' Caroline Searle and Bryn Vaile I was told that I could start work with *Matchtight Media* from February next year on a two month trial period. It was agreed that I would initially do three half days a week. My initial excitement was soon tempered by a need to quickly learn a skill that for too long I had an absolute aversion towards – computer literacy. At the time of the interview I had exaggerated my competency. The truth was, I had only recently enrolled on an open access course at a local drop-in centre and was still at a stage where, contrary to all assurances, I was petrified that if I pressed the wrong button the computer would bite.

1999

When I stepped into the office on that fateful first morning, there was little time for polite pleasantries. The phones were hot with news that Glenn Hoddle, the England football manager, had just resigned. Questions needed to be answered, press releases written. Though there were one or two faceless colleagues at a sister office in Bath, my presence made up one quarter of the on-site work force in an office that was in essence only a compact converted wooden shed. It was sink or swim. I virtually drowned in my own sweat, and would surely have done so but for the wonderful caring interventions of Pauline, the office

181

manager who took pity on me and helped whenever possible. Once she pointed out where the *on* button was on the laptop, she repeatedly and discreetly showed me how to bring up a blank word page and save a document. Use a touchpad? I had never seen one before, let alone use one under pressure of work, and where was the mouse that I needed to click? My fear that the laptop was also going to blow up in my face was never far from my thoughts. I felt Bryn's eyes burrowing in the back of my neck as I fumbled to remember the most rudimentary skills.

Fortunately, things got sufficiently better for me to at least be asked to stay on for an extra month beyond my probation period. In addition to their ongoing work with the English Commonwealth Games Council, I assisted with PR and marketing work of clients at several British and English associations including the Paralympics, judo and netball. Until I did the necessary research, I knew nothing about netball when I was given the directive to visit Fairfax school in the West Midlands and ultimately produce a two page magazine article on the girls playing successes. My time at Matchtight came to a natural end when I was told they were relocating their central office to Bath.

A few months later I was pleased and excited to be asked by a national sports publication to be a guest columnist. My brief was to interview and write articles on an international table tennis player and a young female rower with Olympic ambitions. With no kit sponsor since 1995, the £100 payment received from the publication of both articles helped pay for three new pairs of training shoes. Once in a while, I was paid a similar amount to write more articles. It all helped, particularly as three part-time jobs quickly became one.

The owner of the Plymouth Health Studio said he no longer required a manager. He planned to take over the duty as his private building work was going through a lean period and the gym was not making enough money for him to keep me on. Though he offered the promise of ad hoc managerial work as and when required, technically, I was being laid off for a second time in a matter of months. Work at the vet surgery alone would not pay my living costs. Bill Lawrence, my club mate and friend from Bristol came to the rescue again when he raised nearly one thousand pounds of sponsorship funds to help keep me going. Meanwhile I was periodically meeting the Mayor of Plymouth at City Hall and talking about my Olympic ambitions. He and his financial advisers said that they were interested in helping me and were impressed by local press reports of my racing successes.

By the end of the season I had completed seven 20km races in all, five of which saw me walk consistently good times of between 86 and 87 minutes. It was unfortunate that the one significant *blip* occurred during a World Cup race at Mezidon in France when I was ill with a stomach bug. In spite of that, and more because I'd won both the national championships and a Grand Prix race at Leamington, I ended the year ranked British number one for the distance. A pulled hamstring towards the end of the season meant that I had to abort any plans at increasing the volume of my training for an attempt at a sub four hour 50kms. The injury occurred during the first of two races at Gateshead where I had bowed to

182

persuasion and agreed to compete in the World Veteran athletics championships.

Previously, and for no reasons other than vanity, I said that I had no desire to participate in any veteran only competition where men aged 40 and over and women over 35 years took part. I changed my mind with the clear understanding that my main goals still lay ahead. A gold medal won in the road 20kms came at a cost. My brother Peter's continual roadside shouting stopped me from dropping out even though I knew my strained hamstring was worsening with every stride. Five days later under floodlights, the injury held up sufficiently for me to win the 40 – 45 age category track 5km walk in a little over 21 minutes.

There was no disguising the sense of pride I felt at becoming a double world champion. To this day the medals won are among a select few hanging around the neck of my old university teddy bear, now sitting comfortably in a corner of the small bedroom at home.

Of the many athletes I tried to help through the years, most stepped on and off the Maddocks' coaching conveyor belt with conspicuous speed and frequency. My training methods were deliberately hard. They needed to be if best possible results were going to be achieved. Though the training schedules I set for some were possibly too hard, I do believe that the friendships formed have been lasting. Niobe Menendez was so determined and yet our relationship ultimately suffered by our dogged clash of personalities. During the course of the year she visited me on a number of occasions, the last time armed with the most unusual *thank you* gift – a five litre can of extra virgin olive oil, more evidence of her Spanish roots rather than any covert message.

Every now and then, my thoughts turned to how Nan was coping with her declining health. I had visited her in the summer at a nursing home in Cullompton where it was sad to see her in a room, surrounded by a few familiar personal possessions talking about how she was ready to die.

Ninety-two and confined to a wheelchair, she spoke with a sobering dignity and contentment about her early life, raising seven children and how blessed she felt at having so many grandchildren. I struggled to contain the tears when she said she would not be around if I ever were to add to her growing number of great grandchildren, but said how proud she was of my other accomplishments. It was obvious that she loved my stubborn old Grandad and missed him deeply since he passed away. I recalled happy childhood memories of holidaying with them at their dairy farm in north Devon. Seeing her smile at my recollections made the visit all the more poignant, particularly when the veterinary nurse poked her head around the surgery door one evening and said that I should come to the phone.

Toby had rung and said that Nan was very poorly and that Mum and other family members were already there comforting her and not to worry if I could not make it. My head was in a spin; unsure what to do next, I rejoined Edmund who was talking to clients about inoculations for their new puppy. He looked up, saw me and immediately excused himself before leading me into the pharmacy for a whispered chat. I was told that it was alright to leave straight away and if I wished I could borrow his car as he knew mine was proving unreliable.

An hour later I was ringing the bell of the nursing home. The relief was immeasurable when a member of staff answered and said she had been made aware that I might arrive and that my Nan was in her room and it was okay for me to go in and see her. Reminded where to go, I was told that the others had already left. My walk down the carpeted corridor was made with a degree of indecent haste until the moment I paused at the door before tapping gently and stepping through.

Lying in bed, Nan's face was partially illuminated by the table lamp next to her. Eyes closed, she appeared to be peaceful. I sat down in the chair opposite, looked across and gathered my thoughts. Apart from the sounds of my breathlessness and occasional distant chattering voices outside, it was serenely quiet. A minute or two passed before I began to question the implications of the tranquility. Tentatively I rose from the chair, stepped forward and momentarily hesitated.

'Nan,' I whispered. Disturbing her did not seem right, but I was desperate and hardly thinking straight. There was no response, so I reluctantly raised my voice a notch, 'Nan.' I waited and waited before reaching out and lightly stroking her cheek.

Oh God! I stepped back and sat back down in the chair.

I'm not sure how long I sat there, but when I felt ready and had regained some semblance of composure, I got up, opened the door and walked out. There was no one to be seen in the corridors, so I followed the sound of voices until I saw through an open door two ladies chatting over tea.

I tapped on the door and leaned in. 'Excuse me,' I said. 'Is my Nan dead?'

Two days later, I was alone pushing my Capri and bump starting it down a hill. Ordinarily, this kind of soul destroying act first thing in the morning was enough to see me embark on a drive into the countryside, only to decide that I could not face a single step of training. That day would be different. I parked up at Yelverton aerodrome, turned off the ignition key, heard the birds singing and thought to hell with the consequences of whether or not it would start again on my return from training. Three and a half hours later I had completed my best 45km walk in years. Mercifully, the engine fired up when I turned the key.

PART SIX

Part 6. The final push: 2000

Dartmoor hikes with Richard Pannell, with or without either of his kids, Katie or Greg were always enjoyable. More often than not, they proved to be both physically and mentally therapeutic for me, as they were usually undertaken within hours of completing a particularly hard morning training session. It gave us a chance to chat about all other matters on our minds whilst soaking up some of the most glorious views in the region. Occasionally some hikes seemed more memorable than others, as was the case in early March one bright Sunday afternoon.

After completing the ascent to the summit of Sheepstor, it was time for a well earned rest before contemplating the next stage of our trek across the moor.

We sat back, looking out over the vast landscape before us, filled with wistful melancholy. Overhead, soaring high circling on fluttering wings, the skylark's flight call, full of liquid warbling notes and short trills filled the air. Perched by our sides, panting and looking like he was in his element lording it over his kingdom was Horace, Richard's short-legged little black and tan dachshund, his long soft ears billowing gently in the light breeze. Polly, the family's rough haired terrier was down amongst the yellow gorse foraging, visible only by her rear end and wagging stubby tail.

While we sat in reflective mood I recall being mesmerized by shadows from cloud formations reflecting onto the moor and rolling down the scrubland like creeping fog. Our panoramic view aloft the huge granite rock of Sheepstor was both spectacular and awe inspiring.

'Isn't it just fantastic, Rich,' I said.

'On a beautiful afternoon like this, I don't think there's anything to match it.'

I nodded and looked over and down to my right deep into the valley below, to where Burrator reservoir nestled like a giant pond in amongst dense woodland. My attention drawn by the sight of a vehicle moving along a section of the four mile perimeter road until it disappeared behind a line of trees. 'I reckon you can see at least three-quarters of the race circuit from here.'

Richard looked down towards the reservoir and said, 'You didn't get sick of it then when you had to walk eight times around it?'

The comment made me smile. 'Blimey, that race was *ten* years ago,' I said. My thoughts fleetingly went back to that cold rainy day in October 1990 when I recorded my British 50km record. 'Three, fifty-one,' I mumbled. 'Christ, I'd love to do something like that again.'

'Well, in two weeks time, that's the score, mate. If you want to make the team for Sydney, that's what you gotta do? We'll start walking again in a minute.

You're probably seizing up.'

'Yeah, I am a bit. My bum is too bony to sit on this rock for much longer.'

Pointing in a north-westerly direction Richard suggested a hike over towards Crazy-Well-Pool and onwards to the rutted track running alongside the leat leading through Blind-mans wood before heading back to Norsworthy Bridge where, one hour earlier we had left his car.

In spite of all the hard work, I was still troubled by self doubt. It made little sense. Richard had just heard about another mid-week 45km training session. Three hours 24 minutes made it easy for him to be optimistic – the best I had ever recorded on the Yelverton aerodrome circuit.

'Forty-five kilometres, that's 28 miles in 3.24. That's world class.' he said. 'World class,' he repeated.

Richard's pep talk went on. He told me to ignore the cynics prone to suggestions that I was too old to walk another sub four hour 50kms, or that the selectors would not want someone of my age on the team. The Isle of Man race in February had been a success, particularly as it had been done during a period of heavy winter training. Faster sessions had included a hilly 10 mile walk in Central Park in 68 minutes. He reminded me of the recent good training walks with Steve Hollier and all the other solo sessions of 25 miles or more completed over the past few months. Richard said in no uncertain terms that I needed to believe in myself; be confident and heed Edmund's advice and ease back occasionally in order to give my body a chance to recover from the long hours of training. If I produced the right result in Holland, and no more than two other British men achieved the qualifying time, the selectors would not be able to ignore me.

Richard's clenched fist and words said through gritted teeth, suggested that he meant every word, 'C'mon, you gotta think big now. You can not only qualify for Sydney, but get there and have a bloody good race. The form you're in, who knows what's possible?'

Those final emphatic words sent a shiver down my spine. It was enough to bring an abrupt halt to our conversation. We took in the views for a while longer before rising to our feet and setting out across the moor.

I knew this would be my last shot at competing on the world's biggest sporting stage. *Yes*, I was in great shape, the best that I had been for years. And yet, it still rankled that my efforts in reaching the pinnacle of sport had not brought a greater sense of worth and reward.

The return journey to Holland needed to be done as cheaply as possible. It was all planned. Richard would use his own transit van and tow a borrowed caravan. There and back, it would be a five day trip; we could rest comfortably when required, and having use of a cooker and toilet facilities meant that accommodation costs could be kept to a minimum. Friends would put the three of us up at their place prior to our morning ferry crossing from Dover to Calais. Once we arrived at our destination in Sint Oedenrode, Theo Tromp, the local race organizer would accommodate us at his home for the two nights before race day. I had already talked to Steve Hollier about us meeting him en route. Young, and not long out of university with typical post-graduate debts, he was an athlete with potential, and as a consequence qualified for a modest level of lottery funding, some of which was going towards his share of the travelling costs. Though I had made all the usual enquires, I had been told that it was unlikely that any similar funding was coming my way. It stuck in my throat, but what more could I do?

Discussions with the Plymouth Mayor were initially promising. I made my pitch for local funding and the prospects appeared good. I explained how as far back as 1980 the British Ice dancers Torvill and Dean had famously been supported by their local authority in Nottingham. I thought the Mayor would be more prepared to offer similar assistance if I offered to work as an ambassador for health and fitness in the community. The Mayor had not wholly dismissed my idea of visiting schools and clubs on behalf of his office, but conversely thought that an aspiring five-time Olympian had enough on his plate without that added distraction. The truth was that I would have liked the challenge of such a responsible ambassadorial role, but, back then it was music to my ears to hear the Mayor acknowledge that anyone with Olympic ambitions should retain their real focus.

The Mayor suggested that my approximate budget of £10,000 for the year leading up to the Sydney Olympics was in all probability an underestimate. He considered that if the City was going to assist with my finances, a figure three times that estimation was surely more realistic.

I was told to go away and re-evaluate my budget. In particular, itemize living costs a full-time athlete might need for the following year, cost the desired trips for training overseas, and note all anticipated peripheral extras for clothing and medical expenses before submitting the new figures for consideration. I remembered licking my lips with anticipation and recalled how the coffee and biscuits tasted particularly sweet at that time. Although it was reasonable to believe that international athletes lived and prepared for world and Olympic competition on the kind of money we had talked about, I hardly dared to think in those terms for myself as it was so far removed from anything that I had ever had before.

Refreshingly, the Mayor appeared to be a man who recognised that big ambitions cost money. He was in the last year of his office, and I assumed he would try to offer any reasonable assistance if warranted. He acknowledged that any person with measurable talent who wished to commit to being a full-time athlete and who had to travel ought to live in reasonable comfort and be able to pay the bills.

As it turned out, I failed to understand why it had become necessary for me to attend monthly meetings with council staff in order to implement the new itemized budget requested by the Mayor, only to repeatedly hear how funds from the Plymouth Arts and Heritage Committee two million pound pot might be released. I did get to know a *nice* lady called Helen who had effectively become my case officer. Our early meetings before Christmas were amicable but later soured when it became apparent that discussions had reached a stalemate. Initially I had to accept her compromise suggestion that the £30,000 be reduced to a more attainable £8000. That *offer* only lasted for one of our Friday coffee afternoons. The first meeting in the new millennium saw Helen reduced to discussing which shops in town might be able to provide me with shoes and which fitness club could offer me free membership. It did not seem to matter that I told her I had already bought a stock of discounted racing shoes and that I preferred to train at my regular gym. Cut price air tickets were suggested as a sweetener, but that only served to frustrate me more. Valuable time had gone by and all I had got from the council was a monthly cup of coffee and a few biscuits.

It was a sharp, rocky descent from Crazy-Well-Pool down to the base of the leat. With the rugged ground behind us, Richard and I followed the line of the man-made water way for almost half an hour, exchanging few words. He pointed out occasional landmarks spotted across the rolling landscape of the breathtakingly beautiful National Park.

'Blimey,' I said. 'Some of those rocks were slippery. My legs were a bit shaky going down there.'

'If you like, I'll give the ole pins a massage when we get back. Janet's going off to rehearsals at six. Oh, by the way. I've picked up four tickets for the show for me, you, Greg and Katie. It should be good.'

'I'm looking forward to it. I overheard her singing the other day in the kitchen. She was singing, *Girl, you're a woman*. It was fantastic.'

'Oh, God, don't tell her that. She'll be acting like a right diva.'

'I already did. I asked if she was also singing, *I will always love you*.'

'Ah! That confuses a lot of people. Because Dolly Parton sung it in the film version of Best little whorehouse in Texas, folk are surprised and disappointed when they don't hear it in the stage production.'

'Yeah, she told me.'

'Good. Anyway, about later...she told me that there was enough roast dinner for two extra. So, should be just enough for you.'

'Great, I'm starving.'

'Did you weigh yourself yesterday at the gym?'

'Yeah, 147 pounds, although after this morning's walk I'm probably down to 140. I'm feeling as weak as a kitten at the moment.'

'Don't say that too loud or Horace will be chasing after you.' Richard looked around the surrounding moor and asked, 'And where is the little rat infested turd now?'

In the time it had taken me to dunk the fourth digestive in my tea, Steve Hollier had spooned in a bowl of porridge and scoffed the last segment of his toast. His mouth was still full of crumbs when I saw him look again at the note left on the breakfast table by Theo Tromp. I was sure he was about to say something until perhaps he thought better of it. We were in Holland. If the day went well, an Olympic qualifying time was within our grasp.

All discussions about race tactics, pace judgement and the likely opposition had been concluded in the days leading up to this important time. Any topic relating to these matters was strictly off the agenda. Staying relaxed was all that was important now. I glanced out of the window past the potted plant resting on the sill and saw Richard out there beyond the patio. He had insisted Steve and I stay inside and that he would manage. Watching him, I wasn't so sure.

Despite the early morning chill he had cast aside his woolly hat and fleece and looked as if he was about to brace himself for one more monumental effort. Heaving the caravan back and forth until it lined up with the transit van's towing hitch was obviously proving irritatingly difficult. A neighbour's car, parked too close to the transit sometime late on Saturday night, had been an unexpected obstacle that all of us could have done without. I watched and saw Richard take a sharp intake of breath before his face became bloated again by the extreme effort. A top section of window had been left ajar. I could just about hear Richard's take on proceedings: 'C'mon you bastard…move!'

It was painful just to watch. I caught his forlorn glance back at the kitchen window. His thumbs up belied what I thought may have been his true feelings at that moment. I put a hand up and smiled rather pathetically, as if to say *well done*.

Steve appeared oblivious to the physical effort occurring thirty yards away in the cul-de-sac outside. He sniffed and said, 'Following Theo would've been easier.'

The note on the table contained written directions to the race venue which, according to Theo was about a twenty minute drive away. He had left earlier so as he could start setting things up for the race and coordinating marshals and other officials.

'Don't worry,' I said. 'We'll find it. Stay cool. Let's just think of it as a hard training day and by three o'clock it will be over.'

'Okay.'

'Good. Grab your tea and we'll go and see how Richard's getting on.'

Outside, our man was sitting rather uncomfortably it appeared, on the transit's secured towing hitch, mopping his brow. I thought it was quite cold so zipped my tracksuit top up under my stubbly chin.

Steve cradled his mug of tea and said, 'Alright Rich? Looks like it's going to be a sunny one – a great day for a hard training session.'

I ignored my lanky friend's veiled sarcasm and asked Richard if he was okay.

'I think I've buggered my back. Ah, is that for me, Stevie boy?' And with that he reached out and took possession of the mug. 'Thanks. Well, I think we should hit the road in say, about an hour. That should give you plenty of time to do some stretching in the house before we leave. I'm gonna have a lie down.'

Less than a decade old, Sint-Oedenrode's modern sports complex bore the name Frederikstraat 41. When our transit and caravan veered sharply into the car park I caught a glimpse of Mark Easton loosening up, whilst a group of other fast moving athletes appeared to be in the throes of a race that I assumed to be the men's 20km event, scheduled to start at ten-thirty.

Earlier, Richard had fallen asleep and, handicapped by a chronic backache, had been slow to move. Leaving Tromp's home late and getting lost en route meant there was little time to lose. Steve and I already had hold of our kit bags and were leaping out of the van before Richard applied the handbrake.

The moment we crashed through the changing room doors and for the umpteenth time since leaving, I anxiously checked my wristwatch. There was exactly 22 minutes to the start of the 50km race. Our kit bags slung to the floor echoed round a bare room, reeking of fresh chlorine.

'I've no idea if we're in the right place,' I stressed. 'Is this a male or female changing room?'

'Who cares, we're here now. Bit tight, wasn't it?'

'Yeah it was. But hey, we've both trained hard. Let's get out there and do it.'

Steve nodded, peeled off his tracksuit top, looked across at me and said, 'Max, is that my race number that you're pinning on your vest?'

'Oh shit.'

The wraparound sunglasses were dropped into place moments before the gun was fired at eleven. Up to speed within seconds, I shot away from my rivals. I was a man with a job to do, and thousands of miles covered in preparation, determined that nothing would disrupt my concentrated goal for the next four hours.

With an afternoon temperature rising to a high of twelve degrees, the light wind and cloudless sky meant racing conditions were perfect. Sporadic shouts of encouragement came from the more enthusiastic spectators lining the route through the housing estate. Connecting roads had been closed to traffic. Though local people were accustomed to the sight of walkers appearing annually on the scene, some nevertheless looked bemused at the sight of men and women hip-swinging past their windows.

As the time approached one o'clock, my unwavering pace close to 13kms per hour meant my steely focus had remained firm for nigh on two hours. With each passing kilometre my green Plymouth club vest had became increasingly damp. I deviated from the kerbside racing line only when striding past slower lapped walkers. A few of whom, much to my frustration, choosing to race three or four abreast, causing me to go extra wide and adding precious seconds to my time.

Turning left into the road running parallel to the town's senior high school, I sighted the Irish walker sitting on a bench seat with his head in his hands looking disconsolate, his latest Olympic dreams seemingly over. Bobby O'Leary had aborted his 20km race at half distance, complaining of a knee injury. The 1992 Olympian would as likely have to content himself with the once in a lifetime experience. The sad sight was a sharp reminder for me to push on, stay strong and seize the day.

I glanced over my shoulder and saw Steve was still little more than 200 metres behind. I considered that the gap was too short at this stage of the race, and significantly too close for my friend's own good. I refocused my attention. In the far distance, just beyond the row of tables, seated timekeepers and lap scorers, I spotted Richard stepping gingerly from out of the caravan. In a perverse way, it inspired me even more, knowing that he was trying hard to disguise his back pain while Steve and I battled to control our own discomfort. Moments later, and for the tenth time, I sped past the electronic clock positioned in the middle of the road.

Prior to the start of racing, Richard had set up a roadside drinks table by the caravan and provided the two of us with sports drink every alternate lap. Handing over a plastic bottle he said, 'Halfway, Max. One hour fifty-six minutes, fifty-four.'

Gulping back my drink, I pushed on ahead and heard Richard shout, 'Bang on schedule, mate. Brilliant! Steve's still not far behind.'

Of course I already knew that, and it worried me. Not because he was a threat, more that he was not keeping to the pace schedule we had so clearly discussed beforehand. I was convinced his time was marginally too fast. I had also seen the judge's disqualification board being updated as I passed through the race recorder's section. A second red adhesive disc was placed against his race number. Steve Hollier had received another warning. One more and he would be out. I had to banish the negative thought and refocus on my own race.

I maintained a metronomic pace, catching and lapping third placed man, Mark Easton by the time I reached the 35km mark. Going into the twentieth and last lap I heard I had pulled nearly three minutes clear of Steve, who was holding onto second position. As great as it was to hear that he was still in with a chance of an Olympic qualifying time, I had my own mission to complete. Onlookers would have been left in no doubt…I was digging deep into every last reserve of energy. I powered on eventually turning the final corner.

At the far end of the road, I could see Richard Pannell at the finish line punching the air and shouting. 'Oggy oggy oggy!' I cracked a smile.

Soaking up the applause I moved swiftly towards the finish line, my legs heavy with lactate, my head full of excited emotion as the ticking clock came into sharp focus: 3:57…and counting. Self-control held firm, seconds later I was through the line arms aloft, screaming 'Yes, yes, yes, I've done it!'

191

Richard wrapped an arm tightly around my shoulders and said, 'Fantastic, mate! You've bloody well done it!'

I was ecstatic. My throat dry and cracking with emotion, I said, 'We've done it. We've bloody well, done it!' I turned and gave him the firmest bear hug I could muster. It was too much for him.

'Agh, my back!' he whimpered.

I released my grip.

Theo Tromp stepped forward and vigorously shook my hand. It was too formal. Embracing me he gleefully shouted words of praise in Dutch, before offering a few congratulatory words in English...'Champion; number one.'

O'Leary stood close by watching and clapping. 'You old fecker,' he said. 'That was bloody fantastic.'

Released from Tromp's grasp, I lifted my sunglasses. There may have been tears in my eyes, but I didn't care. I said thanks to Bobby and turned back to Richard and asked, 'What about Steve? How's he doing?'

The smile dropped from Richard's face as he glanced down toward the pavement. Steve Hollier was sitting despondently on the roadside, his arms wrapped around his knees. My joy was immediately tempered when I asked, 'What happened?'

Steve looked up, his eyes empty of emotion. 'Disqualified at 48 kilometres, mate, with one bloody lap to go. I think I would've sneaked inside four hours if I'd finished.'

Shocked, words almost failed me. To say *sorry* seemed so inadequate. 'Bad luck, mate; hopefully you'll make it next time.' It was the best I could do.

Steve reached up and offered his hand. 'Yeah thanks. Hey, well done, fantastic effort.' I shook the hand and walked away to gather my breath and soak up the enormity of what I had achieved.

The few minutes resting in the caravan was just enough for my body to begin stiffening up. Alerted by the applause outside greeting Mark Easton's finish, I rose gingerly from my comfortable seat just in time to glance out of the window and see him cross the line in second.

From the caravan doorway I raised my plastic mug of water and shouted, 'Well done, Mark, great effort.' Easton glanced up and saw me. Walking across the road, he was followed closely by his wife draping a tracksuit top over his sweat sodden shoulders. We shook hands and he said, 'So, you've done it again? Well done.'

'Thanks.' I watched him walk away leaning heavily on his smiling partner.

Within two hours the prize presentations had taken place in the clubhouse. A limited race budget meant there was no money to be won. I received a small silver cup and certificate. The figures 3:57.10 printed on the certificate were worth more to me than anything money could buy. I made an emotional telephone call to my Mum, and regained enough composure to give Edmund a ring.

The transit van pulled away at five-thirty. Richard repeatedly beeped the horn while I waved goodbye to Tromp and a few new friends standing at the gates of Frederikstraat 41. Steve's wave was mustered with minimal enthusiasm. Watching him slump back on the rear seat, I was mindful to leave him alone with his thoughts, for I knew how gut-wrenchingly disappointed he would be and how he would also be loathe to spoil my special time.

Thoughts of retracing our route back through Holland and Belgium into France and on to Calais docks appeared to hold no fear for Richard. For the first three hours Richard and I whiled away the time chatting, joking and analyzing the day's events until my head began to drop with exhaustion. Steve drifted in and out of sleep on the back seat. With the onset of darkness, Richard finally pulled into a service car park in Belgium. He parked in a secluded corner near dense woodland.

'You two get out and stretch your legs,' he said. 'I'll get some food on the go.'

Both Steve and I nodded. I suspected I looked as pale and pasty as he did; for sure, neither of us felt well enough to face any cooked food earlier. But with the healing power of time, we both become ravenous. We sauntered aimlessly around the car park, waiting for a call.

'Who's for Mum's finest stew?'

Thirty minutes later bread slices were being used to mop up the last remnants of juices on our plates. We sat around the dining table in the dimly lit caravan. Richard had munched on his own mozzarella and olive salad. He popped the remaining few grapes into his mouth as he spoke. 'Well,' he sniffed, 'that's put some colour back into those cheeks. You don't look quite so hideous now.'

'Yeah, that hit the spot alright. Thanks Mum.'

Steve pursed his lips. 'Any of those cakes left? And I wouldn't mind another cup of tea.'

Richard rose from the table, stretched and yawned. He walked toward the hissing kettle in the kitchen area. 'I will be invoicing you for these acts of slavery you know. I don't come cheap.'

Steve said, 'I'd do the same for you, Rich.'

'Can I get that in writing, Mr Hollier?'

I looked at Richard and said, 'You must be knackered yourself. You still up for driving on to Calais?'

Richard rubbed his eyes. 'Oh, I'm okay. You two can clear the dishes while I go to the loo. I reckon it's another 120 kilometres. Probably get there about midnight.'

Richard succumbed to exhaustion 25 kilometers from Calais. He had fallen asleep in the rear of the caravan moments after closing the flimsy wooden

193

doors to his sleeping enclosure, his pneumatic snoring started presumably within seconds of his head hitting the pillow. So long as we left the car park site around eight, it had been agreed that catching the nine-thirty hovercraft from Calais to Dover would pose no problem.

Bedded down at the front end, Steve's ear plugs must have worked a treat. While his sleeping bag barely moved all night, I struggled in the other half of the lounge area tossing and turning virtually all night.

Throughout the early hours I had relived my epic race over and over again. I finally gave up around six in the morning. Thrusting off the covers I wriggled out of my sleeping bag. Wearing tracksuit and socks meant I only had to slide on my shoes and locate my padded winter coat, scarf and gloves.

Stepping outside, my breathy expulsions appeared like puffs of cigarette smoke in the murky light. Surveying the surrounding landscape beyond the near deserted car park, a serene stillness was broken only by the distant drone of occasional motorway traffic. Taking a deep breath, I filled my lungs with the cool fresh air and in spite of every bone in my body aching, I felt an overwhelming sense of exhilaration and a desperate need for a pee. Beyond one side of the car park and a stretch of scrubland I was drawn to the rutted country path running parallel to a river.

Picking my way through knee-high brambles, the frosted grass crunched beneath my feet. Once the path was reached, the traffic noises faded, allowing a joyous dawn chorus to predominate. My sense of solitude was briefly interrupted by jingling bells and two grizzled old men chatting to each other as they cycled past. I wanted to savour every blissful moment. I couldn't recall the last time that I felt so good, a time when I felt so energized. The sacrifices, the hard work that had so affected me, seemed less important now. Where there had been questions, now I had answers. Why did I still race? Why was I still chasing an elusive dream? Contentment felt like a wonderful justification.

I smiled at the thought of my mother sobbing tears of happiness down the phone when I told her the news, and how Edmund simply said, *I knew you could do it*. I relished the thought of sharing the news with others. My mind went to all those family and friends who had helped me through the years. The wistful thoughts stopped the moment I realised that I had arrived at a clearing and a tall derelict brick building standing next to a lock on the river.

In the half-light the old oast-house had an almost gothic like appearance. I looked skywards and jolted back, startled by two bats flapping out of a small window in the spire. My sense of adventure aroused, the front door creaked as I pushed through and looked in, almost immediately backing out, assaulted by the strong musty smell of rotting hay. Undeterred, I wandered around the side. Tucked away at the rear of the building was an old thatched cottage. It looked unloved and uninhabited. Its windows were too grimy with damp moss to see clearly inside. A side door leading into an old utility room was open. I paused before walking in, my heart pumping with nervous excitement.

Cobwebs hung from the corners of the low crumbling ceiling. In spite of the dark, I walked on through to another room. Cupboards lay bare, bar a few rusting utensils. Water dripped from the taps at the sink in the kitchen. Creeping through into an adjoining room where it was noticeably drier, debris scuffed up from the floor caused puffs of dust as I shuffled tentatively forward. In the next room the window shutters were closed and boarded. Too dark to see clearly, I accidentally kicked a discarded wine bottle. The sound echoed around a room where I could only see the outlines of tatty furniture. I turned to leave, when out of the gloom I heard a groan from across the room. From under a mess of filthy cloth sheeting, a large silhouetted figure shuffled and rose to its feet. Momentarily I was frozen to the spot. I gathered my wits and scrambled out of the building into the light.

Disorientated, I frantically looked around before sighting the path alongside the river. My pounding heart settled once I realised that I was not being pursued. My straining leg sinews relaxed again.

Strutting back along the path, I thought, what a fool. Why could I not have just enjoyed the most heavenly walk and stayed out of there.

It was after five-thirty the following evening when I turned the lock and let myself back into the flat. I had time only to dump my travel bags down in the living room, have a quick shower and change into a clean white shirt and dark jeans before walking back downstairs into the veterinary consultation room. The evening surgery was already in progress.

Edmund Shillabeer secured the cat basket and looked at the young lady. 'There you go, all safe and sound. Bring the kittens back in three weeks and we'll give them their second lot of jabs.'

I stood to one side allowing the woman to pass.

Edmund gazed over his half moon spectacles and smiled at me. Stretching out his hand he said, 'Fantastic Chris. Well done. There's a full waiting room out there. We'll talk later. Okay?'

I was sure that Edmund would want to hear a full account of the Dutch trip. I wasn't wrong.

An hour later and as soon as the last client had been escorted to the exit door, Edmund said, 'Right, let's get a celebration drink. Where shall we go?'

By eight-thirty the China House Pub was packed. I warmed my hands by the log fire its warm glow felt wonderful on my face. I looked back at Edmund, and smiled as I saw the waiter approach our table holding two plates of scampi and chips. I sat back down, took a mouthful of Guinness and wiped the froth from my lips. 'Thanks, a lot, Ed. I really appreciate this.'

'That's okay. You've got to keep your strength up. The hard work really begins now. Barbara and I are looking forward to seeing you race in Sydney. Our tickets are already booked. We can't wait. Of course, I've got to organize a locum...'

'What? No, Ed! What do you mean, *already* booked?'

'Didn't I tell you before? I didn't want to put extra pressure on you. If I'd left booking till now I don't think I would have found anywhere affordable. Most of the tickets for the athletics programme have already sold out. I'm still trying to decide if I try to get stadium tickets for the day of your race. I mean, most of it will be out on the roads.'

'Yes, I know, but I haven't been selected yet.'

'You will be.'

I felt my blood pressure rising, took a deep breath, and said, 'You know what the British selectors can be like. They've not exactly been on my side up to now. I've been let down so many times before.'

'I know.' Edmund sighed, put his knife and fork down and paused.

I knew him well enough to know that there was something on his mind and he wasn't saying. 'What is it?'

'I took the liberty of making a phone call to UK Athletics earlier today. I spoke to the national endurance coach.'

'Norman Brook.'

'Yes.' Edmund looked me in the eye. 'Of course I wanted to tell him the great news. You know, about your win and the qualifying time. Obviously I mentioned Steve and how much of a disappointment that was. I also wanted to ask what the chances were of you getting your travel expenses reimbursed. I told him that you made the trip as cheaply as possible but it still cost about...£300. I said £300 but I wasn't sure.'

'It's close enough,' I said rather coldly. I had a bad feeling where this conversation was going.

'I also wanted to ask Norman about you now getting some lottery funding to help with your Olympic preparations. I know you haven't been selected yet but strike while the iron's hot, I say. Well we had a good conversation. He was full of praise for what you've done. Oh, and he passes on his congratulations, says well done, and he'll chat to you sometime. Made some joke about..."So the old boy did it then." Edmund laughed but stopped once he realised that I was struggling to see the funny side. 'Well it seems that he won't, or can't sanction the money being reimbursed. I reminded him that you're doing all this on an absolute shoestring, that you've got no money to speak of.'

'Thanks, Ed,' I said. My level of despondency was rising fast.

'Well, you know what I mean. Anyway, I'm afraid there's still no promise of any lottery funding. It's because you're not a likely Olympic medal contender or have a sufficiently high world ranking. He said, he's sorry but it looks like you're not going to get any money.'

'He's sorry! Oh, that's alright then.' I couldn't stop myself. My voice reached a higher, unsuppressed pitch. 'I know; you know; he bloody well knows that the majority of the British Olympic team are not medal contenders.'

'Shush, shush, shush. Calm down…people can hear.'

Reminded that there were other diners close by, and the drinkers propped up against the bar, were perhaps within earshot, I lowered my voice to a whisper. 'It's bloody true! Of the 300 or so in the British team, probably eighty maybe ninety per cent won't win a medal. And yet the vast majority, in fact virtually everyone who gets in the team, will be lottery funded. Some get thousands of pounds. Some even get tens of thousands. I read some stats recently that said in total around 800 British sportspeople are getting some level of lottery funding. If that's true, it means that there are about 500 athletes receiving money who end up not getting selected for the Olympics. Why should I continue to get nothing when I've got a qualifying time?'

'I know it's not fair.' Edmund paused. 'Finish your meal…before it gets cold.'

'I'm not hungry.' I had a sip of my drink. 'And you're right, it's not bloody fair.' I felt the tears welling up, so paused for a moment to regain my composure. 'There are bloody millions of pounds out there. Why does it have to be such a damn struggle?' The rhetorical question was met with an appropriate awkward silence. 'Did Norman say anything else?'

'Yes.' Edmund gulped. 'He confirmed that you're not selected yet.'

'No.'

'No. But now's not the time to be negative. You've got to believe that it will be alright. I'm sure you'll get the selection nod soon. In the meantime, you've got to train as hard as you can. Then, hopefully you'll be ready for a great race in Sydney. And Barbara and I will be there to see you do it. Okay?'

'Okay, but…'

'No buts.'

'I'm still not confident that they will select me early.'

'What have I said? Have faith. You're the only British walker with a qualifying time. Hopefully there will be more Brits that do it, but realistically who else do you see who is going to better 3.57?'

I pursed my lips.

'I'll tell you; probably no one. Steve *may* sneak under four hours when he has another go. After that, there's three or four other Brits going for the one remaining place, and I'm not sure any of them can do it. If the selectors have got any sense, they'll pick you within the next few weeks and you can concentrate on getting ready for Sydney. Now, eat your food, and I suggest that we finish our drink outside on the veranda. It's a full moon tonight. There's some fabulous boats moored off the quay.'

The level of media interest surprised me. Local press and TV were first off the mark to give extensive coverage to the possibility of me becoming the first man in British athletics to compete at five Olympics. I thought the national press might only show their hand when my selection was confirmed; on the contrary, my phone was hot with requests for interviews, filming and photo opportunities.

Sky News wasted little time in sending their reporter and cameraman to meet me at Burrator. The resultant film that went out two nights later was excellent. Simon Turnbull, writing for the Sunday Independent visited me at my flat and, in my opinion, used the one hour taped conversation to brilliant effect when I read his full page article. It pulled no punches yet was informative and accurate. Through no fault of Simon, there was a downside to the piece. It was also published as a prequel to an eight nation walks competition at Leamington that I had no real desire to be a part of.

Even though I had won two 20km races at the venue the previous year, I made it quite clear to selectors that the prospect of racing the same distance there again held little appeal. It was too soon after my race in Holland, and more importantly, the one kilometer circuit at Victoria Park simply did not inspire me. My preference was to save myself and prepare for the European Cup walks at Eisenhuttenstadt, East Germany in June where I hoped to try and go below 3.55. The rationale was that I keep my motivation levels high in the build up towards Sydney where I aimed to be at my absolute best and perhaps even be in a position to challenge my British 50km record. Committing to this personal plan came with a proviso: In order to race without a fear of negative consequences should something go wrong, I needed to know that I was already selected for the Olympics. My belief was that I should not voluntarily risk doing another 50km race if it meant undoing the strong position I had put myself in.

As no one was prepared to give me these assurances, I felt compelled to race at Leamington, not least because it seemed likely that the names of qualified walkers thereafter could be put forward to the Olympic selection panel. I also shelved any plans to do the 50km event in Germany, and instead only be available for the 20kms. It all felt so meaningless. I knew I could stay at home and train hard over the shorter distance, but the opportunity to walk fast 50km times simply did not happen too often. I wanted to maximize this period of time and I believed it was being denied to me.

I didn't race well at Leamington. I was ill before it, and felt worse afterwards. In fact it would be fair to say that apart from Lisa Kehler, who walked 95.35 in the women's 20km event thus achieving a sub '96 minute Olympic qualifying time, no other British walker performed particularly well that day.

Breakfast in the hotel dining hall on the Monday morning should have been a time for everyone to relax before their respective journeys home. Well, that's what any reasonable person would think. My big mouth however got the better of me. For a time, I had been content to sit chatting with friends, Andy Penn, Rocky Stone, Steve Hollier, and Pierce O'Callaghan, until distracted by the sight and animated conversation of a particular group of diners across the room. I tried to ignore it at first, but it just niggled me. Of the ten or eleven sitting there, at least half were selectors, several of whom had barely taken the time to speak to me over the weekend. That's their prerogative, of course, but short of banging on the table and demanding their attention, I hardly endeared myself to any of them by marching up in order to express my pent up frustration.

I thought it ridiculous that I was not being reassured they would at least be putting my name forward for Olympic selection. No other Brit had come within 10 minutes of the time I had achieved in Holland. The publicity that was being generated was better than any British walker had enjoyed in years. An opportunity, I argued, was being lost if *we* did not at least capitalize on it now. I reminded them that the British marathon runners would all be selected by now, and it made no sense to delay selecting any other qualified endurance athlete. All the leading British walkers with Olympic aspirations had at least two attempts this season to get a qualifying time and most had missed by a country mile.

There was a lot of huffing and puffing and expressions of empathy, but nothing of any substance was said in response to my tirade. Met by a virtual stonewall, I turned and walked away half expecting as I did so, a paper dart or part eaten sausage to hit the back of my head at any moment. The sheepish grins etched on the faces of my mates as I approached their table probably summed up what I had just achieved.

A couple of days later, Peter Marlow rung me on behalf of the walks committee to say there would be no early selections, certainly not until after June 20 and the European Cup walks when everyone would have another shot at getting the necessary qualifying times. Apart from Lisa, who improved her British record again, no one else did. No one else came close.

Steve Hollier at least tried. He was certainly fit enough to go sub four hours in the 50km race, but handicapped by weeks of recurring knee pain, he did well to revert to our plan 'B' and salvage his day with a personal best 4.07.18 clocking – well short of what was required for his dream ticket to Sydney but, as it was marginally quicker than the time achieved by Mark Easton in Holland, it did at least rank him second behind me for the year.

It was more with a sense of relief rather than satisfaction, when my 91.39 time was enough to see me finish first Briton in the men's 20km event, as by then I was feeling completely de-motivated. Of course the performance left me well short of the eventual winner, Robert Korzenoiski, and the likes of Germany's Andreas Erm and Spain's Francisco Fernandez.

In the intervening two months between Leamington and Eisenhuttenstadt I probably had not helped my own cause by doing two other races of contrasting fortune. Mindful that I needed to maintain high mileage in training, I entered the national 35km championships. It was a knee-jerk reaction to the telephone call from Peter Marlow. I was so angry that the following morning I went out and walked 35kms in 2.41.15 at the Yelverton aerodrome circuit. Fueled by frustration, the fast session was enough to convince me that I might boost my flagging spirit by winning another national title. Ten days later I was in London and well on the way to achieving that aim. After almost two hours of racing, I had built up a commanding lead of several minutes, when suddenly, my motivation to keep going, simply evaporated. I stepped off the road and slumped to the grass lying flat on my back feeling utterly fed up.

Katie Pannell's voice was one of the first I heard trying to coax me to get up. 'C'mon, Chris, what are you doing? Don't be a wimp. You're Mad Max…you can't let those others beat you.'

Katie was a first year medical student based in London. It was great to see her again, and though my present predicament was embarrassing, I was devoid of energy and incapable of rising to my feet. Mum, nor anyone else for that matter, was going to persuade me otherwise. Catching a blurred rush of feet and legs going by was enough to validate my position. I was done for the day.

I needed a rest. Not for one day, not two, perhaps a week or more just to recharge my mind and body. Instead, I arrived home and arranged with Edmund to join him the very next weekend on his trip to Valladolid in Spain for the World Veteran road championships. I did not dare mention this to too many people, because those that did get to hear about it thought it was a stupid idea. I think Edmund was so enthused by the prospect of having company that he struggled to objectively consider the implications should I compound the demise of my selection dream.

Adding a third World championship gold medal to the two I had won at Gateshead the previous August would hardly appear to count as a *bad* race. It *was* painful though. I felt so nauseas and dehydrated during the latter stages of the 30kms that I almost passed out at the end. Shortly after crossing the line, I was assisted to the back of an ambulance and placed on an IV drip by a team of medics.

The reverberating sound of the race commentary from outside was adding pressure to my already excruciating headache as I lay whimpering on the stretcher. It did at least allow me to catch Edmund's name announced over the tannoy, confirming that he too had managed a finish in the sweltering heat. In the 60 - 65 aged category he may have missed out on an individual medal for himself by finishing only fourth, but he was more than happy to stay behind and collect mine at the prize presentations. Like some wounded soldier, I was aided back to our hotel room where I curled up until Edmund returned an hour or two later and gleefully hung a medal around my sorry neck.

'Hey, you're a world champion.'

Not long after arriving back from Germany, I was flattered to meet up with award winning sports photographer, Mark Shearman. He had been commissioned to take a series of pictures to accompany an extended article due to be published in a forthcoming edition of *Athletics Weekly*. We were in my living room and partway through discussing the kind of photographs that he envisaged taking during the day when my telephone rang. It was Duncan Mackay, a journalist for the Guardian newspaper. He wanted my reaction to the news that I had been selected for the Sydney Olympic Games. Tears welled up in my eyes.

'Really, they've picked me?' I was stunned.

200

Apparently, a press release made by UK Athletics that morning confirmed what I had needed to hear for the past three months.

Duncan asked me a number of questions about my history. I muttered a few inconsequential comments about how proud I was. The following morning I bought my first ever Guardian. I flipped through the pages until I came to the sports section. *Mad Max takes a long stroll into the record books*, the headline ran. Next to it, a huge racing photograph taken during the Atlanta Olympics, with an article that was crammed full of facts and figures – *Wow!..*I thought.

I was probably on the third or fourth read through, when I heard the familiar sound of my post being pushed under my door followed by footsteps descending the stairs to the surgery below.

Fifteen minutes later downstairs, signs were that Edmund had a busy operating day ahead of him. All six kennels at the rear of the surgery were occupied, the incumbents, perhaps in anticipation of their fate, were creating an almighty din.

In adjacent kennels in the far corner, a Jack Russell terrier vied with an Irish wolfhound for vocal superiority with their incessant yapping and barking. In the next kennel along, a giant lop eared rabbit sought solace half hidden amongst a messy mix of hay and old newspapers. A variety of cats filled the other three kennels. Holding a hand to my face, it took a few moments to adjust to the heady stench hanging in the air.

I crouched down in the narrow dimly lit corridor and looked into the first kennel where two kittens meowed for attention. Clinging vertically to the steel mesh front, their tiny claws were precariously entwined in the metal. I gently stroked the invitingly soft paws. Cowered in the rear of the next kennel was a large black cat. Raising its head, it suddenly showed its teeth and hissed causing me to veer backwards and crash against the plywood door behind me. 'Agh, bloody hell,' I cursed, whilst two frightened kittens squealed and dropped to the floor.

The sheet of white paper that I had held in my other hand crumpled as I broke my fall.

A concerned voice from the other side of the toilet door asked, 'Who's that? Is everything all right?'

'Yeah okay, it's only me, Ed,' I said. 'I just had a little stumble. No harm done. Mary told me where you were. If you're reading the newspaper, she told me to say, *put it down and hurry up*. Hang on a minute.' I stood up and dusted myself down. Turning to face the toilet door, I crouched down on my haunches and said, 'Ed, I'm sliding a piece of paper under the door. It's a letter that arrived for me this morning. I thought you might like to read it.'

Dated 21 June 2000, the headed notepaper from UK Athletics, read:

I have pleasure informing you that you have been selected by UK Athletics to represent Great Britain and Northern Ireland in the forthcoming

XXV11 Olympic Games to be held in Sydney, Australia in the forthcoming event(s).

Men's 50km Walk

Your nomination has been passed to the British Olympic Association who will confirm your selection in due course.

Congratulations on your selection and we look forward to receiving your immediate acceptance on the form enclosed...

I sat down resting my back against the other side of the toilet door, and waited. I thought that I could hear Edmund sniggering, though it was difficult to tell above the noise of the barking dogs. There was no mistaking the shouts of, 'Great, great, great,' each *great* louder than the previous and concluded with what sounded like an excited stamp of feet. Momentarily the barking subsided. I was grinning. A feeble meow from one of the kittens kicked off another rumpus.

Receiving that all important letter was the spur that kick-started me to another level of training. I wasn't interested in racing, only in building up my fitness and strength by working hard on the roads and in the gym. I was both flattered and sometimes irritated by the frequent requests for media interviews. One that turned out to be better than I could ever have imagined was after local man, Phil Stoneman contacted me and asked if he could run alongside me during one of my training sessions. He believed he might write a more informed article if he had first-hand experience as to what it was like to train with an Olympic walker.

Initially, I was cool on the idea. I was assured it would not be as I feared, a waste of my time, as he apparently worked out at the gym, regularly ran on a treadmill and felt reasonably fit for a man in his thirties. So, it was agreed, together with a photographer, we would all meet up three days hence at 7am on the moors at Yelverton. The plan was to have a brief introductory chat, do a few warm up exercises whilst a few pictures were taken prior to me starting one of my more *steady* 20km sessions. Thereafter, Phil would do as much or as little of it as he had time for on the day.

As it turned out, five minutes was all it took before he stuttered to a breathless stop and bade me farewell as I carried on and disappeared over the horizon. Behind me, he turned on his heels and begun what I thought might feel like an undignified cut back across the moor to his friend with the camera.

Front page, back page, two pages inside, colour photographs complemented Phil Stoneman's article that was full of high praise. He wrote that one day he would be able to tell his grandchildren how he managed to keep up with an Olympic race walker. Although he was undecided as to whether or not he would reveal for how long exactly this feat lasted and that he was running.

Less enjoyable was seeing my name in bold print in the Daily Mail under

202

the banner headline, *Path to Poverty*. The article by Neil Wilson was brilliantly written, but touched all my raw nerves. Only my closest friends really knew how tight things were for me, though it was becoming increasingly clear that other people were drawing their own conclusions. In fact a general theme appeared to be developing with sections of the media. The historical significance of me competing at a fifth Olympics was being overshadowed by the apparent *shameful* way in which I had been ignored by my own athletic federation with regard to funding. I recall my brother Pat ringing me up the same morning and asking me if I had seen the newspaper article. He struggled to understand how embarrassed I was by my lack of funding being so publicly flagged up. Pat preferred to believe that my phone would be *hot* with people wanting to make donations to help my cause.

The phone did ring...once! It was from Neil who said that he had received an anonymous donation of £50 and that he would be sending it on. I also received a short letter from a lady who was a single mother who simply wanted to wish me luck and apologize for not being able to afford giving more than the enclosed £10. Across the road, the local chemists had set up a collection tin on their front counter asking customers to dip into their pockets and help me win a gold medal in Sydney. I was mortified when I heard that this act of apparent kindness was being carried out on my behalf. As soon as I could I politely requested that the message was removed.

Around the same time, the BBC contacted me and asked if I would participate in a television item for the nine o'clock news. They wanted to highlight the fact that there were a number of British athletes selected for the Olympics who did not receive lottery funding and of those I was considered one of the most high profile. By then, I had just about had enough of talking about it, so it was only after considerable persuasion that I agreed to meet them.

The interview and film of me training in Central Park together with an accompanying clip of me lending a hand to Edmund in the surgery whilst he de-scaled his own dog's teeth was aired soon after. After watching it, I felt sick. Why, I'm not sure. It was, after all, only broadcasting the kind of information I had known about for years.

UK Sport had been responsible for distributing tens of millions each year, and although the amount at their disposal in recent times may have decreased slightly, questions were being asked about where it went exactly. Administrators argued that when lottery funding started in 1998, 240 track and field athletes received lottery cash. By the following year that figure was down to 160. By 2000, they claimed it was down to 91. A prominent athletics chief said he believed that for the first time in history, athletes were adequately funded and that *we* were on a par with countries like Germany, France and Spain.

The following morning I was parked up on the moors, rooted to my seat contemplating the worth of stepping outside. I was cold and beginning to stiffen up. Whilst the howling wind and rain buffeted the car, the facts, figures, and statements from the previous evening's broadcast ate away at my soul. The windows were thick with condensation, the floor sodden by damp through leaking sills. My beloved, occasionally maligned Capri had failed its last MOT and was headed for the scrap yard. I could not cope with continually borrowing my friend's vehicles. Needing to be independently mobile, the £230 it cost me to buy the Ford Escort meant that I just had to be even more frugal, keeping my daily food bills low during the last push towards Sydney.

A blast from the car heater might have offered some crumb of comfort, but to do that I would have needed to turn the ignition and restart the engine, and the battery was already showing signs of being dodgy. I also knew that if I started the engine, there was little chance I would actually start any walk, let alone the longest and hardest one. *Just get out there and do it,* I thought to myself. *This session is important.*

Completing it always gave me a sense of achievement and a boost to my confidence. There were only so many 45km sessions that I could do before a big race. More repeated deep breaths, I willed myself to summon up a surge of energy. Half-heartedly I reached for the door handle before deciding against opening it. The clock on the dashboard clicked over to seven. I had been sitting there for 40 minutes. I needed to get out and move around- either at home, or *out there…* in the rain.

Above the whooshing sound outside I heard distant lamenting cries. My hand reached for the key in the ignition, for a moment I thought I'd risk the car battery. One turn of the ignition allowed me to flick on the windscreen wiper switch. I wiped the inside of the screen with my hand and flicked away the excess moisture. The moors looked desolate. The cries continued, until out of the gloom, I caught a glimpse of a lone foal calling for its mother. The poor animal looked pathetic as it cantered into view, slowing to a standstill and crying plaintively. I stared, feeling even more helpless than before. The forlorn cries abated when the mother reappeared and I bore witness to a happy reunion. I smiled for the first time that morning.

Putting my hand to the door I paused, took more deep breaths and pushed the door open. 'Bloody hell,' I squinted, my face assaulted by the force of the rain my hair blown every which way. I slumped back in, slamming the door shut. 'Shit!'

I turned the ignition key one more notch and the engine spluttered. Frantically, I tried again and again. 'C'mon you, bastard. Start!' Finally, the engine roared. I pumped the accelerator and steered away, the wheels skidding on the gravel. 'Tomorrow,' I said. 'Absolutely no pissing about tomorrow.'

'Git!' I snarled at the passing driver. Another car had sped by throwing up a spray of water and drenching me as I lapped the aerodrome for the ninth and final time. My eyes refocused on the distant sight of the cattle-grid road sign that signified the imaginary finish line. Parked nearby in the dispersal bay opposite, was my Escort, its wet rusting metal supremely highlighted by rays from the sun that had finally broken through the cloud.

On the horizon ahead, I saw the top of St Paul's Church. Fleetingly, I recalled the legend of the Typhoon pilot who died when he crashed through the church spire. Following that fateful day, the height of the church had been reduced. Today, the bells were chiming. As a rule, the sound inspired me. Not so this morning. It irritated me that I had not achieved my aim to be back at the car before the start of the Sunday service at eleven. Three and half hours earlier, I had set that target and started my stopwatch. Already saturated, I didn't care about splashing through the last few puddles.

Closing in on the road sign, the last strides were done with the stopwatch showing 3.33.01. It mattered less that I had been faster on previous occasions. In all the testing circumstances I had to be satisfied.

I trudged over to the car and reached for the last remaining bottle of isotonic drink resting on the bumper. I swigged down the drink while glancing across the moor and catching sight of the silhouetted figure on the brow of the hill. Edmund had walked in the opposite direction and was slowly but surely working his way back towards me to complete his seventh lap. I looked at my watch and estimated that he would be finished in less than five minutes and before 3.40 registered. Ed would be elated. I turned away, unlocked the car and peeled off my t-shirts. Everything ached, though it was a pain I could live with.

The BBC rang again. This time I was excited by their proposed visit to meet me in Plymouth. I was to be featured on Grandstand in their Saturday afternoon *Athletics Focus* programme.

Three days before the film crew were due to arrive I was out walking in Central Park, the wind in my hair and well on course for a fast six mile time, when it happened: BANG! I reached back, grabbed the back of my right leg. It hurt like hell.

As soon as I got home I called Richard. Within the hour he was massaging the damaged area. We thought I might have pulled a hip or hamstring muscle. I did not want to cancel the BBC appointment, so in the interim decided to rest and not attempt any walk at speed until the cameras were rolling. I was determined that I should appear very positive when talking about my race prospects and that I had out of necessity risen above the issues surrounding the much publicized lack of funding. With only a matter of weeks to go, I had already reasoned that there was no point in dwelling on this anymore. Had someone handed over a million pounds, it would not make one jot of difference to how fast I might walk in Sydney.

I had no sponsor to advertize, so I was pleased that there was no objection to me wearing a t-shirt supplied to me by a charity called, *Hope and homes for children* who I promised to assist with their own fund raising.

Christina Boxer and I had previously been part of the same British

Olympic team; now retired and working as a journalist for the BBC, the former 1500m runner chose to do part of our interview whilst we were filmed seemingly training together along a rutted path that passed through a particularly scenic wooded section surrounding Burrator reservoir. Completed in one take, disguising my discomfort was fortuitously easy. Apparently they already had plenty of archive footage that would be edited into a final four minute film to include two of my Olympic finishes and a clip of my hero Muhammad Ali lighting the flame in Atlanta.

As pleased as I was with the film, my primary concern was recovering from the injury as quickly as possible. I simply had to hope that it was not serious. During the following few weeks, I lay on a succession of medical treatment tables while tumbleweed blew over my training roads. It *was* serious.

Richard had several attempts at deep massaging my right hip, my right buttock, and my right hamstring. With each successive treatment session I was subjected to increasing levels of excruciating pain. At Kevin Kelly's clinic, my spine was the focus of attention. Regularly strapped and stretched on the chiropractic table, I may in all possibility have grown an inch or two, but one thing was for certain, the pain failed to dissipate.

An MRI scan showed the true extent of the damage…a torn gluteus maximus muscle. The injury would require at least six weeks of rest to heal. There were three weeks to my departure to Australia, and five to race day. Medical opinion suggested that I should withdraw from the Olympic team. The alternative was to battle on, utilise my hard earned fitness, and leave no stone unturned in an attempt to get to the start line in the best condition possible.

I became a familiar figure at the Mayflower Centre pool doing up to seventy lengths, against the clock. The early morning bathers became used to my manic endeavour. Once word spread who I was and what I was trying to do, they gave me space and encouragement. It helped drive me on. The self help with ice-packs, ultrasound and remedial stretching brought minimal pain relief. In the gym, from the waist up, I had never been stronger. But I needed strong healthy legs. Richard and Kevin alternated their efforts. I surreptitiously knew that I was on a wing and a prayer. To me, the choice remained a simple one, keep going, or give up on one last Olympic dream. I wasn't ready for that, neither were my best friends.

Richard reminded me that I had earned the right to compete. No other man in Britain had qualified. If I withdrew, Britain would have no representatives in either of the men's Olympic walk events for the first time in its history. Edmund simply wanted to see me compete. *Have faith*, he said. *And, why not ask God for help*, he suggested. I could not promise that, but did say that I would look forward to meeting him and Barbara out there in Australia.

At sunset on Friday September the fifteenth, conservative estimates indicated that four billion people worldwide tuned in to watch the opening ceremony of the Sydney 2000 Olympics. The epic pageant of Australian culture evolved into a jaw-dropping spectacular. The evening started with a lone rider on a chestnut stallion galloping into the centre of the arena. The horse reared up onto its hind legs, the horseman cracking a whip and signalling the charge of 120 horses and riders into the ground. In front of 100,000 spectators in the stadium and millions more viewing from all around the world, the greatest show on earth began.

During the opening segment, a thirteen year old blonde-haired girl was hoisted forty metres into the air, swooping and diving on an unseen harness. The choreographed special effects transformed the Homebush athletic stadium into a three-dimensional space, with the crowd enveloped in a sea of blue light representing the brilliant blue ocean surrounding the Island continent. The girl floated amongst exotic sea creatures resembling giant luminous jellyfish, seahorses, and plant-like anemones, all hovering high above the ground, while the imaginary sea floor flickered with schools of human fish.

The show evolved into a visual tapestry of Australia as thousands of dancers and acrobats twisted and turned every which way, while other performers breathed flames recreating a bushfire. The 2000 strong marching band led the parade of 12,000 participating athletes from 200 countries around the globe, played stirring renditions of Waltzing Matilda and Chariots of Fire. Australia was represented as an energetic, multi-cultural country that has become technologically sophisticated, and most importantly, reconciled with its Aboriginal population. The seminal moment came with the lighting of the Olympic flame. Speculation was rife as to who would have the prestigious honour.

When the torch was carried into the stadium by Australian running legend, Herb Elliot, statistics ran across television screens worldwide: *The Sydney Olympic torch relay is the longest and most spectacular in the history of the event. The Olympic flame has been carried by 12,000 people over 60,852kms around the world, and across Australia for 100 days arriving today.*

One by one the torch was passed relay-style by generations of famous Australian sports stars, each running a short section of the track before handing it on. With the spotlight introduction of each successive sporting legend, the applause grew. Elliot passed the torch onto Raelene Boyle and Jill Cuthbert. Then on to Dawn Fraser, Shirley Strickland, Shane Gould and Debbie Flintoff-King until, finally, the world's most famous baton was passed to the *chosen one.*

Dressed in a pristine white jumpsuit, Cathy Freeman, an aboriginal runner and current 400 metre world champion, appeared to a rapturous reception. She stepped into a pool of water holding the flame, as a huge thundering waterfall cascaded down the stand in front of her. Out of the water, she ignited a circle of fire, which ascended onto a giant cauldron. As the flames leapt, the cauldron slowly made its way up the steep incline to the top of the stadium.

I was just one of many people gazing up in awe at the live spectacle showing on a multitude of television screens all around Singapore airport. Like most men, I am inept at multitasking. So, it proved far from easy trying to soak up the true splendour from a corner of the busy waiting lounge, whilst trying to appease the wriggling child sitting on my lap.

In desperation, I looked across to Lisa Kehler. The smell emanating from the baby was turning my stomach. Holding the restless boy was becoming a challenge too far. His mother sat a few feet away, frantically delving into her hand luggage for a clean nappy.

At Heathrow Airport several hours earlier, I had learned to my dismay that little Kai was not staying with daddy and grandma who were there to bid them an emotional farewell. Instead mother and baby would re-unite with them three days later in Sydney; Lisa unwilling to be parted from her baby for that length of time, race or no race.

The flight had touched down at Singapore airport for refuelling and a crew change. Lisa and I, together with brothers, Steven and Andrew Train, the only other British Olympians on the flight from London to Brisbane were resigned to missing the opening ceremony. As we walked through the concourse we gazed up at the giant overhead television screens.

The final leg of their journey across the world saw us touchdown at Brisbane airport just before light at five in the morning. There, we were met by a handful of personnel from both an Australian delegation and from the British Olympic Association. The transfer by mini-bus to the training camp took two hours. The Train brothers were whisked away, bound for a water based camp for fellow canoeists.

Room allocations were followed by a guided tour of the camp. With baby Kai in tow, our arrival at breakfast in the cafeteria was greeted with a modicum of bemusement by the rest of the athletic squad. Lisa's healthy mix of motherly pride and thick skin prevented any negative reaction becoming a problem. After breakfast we climbed aboard another bus to a local school used temporarily as a holding bay for all the British team clothing. Following the fitting and acquisition of several bags of new athletic gear we returned to base camp to meet more team-mates.

The jet-lag started to take hold during the afternoon stroll around town. Feeling woozy, I found the physiotherapy room located on one side of the camp and booked an appointment for the following day.

Lisa and I agreed that we would attempt to shake off the travel stiffness by squeezing in a light training session before the British team meeting that evening.

I held the baby close to my chest, muffling the incessant crying against my new fleece sweatshirt. 'Shush, shush, shush,' I pleaded, over and over again. Behind me, a stream of light shone down from another curtain pulled aside to trace the source of the noise.

I would have preferred not to be seen. Furtively I stepped into the darkened shadow of one of the trees lining the Hotel Radisson golf course. Dry kindling snapped underfoot as I cowered amongst the undergrowth. I realised that I would just have to muddle through with Kai's displeasure until Lisa returned from her short walk.

I slackened my grip just enough to allow me to push the fluorescent light button on my wristwatch. It was nearly seven in the evening. In ninety minutes time the British team was expected to assemble in the hotel's function room for a final squad meeting. I decided that when Lisa reappeared out of the darkness, I would suggest we call a halt to our bizarre interval training session. After four, five-minute walking efforts my jet-lagged body was telling me to stop anyway. We had taken turns to hold Kai while the other walked out-of-view along the moonlit paths entwined in and around the golf course. Kai's contribution was to cry for the full five minutes while his mother was away, and to immediately start to gurgle and coo contentedly when placed back in his mother's arms while I disappeared into the darkness. I breathed a sigh of relief when I heard Lisa approaching, her puffing and blowing steadily increasing in volume the closer she came.

Finally, a silhouetted figure emerged from the dark tree-lined shadows. 'Ooh, ooh look, Kai,' I whispered. 'It's your mummy again. Here she comes. C'mon, just once,' I pleaded, 'Stop crying you little, you little… shh…' Lisa walked past, slowing to a stop a few paces on. Breathing heavily, she walked back, hands on her hips, smiling and reaching out for her baby. Without hesitation I handed him over.

'There, there,' she said. 'Come to mummy.' Kai immediately began to settle. 'Was he any better that time?' she asked.

'Well,' I sniffed, 'a little bit.'

The Queen Elizabeth room was awash with new blue tracksuits. The notice board had stated that immediately following the final full squad get-together, the obligatory team photograph would be taken outside on the grand staircase leading up to the function room.

One hundred athletes crammed into a room with a maximum seating capacity of eighty. I stood at the rear, my back pressed against the wall next to Kevin Hughes, a pole-vaulter and my room-mate at the training camp. Lisa sat just in front of us. She looked over her shoulder and said something, but I couldn't hear her above the chattering noise. I shrugged and smiled, as if to say it didn't matter. Stroking her hair, still damp from her shower, she put a reassuring hand down to her baby. In spite of the commotion, Kai remained blissfully asleep in a child-carrier at her feet.

I scanned the room. The unfamiliar faces would be the first-time Olympians, their excitement it was reasonable to presume, mixed with bewilderment and degrees of trepidation. I doubted any of the new people would know who I was. So, spotting those who had also competed before was both comforting and reaffirming. It felt good to be amongst established achievers, some of whom had assumed star status. At the front of the room near a screen projector were the team coaches, Max Jones, Tudor Bidder and John Trower, in conversation with David Moorcroft the UK athletics' Chief Executive. Seated near the front, I could see Kelly Holmes tugging at her coils of ringlet hair and laughing to a blonde woman sitting next to her. When she turned I recognised the profile of Paula Radcliffe. A loud raucous guffaw drew my attention to one corner of the room. Few people laughed as loud as decathlete Dean Macey. Triple-jumper, Jonathan Edwards, and the javelin trio of Steve Backley, Mick Hill and Nick Neiland, appeared to be in on the joke. I grinned contentedly, revelling in the exalted company. Unconsciously, I rubbed my sore hip as the assembled athletes were called to order by Tudor Bidder banging on the table.

'Okay, guys,' Bidder raised his hand. 'Can I have some quiet please?' The room descended into a hush, bar a few nervous chuckles. 'Thank you.' Bidder smiled, stroked his grey moustache and waited for complete silence. 'Thanks to you all for being here, our last get-together before many of you move on to Sydney tomorrow morning, where…' Bidder paused, and with a wry smile he appeared to deliberately speak deeper and more slowly, '…the games will start in earnest.' Given the mixed response of whooping, clapping and hesitant laughing, his words had the desired effect.

Bidder glanced at his fellow coaches. '*We* won't keep you too long. No doubt some of you will still have some packing to do. The early departure times are on the notice board in the foyer. They'll tell you the bus times to the airport, transfer details and your scheduled arrival time at the Olympic village. Please check them if in doubt. And that applies to the rest of you who leave with each successive day.

'As you can see, we have been joined by David Moorcroft, who arrived earlier today. Also some of you will have seen at breakfast the arrival of our final two athletes at the camp…Lisa Kehler and Chris Maddocks. Lisa is our sole representative in the twenty kilometre walk. This is her second Olympics. Lisa *and her baby boy* are only with us for a couple of days before she moves on to meeting up with some of her family. We'll see her again in the Olympic village later. Stand up, Lisa, so we can see you.' She half stood and offered a token rigid wave.

'Thank you, Lisa,' Bidder said. 'What can I say about, Chris? Hopefully most of you know about him. If you don't, you should.'

My heart thumped. The verbal spotlight had moved to me.

Bidder directed his look to the rear of the room and fixed a stare on me that appeared so strong that I felt myself shrinking back into the wall.

'Chris,' he said, 'is one of our walkers and the first British man to become a five-time track and field Olympian.' Chairs creaked on the wood-panelled floor as people turned to stare at me. Each athlete knew what it took to qualify and be selected just once. The applause that broke out around the room seemed a genuine

210

appreciation of my achievement. Bidder went on, 'Obviously he's been around a while, but I can definitely say that he's still young at heart.' The clapping rose to a crescendo mixed with sporadic cheering. Hairs stood up on the back of my neck, tears welled up in my eyes. Several people shook my hand while others patted me on the shoulder. The noise died down, and Bidder went on to introduce an Olympic video designed to inspire. As the lights lowered, my chest felt tight, my spirit soared.

Half an hour later the lights came up. The double-doors were pushed open and I joined the throng of athletes that spilled out onto the first floor landing leading to a wide oak staircase. The photographer was scheduled to assemble everyone at 8.45 for the official team picture. It was 8.35. The spare ten minutes was valuable autograph hunting time. Out came a variety of British flags, books, spare team kit, and scraps of paper to be signed. Clutching my red and blue felt-tip pens, I unravelled my spare t-shirt and the oversized pair of formal white linen trousers I was spared from wearing at the opening ceremony. The trousers would provide plenty of room for an array of star signatures.

I was one of many groping around on the carpeted floor signing anything thrust in front of them. Traditionally, experienced athletes took such opportunities to acquire a host of names and later pass on the signed articles to organised charities for money raising auctions.

I crawled about on my hands and knees, grateful to Bidder for making my quest so much easier. Fellow team members were more than happy to oblige me with a signature for my *Hope and homes for children* charity who had provided me with several additional logo printed t-shirts, one of which I revealed when removing my tracksuit top. The ensemble of athletes was a golden opportunity to have my photograph taken with some star names. By the time the official photographer called, the ink in my felt-tip pens had nearly run dry. I gathered together the t-shirt and linen trousers, already transformed into a mess of patriotic red, blue and white.

The team streamed slowly over the length of the grand staircase. Mindful not to smudge the signatures, I shuffled along at the rear of the group discreetly shaking dry the freshly marked clothes. I manoeuvred and wedged myself into a position at the back near the top of the stairs. On cue we all smiled. The camera flashed. I felt on top of the world.

My world came crashing down again the following day. Up early, the morning road walk turned into a purgatory experience. A short convenient stroll away from the hotel, the mile long stretch of road I found, would normally be sufficient for temporary training purposes. However, the more times I walked up and down the *Radisson mile* the more my right leg, hip and buttock hurt. While the sun rose, my head dropped. The digger engines roared into action on the stroke of eight, immediately kicking up a dustbowl. As time passed, more people appeared,

211

strolling, walking dogs, and tooting car horns as they went by. I felt anything but an Olympic athlete as I dejectedly limped back to base camp.

Back in the Radisson, my hotel room looked sparse. Kevin Hughes had already packed his bags and along with thirty others, was set for their departure to Sydney. The breakfast meal with Lisa and Kai would be our last together at camp before we too were on our way out.

Meeting Edmund and Barbara later that morning would ordinarily have cheered me, but I was still suffering from the results of the *first* scheduled meeting that day with the physiotherapist. The injury refused to clear. It was agreed that while I attempted to stay fit, intensive aggressive treatment was required. A second appointment was booked for later the same day. Before that, meeting my friends brought some light relief, typified by Ed's big welcoming smile, standing proud in his new leathery stockman's hat. Once I had arranged a special week-long accreditation for my guests allowing access to most team areas, we left camp and headed for the beach.

While soaking up the sun at Southport beach, I willingly agreed to meet Edmund the following morning with a view to training together on the Radisson mile. This would not transform me back into a fast walker, but the sense of togetherness would help. I felt vulnerable. Akin to a child reaching for its comfort blanket, the familiar hand of friendship would be reassuring.

The second round of treatment later that afternoon left me groaning. Drained of every last ounce of energy, I was exhausted and wet with perspiration, my watery eyes evidence of pain inflicted in the name of remedial treatment. Told to *relax* by the physio, a large clean white towel had been placed over my prone near-naked body while she had a word with a colleague at the far end of the room. Barely able to open my eyes, I watched the tall lithe figure walk away past the four other tables in the room where athletic limbs were being rubbed, oiled and stretched.

She had worked on me for a solid half-hour, probing, stretching and pummelling in a manner that made Richard Pannell's treatment seem like a tickling session. The numbing afterglow of her full weight and razor-sharp elbow drilled into my hip and gluteus muscle area had reduced me to restrain tears, and the chatter and groans around me to a fuzzy, noisy blur.

From the corner of my eye, I saw the small plastic cup of water left for me on the adjacent worktop. A dry throat was my reward for having spent much of the last half hour suppressing squeals of pain. Only a steel crane, I thought, could prise me off the table. A few sniggers greeted my strained effort in reaching for the elusive cup. I sipped the water and managed a wry smile by way of return.

Thoughts of meeting up again with Edmund and Barbara for the second time that day helped clear my head. Our evening rendezvous time was less than an hour away. Imagining the smell of the promised barbequed steak had me licking my lips in dreamy contemplation. My wistful grin evaporated when I saw the physio striding purposefully back towards my table. She was smiling. I found it quite disconcerting.

Standing tall and erect, the ears from the six grazing kangaroos twitched like antennae. Poised, they appeared ready to scatter at any moment. The loud echoing laughter from the kookaburra carried across the Currumbin wildlife sanctuary. Undeterred by the familiar distraction, the khaki-clad female member of staff stood in the cordoned off enclosure and beckoned Barbara Shillabeer and the two young girls to move closer. Like stalkers they edged forward clutching handfuls of plant leaves to tempt their hungry prey.

Twenty-five yards back and standing behind a wooden handrail, a hushed line of people watched the afternoon feeding. I found myself sandwiched between an elderly man and woman, my eyes fixed on the action. I was by then habitually rubbing and prodding my gluteal muscles and right hamstring.

The few hours of relaxation at the Currumbin wildlife sanctuary were a welcome diversion from the frustration I had endured at the training camp. The morning walking session with Edmund had been aborted after only six slow kilometres. The hard fast lengths of the Radisson swimming pool did more for my hunger at breakfast than it did for my increasingly challenged fitness schedule. Getting close to koalas, wombats, wallabies, snakes and crocodiles was a gratifying tonic for a waning spirit resulting from my name appearing daily on the physiotherapist appointment sheet.

Applause signalled the end of the feeding session. I looked across to the opposite side of the enclosure and saw Edmund clapping enthusiastically and catching his approving eye-contact with his wife. I smiled as he looked back and gestured for me to come over. I walked round, mindful to dodge the dispersing crowd. Sidling up alongside I asked, 'Well, Ed, what did you think of that?'

'Excellent.' Edmund leaned on the handrail. 'How's the leg? Still bothering you?'

'Yes, a bit. But I think it's improving. I'm not sure really.' I could see that my friend looked unconvinced. 'Ed, you know that I appreciate your company in training. It's no disrespect, but training with you, well it's not exactly preparing me for an Olympic 50km race that's in...' I paused and calculated the figure in my head, '...oh God! That's in *nine* days time.'

'I know that,' Edmund replied. 'Maybe you should just rest it for a few days,' he said. 'How many times do I have to tell you? You have miles in the bank. You'll be alright. And let the physio' do what she can. You've said yourself she seems to know what she's doing.'

Consumed by pangs of selfish guilt, I nodded, realising that I must have sounded negative and uncharitable. 'I've got to try and keep my fitness up. I do appreciate you being there. I just don't want to train on my own at the moment.' I felt desperate, and must have looked desperate when I virtually pleaded with him, 'So, tomorrow morning, we'll still meet usual time before breakfast. Only this time, let's not go on that bit of road we've been using. It's doing my head in. There are some good tarmac paths in and around the Radisson golf course. I doubt anyone else will be there that early in the morning.'

Edmund concurred. 'Okay, that's fine. Remember though, at ten-thirty tomorrow morning we're driving up to the Tambourne Mountains. I've heard that it's great for bush walking. I've got it all mapped out. Don't worry about lunch. We'll get it there. And before we come back, there a wine making distillery that should be interesting to visit. Sound good to you?'

'Yeah.' I'm sure my smile was quite unconvincing. The excursion was something to look forward to, but the nagging doubts over my fitness cast a heavy shadow over any joy spent in the company of such dear friends. They would be gone soon; onto Sydney where their Olympic experience would start in earnest. In addition to supporting me near the end of the Games, they had tickets to watch other sports including hockey and the three-day equestrian event. It meant I only had two more early morning training sessions with Edmund; two more sessions in which I could draw on the wisdom of my older, wiser friend, a man who had unquestioning belief in me – a belief conveyed with such conviction that it was impossible to ignore, as difficult as it was to accept sometimes. As Edmund had reminded me, I had *the miles in the bank* – more than 100,000 of them. At that time I only wished the bank had not been broken into. My body was letting me down at a crucial time. It was time to at least take on Edmund's positive attitude.

Walking across the grass towards the reptile house, I felt the warmth of the mid-day sun and glanced up at the cloudless sky. It was a beautiful day and I did not want to spoil it in any way for my friends. Their suggestion to visit the wildlife sanctuary had proved ideal relaxation time that we assumed would be a one-off experience. But, as embarrassing as it was, I had to tell them some news and trying to find the right moment worried me. Another interview had been lined up for two days time. A journalist from the BBC had made contact and a meeting point had been agreed. My concerns over how they might react, was typically wide of the mark.

'The BBC…that's great.' Edmund said with a huge grin.'

'Where are you meeting them?' Barbara asked.

'At the Radisson,' I answered. 'Then they're taking me to a wildlife sanctuary. A place called, Fleays. I think they want to do an interview with me while I'm holding one of the animals. Something like a cuddly koala bear?' So I thought.

As the fifteen foot long python was carried over by a grinning gamekeeper, so the three man BBC crew gingerly backed away. I smiled inanely, cursing myself for the moment of stupid bravado that saw me agree to the snake being wrapped around my neck while talking about my forthcoming race.

Reminded beforehand that snakes like *Jackson* usually only feed on small animals and killed their prey by squeezing or constricting until it suffocated, suddenly, felt like too much information. I was hardly reassured by being told that only larger species fed on creatures like goats or pigs, and apparently they rarely killed humans.

Reminded to breathe as the python was placed on my shoulders and slithered around my body, its scaly skin felt like sandpaper, its body, hard and muscular. The cameraman adjusted his zoom lens while the sound man shuffled as close as he seemed prepared to go.

The reporter stepped forward. His hesitant steps all too clearly suggested that I was not the only one who was afraid. He sniggered and had the cheek to say, 'Try to relax.'

Whether it was simply a case of taking a leaf out of Edmund's book of positivity, or simple economy with the truth, I was adamant that I should sound upbeat. I said my preparations had been affected by injury but hoped that the great occasion would inspire me to a good performance. And from what I had already seen on the television back at the hotel, the Olympics already looked as good as any I had ever experienced.

I omitted to say, that my injury continued to hurt like hell, and the prospect of racing against the fastest walkers in the world in one weeks' time filled me with trepidation. I saw no reason to mention how tired I felt through worry and lack of sleep. Disguising the usually outwardly visible signs of fatigue, the experience of having an enormous snake wrapped around my neck probably worked better than any temporary face lift.

I repeatedly punched the air and shouted at the screen. 'Yeeesss, yeess, yes! C'mon, c'mon, pull, pull, yeeesss. C'mon, you can do it...'

My voice was one of many heard that glorious day in the Radisson lounge that rocked with excitement as men and women leapt from their comfortable seats, screaming encouragement at the television screen. Amid the pandemonium, manic expressions of joy and concern were stamped on all our faces. Watching the British coxless four rowers closing in on the finish line in pursuit of an Olympic gold medal was so exciting. With every stroke, the Italian crew pulled back into contention. Inches separated them. The tension was almost unbearable. The volume was high on the television yet barely audible above the frenzied screaming for the British team.

Ecstatic smiles, high-five slapping and double arm raises greeted Steven Redgrave winning his fifth gold medal. His team had narrowly beaten the Italians with four other finalists trailing in their wake. On the TV, Matthew Pinsent un-did his foot straps and clambered over an obliging Tim Foster before embracing Redgrave in an exhausted hug. Behind them, James Cracknell wearily patted them on the back. I slumped down in my chair and laughed as a red-faced Pinsent tumbled out of the boat into the cool rippling waters.

The historic win kept everyone buoyant for the remainder of the morning. Opinion abounded on the significance of the race; how exciting it was, and what it might do for British confidence halfway into the Games. On day one, Jason Queally had set the standard with his surprise cycling gold medal. Shared success guaranteed a blossoming sense of team unity.

A more sombre air returned once the suitcases in the foyer disappeared, leaving the Radisson distinctly quieter with even fewer bodies gracing the dining halls and corridors.

The two days following Edmund's departure, I had managed successive sessions of twelve kilometres, the second one faster than the first. With a heavy dose of irony I tried to convince myself that I was at least improving.

I had one last session to do before I left for Sydney. It was disappointing to think that I would be making the flight alone. Most of the team members had already departed. Of the athletes remaining, only me and the marathon runners were left, and as they were due to compete on the last day of the Games, they would travel on later. The best I could hope for was that my final training walk would be a good one.

Breathing like a matador about to face his nemesis, I looked to the far distance before setting off down the road. Beads of sweat had formed on my brow caused by heat from the morning sun. Focussing my mind, I flicked my legs to release any tension.

A glance at the stopwatch revealed my time recorded from the previous day's 12km road session. 58 seconds over the hour had been encouraging. I challenged myself to beat that time. With a press of a button the 1.00.58 figures were zeroed. A confidence boosting walk, days before the big race, was what I needed.

Within a few strides a car sped by honking and kicking up a cloud of dust in its wake. Doing my best to ignore it, I pushed on.

The water was surprisingly cold as I eased myself into the Radisson pool. Waist high, I tiptoed around like a drunken ballerina. Droplets of water obscured the latest figures on my wristwatch: 0.02.30. The two and half minutes I took to walk the estimated quarter mile that morning was my slowest for a long time. The first part had been blindingly quick. Then, the pain in my buttock and hamstring flared like a dagger causing me to slow sharply. Grinding to a halt a few strides later, the trudge back to the Radisson pool was done with the heaviest of hearts.

Ignoring the smells of cooked breakfast wafting from the hotel kitchen, I dipped below the waterline and pushed away.

Pausing amongst other commuters, I leaned on my luggage trolley, looked up at the airport clock and adjusted the time on my wristwatch to 1520 Sydney local time – one hour ahead of Brisbane. Following the signs to the taxi rank I strolled on, confident in the knowledge that an Olympic volunteer was scheduled to meet me at the airport and ferry me to the athlete village at Homebush Bay.

216

Olympic paraphernalia were everywhere. Most prominent was the Sydney 2000 logo together with iconic illustrations of The Sydney Opera House, and glossy images of sun, red rock and beaches. Three colourful cartoon mascots symbolised the spirit and character of Australia: Millie, for millennium, was a spiny anteater; Olly for Olympic, was a kookaburra, and Syd for Sydney was a duck-billed platypus. Pictures of Olly, Syd and Millie smiled and waved from every corridor and shop window.

Like most volunteers, my taxi driver was identified by Christian name only on a lapel badge. William talked all the way to Homebush. I flitted between humouring my jovial driver and staring out of the window to take in the sights during the half hour journey.

William explained that Australians, in particular the Sydney residents, had been slow to embrace the spirit of the Olympics in the years and months leading up to the start. He spoke of cynicism about the spiralling costs. Questions had been posed in the media about the wisdom of staging such a monumentally costly venture.

In 1976, Montreal had staged the games and local tax payers were reputedly still paying for it. Assurances had been given to the people of Sydney that with improved planning that kind of burden would not fall on them. Once the Games had started though, the lighting of the Olympic flame had inspired most people. National pride was also helped by Australians winning an abundance of medals.

'I tried to get tickets for the swimming,' he said. 'Bloody impossible. They sold out in no time. Our boys though were bloody amazing. You've heard of the Thorpedo?' I saw William check his rear-view mirror. 'Ian Thorpe,' he said. 'You'll see him on loads of billboards.' I looked back and nodded. 'What a man,' William added with an obvious sense of national pride.

'And what about our Susie O'Neil? She's a real beauty. I've lost count of how many medals she's won. And our relay boys broke the world record.' William continued talking while I soaked up all the sights.

When our imminent arrival at the purpose built Olympic village at Homebush Bay was announced, my heart pounded a little harder. William pointed out the athletic stadium on the brow of the hill. I stared out of the window and saw beyond the village rooftops the distinctive arena with its sweeping arched roof.

'Hard to believe,' William said. 'Just four years ago, all this was a bloody great building site.'

Constructed around wetlands, the developers with a keen eye on the future had ensured the natural resource would be utilised by the village and used as a natural water recycling plant. Going right through the middle of the Olympic Park complex all kinds of sports arenas had been built off a mile long boulevard, allowing easy access to all venues within short walking distance. There was the magnificent Super Dome playing host to the Basketball, gymnastics and trampolining events. Already underway at the aquatic centre were the swimming

217

and diving competitions. Other centres included those for tennis, archery, and hockey.

The taxi eased to a crawl behind a short queue of vehicles approaching the village's south side entrance. Over by the entry gates were a number of volunteers all attired in the same blue and white polo shirts with yellow trim and cream trousers or shorts. A friendly face checked the taxi authorisation before directing it forward into the village disembarkation area.

I put a hand up to wave William off as the taxi pulled away. The big thumbs-up confirmed his appreciation of the British Olympic team pin secured in place and already lost in a sea of other badges on his old hat.

I gathered up my bags and walked on. Beyond the security gates and the scanning checks, the accommodation blocks stretched out in front of me, sunlight bouncing off their solar panelled rooftops. Advertising proclaimed that these would be the most environmentally friendly games ever.

The site would house over 15000 athletes and officials during the Games. Once the Games were over, the world's largest solar village would be available to residents as 2000 executive standard courtyard homes. The three or four bedroom houses each costing between 350,000 and 500,000 Australian dollars.

I was ushered through into a room where my ID was processed and passport style photographs taken. I sat and took my turn along with other arriving athletes and officials. Armed with an ID tag that would hang around my neck for the best part of the following week, I sauntered forward and was greeted by two strikingly attractive volunteers. Blonde, tanned and curvaceous they were ready to escort me to the British team accommodation block. I willingly accepted the invitation to step aboard their electric powered buggy similar to those used on golf courses, while squeezing my luggage on the back seat next to me. The British base was only five blocks away. The girls suggested we take the scenic route around the village so that I might familiarise myself with my new surroundings.

Meandering along at no more than 15 miles per hour, their youthful exuberance shone as they enthusiastically pointed out various landmarks as other buggies trundled pass the maze of smooth tarmac roads. Track-suited and t-shirted people of all nationalities and sizes sauntered along the pathways. Cyclists in training shot pass. Joggers went by chatting while more focussed runners paced with gritty determination along the village paths.

Most of the homes were two storey structures painted in pastel shades, each with its own courtyard space. Athletes sat around chatting and enjoying cool drinks, while in other courtyards more active pursuits included group stretching, bicycle maintenance, weight lifting and general socialising.

National flags hung from balcony ledges, giving a clear indication as to who had taken up temporary residence. Pumping Reggae emanated from a cul-de-sac draped in Caribbean flags. Turning away into another street the flags and music changed to those of China and the distinctive sound of the Orient dominated by the new film soundtrack of *Crouching Tiger Hidden Dragon*. Moments later, my attention was drawn to a particularly busy courtyard in what was obviously the Cuban quarters. A group of men stripped to the waist were grunting their way through various boxing drills guided by their trainers. The impressive mix of shadow boxing, glove shots, skipping, and punch-bag work had me recalling memories of my brief meeting with two great Cuban boxers in Atlanta four years earlier. Felix Savin and Tefillio Stevenson had each won three consecutive Olympic heavyweight gold medals in their respective eras. Photographs taken with them together with the ones of me and Muhammad Ali were treasured items in my album back home.

As we trundle on, roadside trees rustled in the buggy car's slip-stream. The girls who were Sydney based students, explained how the strategic positioning of decorative Pergolas and deciduous trees would allow winter sun to permeate through and warm the houses, while offering shade during the summer months.

The girls said they had heard complaints by some athletes about the overcrowded conditions. The homes were being used as apartments for up to twelve athletes at a time, with garages even modified for use as bedrooms, leaving many to feel the confinement all too claustrophobic.

I nodded. I was aware that the complaint was a familiar one heard on other championship occasions. Accommodation was seldom ideal and experience had taught me to be reasonably philosophical and to make the best of it.

They drove on past the huge marquee being used as a 2000 seater dining hall. Further on, a shopping mall included a communications building where athletes could access the internet and a choice of games rooms including a bowling alley. The buggy swung into a long cul-de-sac where row upon row of houses had union flags draped from windows and balconies. We had entered the British section. I was despatched with the warmest of good luck wishes.

I stood in between the twin beds and sighed heavily. Both were cluttered with athletic kit, one bed more dishevelled than the other. I placed my bags down and removed kit from the marginally tidier bed and transferred it across. It just had to be *Bow* I thought, the team joker, who I had to be sharing a room with. My philosophical well had run dry.

My late arrival had meant I had drawn the short straw and with it the last available bed. Arriving late meant that I had little or no choice in my room allocation or room-mate. Usual practice was for close friends and event team mates of the same gender to be roomed together by management administrators. I had been paired with a man whose gregarious nature had apparently worn thin at the Gold Coast training camp. I could only guess that few wanted to prolong that experience by sharing a room with him again in the Olympic village. Already eliminated in the first round of his event and therefore released from the need to rest well before competition, he was, by all accounts, in party mode and hitting the town.

219

It was almost six o'clock, a little more than an hour away from a potentially great evening of athletics. The apartment was virtually empty bar two team coaches downstairs who were preoccupied deep in discussion. For the time being, I was on my own. It would be tight, I thought, but I decided: A freshen-up in the shower, a quick bite to eat and a bus ride to the stadium was just about possible.

I knew that I could get easy access to see the athletics knowing that all those athletes wishing to spectate at their own sport venues were permitted free priority entry by their accreditation ID tags. The imminent evening of athletics was destined to be a sell out. The woman's 400 metre track final with Cathy Freeman was one race touted as a must-see event.

The evening stroll through the bustling Olympic Park Boulevard was awe inspiring. Stadia peppered the area like landed spacecraft, each sign-posted and reverberating with crowd noise. The athletic stadium was jaw-droppingly beautiful. High sweeping roof arches enclosed the arena like the smooth lines of a giant sea shell. The crowd noise rose and fell in sync with athlete action. I heard the evolving sound as I shuffled through the crowded stone corridors towards the block reserved for spectating athletes.

An obliging steward directed me to a seat. I cupped an ear to hear the instruction partially drowned out by the deafening roars and rhythmic clapping and stomping of feet. My adrenalin level rose with each step up the stairway towards the increasing swirl of fresh air. I paused at the top. The stadium was packed to the rafters and positively crackled with human energy.

I took my seat while the capacity crowd applauded a successful pole vault of Australian golden girl, Tatiana Grigorieva. Her smiling face was captured on the two giant LED screens positioned high each end of the stadium. The former East European appeared to be in a two way battle for gold with America's Stacey Dragila. The crowd settled. Attention diverted to the track and the second of the men's 110 metre hurdle semi-finals.

The sun had set and camera flashlights sparkled around the arena. The hurdlers were peeling off their tracksuits in readiness for the call to their blocks. Long lens cameras pointed down towards the trackside action.

Stadium announcements were made in French and English. Programme notes said that Jean Francois Raffaell shared commentary duties with retired wing commander Alan Warner. I listened attentively as each hurdler was introduced to the crowd. As they came under starters orders a respectful hush descended over the stadium. I noticed both LED screens instantly flicked to a wide shot of the eight hurdlers. They rose, paused, and on the *B* of the race starter's bang surged out of their blocks.

A deafening roar from the crowd followed the eight runners sprinting down the length of the track. I shouted support indiscriminately. Thirteen seconds later the cheering began to subside. I watched an aerial camera replay on one of the LED screens and had barely gathered my breath before I was drawn by the loud rhythmic clapping indicating that Stacey Dragila was running down the pole vault runway. After watching the American clear the bar I ran my index finger over the programme resting on my lap. The remaining event order read:

1903:	400m Hurdles Semi-finals Woman.
1915:	Discus Final Men
1945:	400m Hurdles Semi-finals Men
2000:	Triple Jump Final Men
2010:	400m Final Woman
2025:	400m Final Men
2040:	110m Final Men
2055:	5000m Final Woman
2135:	800m Semi-final Men
2215:	800m Final Woman
2245:	10000m Final Men

When the last of the 10,000m runners had crossed the line, I joined the masses slowly making their way out of the stadium. Grinning from ear to ear, my first live experience of the 2000 games had been enthralling.

Australia had won their first athletics medal of the games with Gregorieva's silver behind Dragila. Jonathan Edwards had given the hordes of union jack flag wavers the chance to sing the British national anthem. But *the greatest night in athletics history* would be remembered principally as the Cathy Freeman night. Prior to the start of the woman's 400m race, the air of expectation had been palpable. Every tension filled moment had been captured at close quarters and relayed up onto the LED screens.

Wearing a hooded lycra cat-suit for a streamline affect, Freeman had crossed the line ahead of Jamaican Lorraine Graham and Britain's Katherine Merry. Freeman more than won a race. At that moment, she had united a nation. Her race with destiny was over in less than fifty seconds, and in a blaze of flashing photography the applause evolved into possibly the longest standing ovation in sporting history. Sitting on the track at the finish and pulling back her hood and seen in close-up on the LED screens, it wasn't difficult to sense her relief.

By comparison, the men's 400m final featuring Michael Johnson was almost an anti-climax. The American had nevertheless reinforced his superstar status with another Olympic gold. The 10,000 metre race had been a fabulous finale. Running hard off the final bend and away from the chasing pack, Haile Gebrselassie and Paul Tergat had entered the last 100 metres side by side. The diminutive Ethiopian's duel with the taller red vested Kenyan resulted in Gebrselassie edging a win by the thickness of his green vest. Gebrselassie's sweat saturated smile was infectious and ensured that fans such as myself left the stadium with joy in our hearts.

I smiled and fantasised about walking into that magnificent stadium with

221

the crowd cheering me on. I was jolted out of the daydream by an overzealous spectator barging past on the stairs. Wincing with pain I snatched at a handrail, the sudden movement had caused a painful tweak in my gluteal. I resolved to make time for another physiotherapy appointment.

After several nights of interrupted sleep, I felt justified in asking management if I could move to another room. The option to move into a *safehouse* the night before my race held little appeal. I said as much when one of the team managers offered it. I had moved to a room and bed away from noisy village life at previous championships and had not found the upheaval outweighed the potential benefits. The promise by one of the team coaches to get me a room key in an adjoining athletes block attracted me more, even if it had resulted from another's misfortune. A family bereavement meant Jonathan Edwards would leave for home early.

I was told that I could collect my new room key in the British Hospitality lodge the evening before the woman's walk, and *two* nights before my own.

'Well, that's good news,' Michael Lane said.

Over lunch it had been great catching up with an old friend and racing adversary. Lane was now retired and well and truly ensconced as one of the most respected Irish team coaches, a man who also shared my love of talking in infinite detail about all aspects surrounding the Olympics. Conversation flowed, virtually unaffected by a succession of other track-suited athletes occasionally pulling up chairs, sitting down and departing after their meal. Only the sudden clatter of smashing dishes and spiralling cutlery caused a brief interruption. Though it had been difficult to locate the unfortunate culprit, we, in the spirit of United Nations joined the spontaneous cheering and thudding of tables that had broken out around the marquee. Once the noise died down, most Olympic events continued to get dissected, none more so than the men's 20km walk where Daniel Garcia had crossed the line one second ahead of Poland's Robert Korzeneowski.

Still basking in the glory of his win, the Mexican learned of his last minute disqualification while receiving telephone congratulations from his nation's President. As heart breaking and controversial as that was, both of us agreed that the Pole was a worthy champion. Lane had enthused about his own protégé Robbie Heffernan who had finished inside the top 20, confident that he was coaching a star of the future. Their hope was that the woman's walk would be just as exciting but escape similar controversy.

Almost three hours after sitting down, we finally got up and left, satisfied that in time honoured fashion most issues had been covered in appropriate infinite detail.

Such was the size of the Olympic village that I only bumped into Lisa Kehler fleetingly. We had a short staccato type conversation whilst lying on adjacent beds in the physiotherapist quarters during a simultaneous pummelling massage. Catching up with her again in the British hospitality lodge the evening before her race, had at least presented a better opportunity to wish her luck. She had her own injury worries and looked nervous as I watched her leave.

The lodge was located just across the road from the Olympic village. It was a popular facility provided for by the British Olympic Association as a meeting place where team athletes could relax with their family and friends. Comforts included sofa chairs, a free bar and refreshments, with a big screen continuously showing BBC Olympic coverage. Throughout the day athletes dropped in to meet pre-arranged guests. Open from mid-morning until late at night, it proved to be a conveyor belt of people coming and going.

I had arrived early that evening. Edmund and Barbara's late rendezvous with me due to traffic problems was quickly dismissed. I was just pleased to see them again. A bonus was seeing another old friend from Plymouth turn up at the lodge entrance; Dave Fox, looking every inch the holiday maker, beaming smile, complete with sun hat, shades, backpack, bum bag, shorts. Tipped off by Edmund, he had made his way over from the action at the cycling velodrome and prepared to miss the early part of that evening's athletics just for the chance to call by and share some time with us. His accreditation was sorted in no time.

No sooner than they had all sat down, Foxy had extracted a crumpled map used by spectators at the men's twenty kilometre walk earlier in the week. His enthusiasm saw him explaining all that he'd learned from his *exciting* day at the race. I already knew much of the detail but allowed Foxy time to share his thoughts for the benefit of his two other friends.

Each of the three walks started with five laps of the athletic stadium. After exiting the stadium, it was about a half mile to the two kilometre road circuit where the appropriate number of laps are completed, eight for the two 20km races and twenty-three laps for the 50km event, before returning to the stadium and finishing on the track. On paper, the 2km circuit looked T shaped; the walkers joined the lap at the head of the T before heading down the length of the T and turning around cones at the far end and heading back up towards the head again for one complete circuit. I expressed no desire to dwell on Foxy's reminder that I had *twenty-three* laps to look forward to.

Foxy pointed out that the circuit appeared to have no shaded areas, and could be exposed to strong westerly winds blowing in across the Great Dividing Range, Australia's largest mountain range. Stabbing the map, he said how detached he had felt from the walkers by the three metre high wire fence erected around much of the lap. He recalled how for a time he had mixed with picnicking masses on Olympic Park Hill – a large grass banked hill in the shadow of the stadium. Although a short distance away, he suggested that the best panoramic views of the circuit and much of the racing action were possible from that higher vantage point.

Foxy explained how he had since heard that those people wanting to get closer to the action had set up *camp* along the quarter mile stretch of road south of the athletes' drinks zone that led down to the turn at the tail of the T. Edmund intimated he would check it out during the woman's walk and if he agreed with Foxy's assertion, then that's where he too would base himself during the men's fifty. He and Barbara would be easy to spot. Edmund had said with a proud smile that their son had made a special flag for the occasion, and hoped it would meet with my approval when I saw them come race day. I asked, but received no more information, much to Edmund's amusement.

The two hours spent chatting had flown by – too quickly for my liking. As my three guests got up to leave we rationalised that there was only a remote chance that we might see each other the following day during the woman's walk, and if not, then it would be out on the course the next day for the fifty kilometre race. My weak smile probably betrayed me. Edmund hung back.

His parting pep talk was brief and to the point. Reminded of all the hard work that I had done, Edmund asserted, that *now* was the time for me to have faith and believe in myself. We shook hands as if to seal the deal.

The lump in my throat saw me reach for a can of coke from the cooler cabinet and take it back to my seat in the corner. I was keen to avoid eye contact with anyone. My legs felt weak as I slumped back into my chair.

I'd all but finished my drink when I heard a voice ask if he could sit down. I looked up. I had seen the man plenty of times before without actually knowing who he was. Mark McCallister smiled, offered his hand and introduced himself.

At no time during his twelve years travelling with the British athletics team as part of the Christians in Sport organisation could McCallister recall our paths crossing. It was no surprise; His duties included leading prayer and Bible study and offering support and encouragement from those who sought it. I had no previous inclination to do so.

McCallister's distinctive Liverpudlian accent helped our conversation move from Olympic interests to our shared passion for football. Though we shared a few laughs, I can only assume he detected that I might be preoccupied with other matters. In view of the lateness of the hour, we agreed it was time to leave, but he suggested that before we did we might pray together. Caught off guard, I had not seen the offer of spiritual help coming. The number of people remaining had dwindled to a few, and none, I deduced, were within earshot. As uncomfortable as I felt, I said, 'Okay,' and followed the Chaplain's lead by bowing my head.

It was eerily quiet in the apartment as I tip-toed up the stairs. Dark, bar a light left on in the living room below, I presumed my new house-mates were either out or tucked up in bed. First room on the right past the bathroom, I had been told. Holding my breath, I placed the key in the lock...*clunk*. Exhaling quietly, relieved, I stepped inside placing my kit bag on the floor.

I reached for a bedside lamp and sat on one of the two twin beds. I had been assured that the room would be empty as my new room-mate would be out of the village for a day or so. The only visible sign that Steve Backley had been in the room were the two pairs of size twelve trainers and the thin elongated case poking out from under the other twin bed – presumably, I thought, a case containing his javelins. Any temptation to poke around for signs of the silver medal he had won a few days earlier was easily resisted. It was past midnight.

In double quick time, I had brushed my teeth, peeled off my clothes, flung back the duvet cover and was resting my head back on the pillow with a heavy sigh. Flattered that McCallister promised to watch my race I switched off the light, closed my eyes, and tried not to think about it.

The following morning I joined 30,000 other spectators in the stadium and watched the fastest female walkers in the world complete their five laps of the track before heading in a long line out towards the 2km road lap.

By the time I had reached the road circuit, the intrusive rumbling sound of an overhead media helicopter had grown ever louder. An Italian was forcing the early pace closely followed by three Chinese woman and three Russians.

During the following hour, other walkers flirted with the lead before fading back into the chasing pack. In order to witness the end of the race, I knew I would have to leave the racing action and make my way back to the stadium.

The dash back from the road circuit to the stadium had taken me more time than I had bargained for. Scared of aggravating my suspect muscles, I tentatively negotiated my way through the crowds. My ID tag ensured easy access back into the stadium. Guided towards block F, I spotted a spare seat at the far end, just three rows up from trackside. Perfect, I thought, the seat would provide an unbelievable birds-eye view of the action.

Directly in front of me on the track, a line of traffic cones led from a tunnel leading to the road. Standing close by a handful of race stewards waited for the return of the walkers. On the infield at one end, women were in the final throes of high jump qualification. At the opposite end the decathletes were flexing their throwing arms and taking their turns in the discus circle

I sidled past a row of smiling preoccupied spectators; they were clapping, cheering and stomping their feet in unison with a crowd that had swollen to more than 80,000. Most eyes were drawn skywards towards the two LED screens; one looming large over and above my shoulder.

'Excuse me,' I said. 'Huh, excuse me. Thanks. Oh, sorry!' My small backpack snagged on someone or something. No matter, they barely noticed me. I looked up at the screen. My eyes popped. *Fantastic*. A surprise, and not the fast walking woman I had expected to see at all.

On the LED screens the leading female walker out on the road fast approaching the stadium was the Australian, Jane Saville. The noise soared ten-fold. The stadium was rocking. Excited, hairs bristled on my body as I joined in with the rhythm of the clapping.

Australians loved their sport. Australians also loved nothing better than to see their own competitors win. It was beyond my comprehension that a walker could receive such an amazing reception, though I recalled Rome '87 and the World Athletic Championships when Maurizio Damilano walked his way to gold in front of his countrymen.

On the LED screen Jane Saville could be seen descending into the tunnel. No other athlete was in view. With every rapid stride the volume of cheering increased. Then, when she was within sight of the track…disaster struck.

A race judge stepped out in front of her. Brandishing a red lollipop baton, he signalled her instant disqualification from the race. Over exuberance had led to her transgressing the walking rules. She had been judged to have lifted both feet off the ground. She stumbled to the side, crying uncontrollably. Her anguish was shared as the stadium plummeted into shocked silence.

Within thirty seconds Wang Liping appeared on the track. The pony tailed waif-like Chinese girl walked with impeccable style into what must have seemed liked the world's largest morgue. Striding the one hundred metres towards the finish line, she received respectful applause from the stunned crowd. Thirty seconds later Kjersti Plaetzer sank to her knees after claiming a surprise silver for Norway. Maria Vasco maintained a strong tradition of Spanish success with her bronze medal walk. In pinball succession others filtered in. An Italian, a Mexican, a Romanian. Then, in seventh place the *first* Australian, Kerry Saxby, helped bring the stadium crowd back to life.

I was pleased to see the Irish walker, Gillian O'Sullivan, come through in tenth. A few minutes passed before I yelled as Lisa Kehler appeared on the track. 'Well done,' Lisa, I shouted. She was obviously tired and bedraggled but managed to stay seconds ahead of the fast finishing Irish woman, Olive Loughnane.

One by one they finished. I watched the final woman cross the line. I did not feel like watching the second pool of decathletes in the discus. From the look of empty seats that had appeared around the stadium, neither did many others. I rose from my seat taking one last look at the vast arena before walking away. Less than a day to go, I thought.

The figures on the digital clock showed 0735. Half of the athletic stadium was bathed in cool sunshine, the other half shrouded in a shrinking shadowy blanket. The LED screens were blank; and, then, cascading down the screen like a tumbling line of dominoes, the order of morning events appeared one by one:

08:00	50km Walk	Men FINAL
10:00	Javelin	Women Qualifying Group A
10:00	4x100m Men	1st Round (5 heats)
10:45	4x100m Women	1st Round (4heats)
11.45	Javelin	Women Qualifying Group B
12:30	4x400m Men	1st Round (5 heats)

Just a few of my scrap-books. My flat above the veterinary
surgery in Plymouth wasn't always this messy.

The transit and caravan used by myself, Richard Pannell and Steve Hollier on our epic trip to Holland and back in 2000.

50km win in Holland 2000.

Startrack coaching in Plymouth with budding enthusiasts.

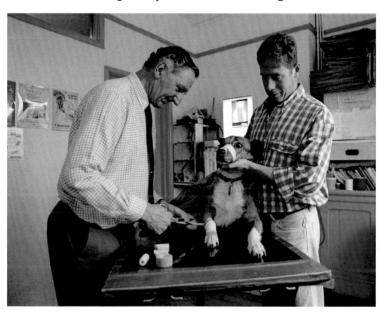

Assisting Edmund in the veterinary surgery.

Journalist Phil Stoneham's idea to try and run with me was short-lived.

With Lisa Kehler and her baby in Australia.

Australia 2000 – BBC interviews.

Racing 50kms in Sydney 2000.

Hunted down in Sydney.

THAT flag, given to me by Edmund, as promised.

With Denise Lewis in the Sydney Olympic athletes' village.

Sharing the limelight with the 'world's greatest walker', Robert
Korzenoiwski during a colourful Sydney Olympics closing ceremony.

Happy days with Fiona and baby Eleanor.

A voice from the main control room reverberated over the tannoy system: 'Now showing on the scoreboard, a listing of this morning's order of events. The first final, the men's fifty kilometre walk, will commence in twenty-four minutes.'

The same announcement was heard in the bowels of the stadium and repeated in French. The sound carried through the maze of hushed stone corridors to the athletes' pre-competition call-up area to where I was one of fifty five men preparing for the 31 mile walk. Looking away from the TV monitor displaying the detail of that morning's athletics action, I was mindful of a handful of officials and stewards respectfully looking on in silence as my rival competitors engaged in a variety of mobility stretches, sprint walks and nervous banter. Several walkers had divorced themselves from any eye contact and were pacing up and down the warm-up area like moody alley cats.

I was in a far corner sitting alone, one racing shoe on, the other in my hands. 'Bollocks,' I whispered with increasing agitation. All fingers and thumbs I nervously tried to secure the small featherweight plastic device to my right shoe. It was my third attempt and still it looked a tangled mess. 'You bloody idiot,' I said to myself.

The digital recording device was the size of a fifty pence coin. Issued two days earlier to each road racing athlete, it had to be threaded onto the laces of one racing shoe. I lost my original device during the apartment move. Anxiously I had acquired another at the race signing in desk. Unravelling the laces, I paused and tried to breathe. I would have to try again. My predicament had apparently not gone unnoticed.

A man in a pristine red and white tracksuit stood over me. I looked up. In broken English the man said, 'Excuse me. Let me help you.'

Robert Korzeniowski sunk down on his haunches, took the shoe, straightened the lace and secured the offending piece of plastic within moments. He handed the shoe back with a half smile and a wink, before getting up and coolly walking away. I called out my thanks.

One by one, competitors began to peel off their tracksuits.

At precisely 0745 ripples of applause greeted the walkers as we spilled out onto the track. Some broke away into fast sprint walking intent on focussing their pumped up adrenaline. Others took a moment to glance around to absorb the magnificence of the stadium from track level. Meanwhile, I readied myself to start my first warm-up walking strides in five days. If, by some miracle, my prayers had been answered, and the enforced rest had done some good, my dreams of a career-defining race might yet be realised. Pushing away, a ticking time bomb activated in my head as I steadily quickened my pace.

Within seconds I ground to a halt, sweating, my heart pounding. The instant pain shooting from my hip, through my buttock and down my leg made me want to howl with anger and frustration. The noise of the media helicopter hovering above disguised my pained anguish.

227

Striding up the length of the track, I kept thinking that I needed to remain positive and walk without fear. Yet, another side of me was loath to try again. I tried to psych myself up, as I did so, Valentin Massana, a small bespectacled Spaniard, shot pass with an effortlessly fluent technique. Paranoia would not help, but I couldn't help thinking that everyone on the track appeared fitter, faster and more bronzed. Fresh from setting a new world record, the moustachioed Russian, Valyri Spitsyn glided by, his face etched with concentration.

Repeatedly they flashed past, a rainbow of moving colours. I'd seen it all before. In the early years I would have been intimidated. Now I was experienced. Richard Pannell would be telling me to be strong and confident. I knew Edmund and Barbara would be out there somewhere on the road circuit to encourage me - if I ever made it that far.

I readied myself to try again. Attempting to banish thoughts of encroaching negativity, my mind became a kaleidoscope of thought: The solitary miles of training on the moors had to count. Some long sessions with Steve Hollier had been awesome. I saw my Mum smiling. Jack Snow on his bike shouting orders to quicken my pace. The Chaplain's kindly face intervened. One prayer answered.

Breathing deeply, I tentatively raised my pace to fast strides. Seconds later I was gasping. It felt as though a rod of molten iron had been rammed and twisted around my hip and buttock. Shuddering to a halt, my mouth felt dry. The prospect was almost too horrendous to contemplate. I had never dropped out of a major championship race. The realisation loomed large. I might not even get out of the stadium let alone walk back into it, thirty-one miles later. The call came to assemble on the start line. One by one, like Formula one grand prix drivers dropping their helmet visors, sunglasses were positioned. There *was* no time left to think.

Minutes later the starter's gun fired. The pain was instant. I felt helpless against the speed of thirty walkers stretching away from me on the first circuit. An effective fluid technique was replaced by a dogged style and determination to cling to the tail of the second cluster of walkers. The awful memory came back. My last walk on the Gold Coast had lasted barely three minutes. Have faith; the rest will do you good, they said. As the laps were counted down, I hoped that I might at least make it out of the stadium. Ten minutes at worst I rationalised. Ten minutes in which to force my leg and hip against the pain and not get disqualified by the judges.

The eleven minutes taken to filter off the track, walk through the tunnel and head out towards the road lap had felt like an eternity. With the burning pain taking my breath away, I was already detached. Ahead of me were 54 men in a tussle for medals and placings in a race that I no longer felt part of. Oblivious to my negative thoughts were the spectators intent on clapping and shouting words of encouragement. It embarrassed me as I pushed on.

The volume of applause and cheering rose as I approached Olympic Park

Hill and intensified as I was guided by stewards past a line of marquees and on towards the first road lap. Racing anti-clockwise, walkers had been directed down one side of a central reservation with the intention of turning at the far end and racing back along the parallel road.

Stretching out before me, I saw the road I had seen at close quarters only the day before. Only then, I was comfortably the other side of the three metre high fence sharing an experience with thousands. Now, I felt exposed. The road looked impossibly longer and less inviting as the bodies ahead of me pulled ever further away. The sun was up, and the sight of limp flags suggested that the only wind blowing in from the Great Dividing Range amounted to no more than a wispy breeze.

By the time I had walked past the row of nationally designated drinks tables, the hazy emergence of flashing headlights from the race lead motorbike indicated that I was about to see those men contesting the medal positions. Sure enough, close behind was the pack of leading walkers, shimmering into view like a posse of cowboys from a spaghetti western. I cast an envious eye across the low steel barrier as they went by. Most faces were familiar to me: Craig Barrett in the black vest of New Zealand; The Fin, Valentin Kononen; two Mexicans; three Russians; the tall fair-haired American, Curt Clausen; Robert Korzeniowski, and Australia's Nathan Deakes. Others passed by in a blur. In twos and threes they went by until it momentarily went quiet.

My head dropped for the first time. The 300 metre stretch of road beyond the long row of thirty tables and canopies looked more desolate, the surrounding area mere scrubland with no visible buildings, bar the distant sight of the Olympic village over to my left. Temporarily marooned, the thinner line of supporters was understandably less vociferous in their support of me as I passed by.

Race fans had either detached themselves far from the anticipated bedlam created at the opposite end of the circuit, or unwittingly found that they were cut off by security once the race started, preventing access to and beyond the competitor's drinks zone. Either-way, that's where I first heard the distant noise of the hunting horn sounded by Edmund. The shock of it had me lifting my head off my chin straight away. I saw he had strategically positioned himself on the road ahead, near the arc of traffic cones that marked the turn-around point. He was leaning on a waist high steel railing and waving, Barbara was by his side and surrounded by other spectators. I heard Edmund yell something incoherent before he offered another blast on the horn. Those stood around him covered their ears.

As I rounded the cones I caught Edmund's stare. It was a caring look, one that recognised my pain, but *not* one that suggested, *stop...its okay; you've tried, you done your best.* I pushed on, sure that I could not survive the hurting for much longer.

Walking beyond the drinks zone, and sighting the first of two disqualification boards placed around the lap, reminded me of the need to walk correctly. Maintaining contact with the ground was not a problem; I wasn't moving quick enough to concern the judges. Straightening my knees on the other hand was proving a hellish experience. The second board was visible by the seated race recorders under the digital clock and gantry. Several red discs were already dotted against various race numbers. I glanced at the board as I went by and saw that number 1808 wasn't one of them. My fate was still in my own hands.

'Just take it, Chris.' At the second time of asking, I accepted the *1808 MADMAX* marked bottle from my personal assistant in the drinks zone. Lisa Kehler had given me little choice. She had demanded it. Dressed in skimpy leisurewear and sunglasses, she might well have looked relaxed, but her recognition that I was in trouble, meant that the threat of dehydration was not going to be on her head.

If I was looking for sympathy, it was also in short supply at the turn. First time round three Australian race marshals had obscured my view of Edmund's English flag of St George. Secured to the steel railing, there was no mistaking it this time. In the four white corners, Edmund's son had inscribed in thick black ink, the words: LA, SEOUL, BARCELONA, and SYDNEY. ATLANTA had been inked down the vertical red line, and written along the horizontal red line was, MADMAX.

'C'mon, Max,' Edmund shouted. 'Head up. The flag...look at the flag.' I managed to return a half-hearted smile as I went past. I noticed Barbara attempt to make herself heard but whatever it was that she shouted was lost amid a random barrage of encouragement from around. The hunting horn was given another airing. Edmund was heard hollering, 'Keep going, Max. You're doing great.'

An hour into the race and the numbers of spectators had swelled to all parts of the course. Enjoying the warm sunshine, the majority had flocked to the birds-eye-views possible from Olympic Park Hill. Virtually every patch of grass had been claimed. Breakfast hampers were out, towels down, flag wavers in full voice. The two previous Olympic walks had attracted big crowds suggesting some to re-christen the free viewing vantage point *United Nations Hill*. With each passing lap the noise grew with fans doing their best to out shout each other. Thousands lined the length of the road leading down towards the turn. Four, five people deep; in places the high steel mesh wire almost bowed under their weight. Children enjoyed some of the best views, held aloft on obliging shoulders. Older heads bobbed and weaved, each endeavouring to glimpse the walkers racing past.

An hour since the start and I could hardly fathom why I was still in the race. Dreams of a great race had gone. With every painful step, I was merely surviving. Thoughts of an escape route were becoming increasingly difficult. If I was to drop out, I wanted to do it quietly, without fuss, without someone trying to persuade me otherwise. Slipping away unseen by the masses would have to wait. The rising reverberations of the overhead helicopter had alerted me to the imminent arrival of the leading walkers coming up from behind. I was about to be lapped.

The lead motorbike trundled past. Riding pillion, a cameraman hung off the back filming, giving me no more than a cursory glance as the leaders closed in. Behind me, the fast moving walkers had already swept past the mass of seated race recorders and dignitaries beneath the gantry. Each of their laps had been covered within a few seconds of nine minutes. The leaders turned right and after covering another 100 yards double-backed towards the sponging station positioned along the head of the T-shaped circuit.

A line of young men and women readied themselves to hand cool wet sponges to me and the other walkers. I held out a submissive hand. Like an injured prey hunted down by a pack of baying wolves I was engulfed by the leading seven amidst a mass spray of water. Seconds later and jostled out of my stride by another group of walkers, they passed in a blur of metronomic legs and fast pumping arms, pulling further away before turning to eat into yet another lap.

My heart pounding, I put a hand to my right hamstring and slowed to a virtual stop. Shuffling forward and shaking my head in sheer disbelief, I reminded myself again that I had never dropped out of a major championship before. My heavy sigh was one of total resignation. At that moment I heard a voice – a familiar voice, shouting above all the noise and mayhem.

'C'mon, Chris. C'mon, you can do it.' David Fox was a distance away to my right standing on a section of Olympic Park Hill surrounded by race fans, all demanding that I should keep going.

It took a few moments before I decided to raise my arms and stride on again. The feeling that I was only delaying the inevitable was never far from my thoughts as time passed and I completed more laps.

Approaching the drinks zone for the ninth time, I sighted the United Kingdom table. The arm of Lisa Kehler was already ninety-degrees bolt straight, bottle in hand. Swamped by passing walkers, I initially failed to hear anything of what she was shouting. The Australians were the first table that I passed. Positioned alphabetically, thereafter organised chaos prevailed. With every passing walker a fresh impetus of grabbing of drink bottles, sponges and instructional shouting ensued, languages all merging into a verbal scrum.

I could see Lisa standing firm. 'C'mon, Chris,' I heard her say. As she did so, she appeared irritated by a man who appeared to be causing a distraction by leaning in close and cupping his hand to her ear. Unable to hear the brief exchange of words, I was more concerned at snatching the bottle anyway. Moments later it was in my hand and I was tilting my head back whilst Lisa screamed at me to drink all the contents.

'I don't see the bloody point,' the man whined. 'He's already so far behind.'

It was a damning comment that I would have preferred not to have heard. But if there ever was an occasion when the truth hurt, then this was it. Lisa shouted at me again to keep going.

My hair was still sodden by the latest saturated sponge when I heard the hunting horn heralding my imminent arrival. I reached Edmund and Barbara Shillabeer and shuffled to a standstill. My shoulders slumped, arms dropped by my side, chin buried on my chest. Sapped of energy, I draped heavily on the steel barrier bearing my name. 'I can't go on,' I mumbled.

In unison my friends responded with: 'Yes you can; c'mon, don't give up, Chris; you've got to keep going.'

I heard similar shouts of encouragement from all around. Mark McCallister was amongst those offering additional vocal support. It made no impact on me. I had walked beyond twenty kilometres – way beyond what I thought possible when I had lined up at the start of the race. Maybe the chaplain's considered words from two nights before had helped me get that far at least, I didn't really know.

'I can't take anymore,' I rasped. Unable to look anyone in the eye, I said, 'I'm in so much pain. It hurts like hell. I'm sorry.'

Spoken with a soft yet very deliberate voice, I heard Edmunds response. 'I know it hurts. Believe me I do. And it's probably going to hurt for a few weeks. But if you stop now...' Edmund paused. 'Look at me; c'mon, look at me,' he repeated.

I raised my head and stared back at him.

'If you stop now,' he said, 'it will hurt for the rest of your life.' He took a deep breath, pointed and raised his voice. 'Start walking. Get up that road and finish this race.'

'But...'

'No buts. Go on, you can do it.'

Barbara concurred. 'You can do it Chris.'

Against any real desire, I felt myself straightening up. My eyes remained locked onto Edmunds'. I heard Mark McCallister's intervening voice, 'Yes Chris, you can do it.'

I said nothing, turned and started to stride slowly away. 'Yes, that's it,' I heard Edmund cry out. 'C'mon, head up! You can do it. Walk tall.'

Sounds of whooping and cheering erupted from all around as I pulled away. Before I could raise even a modicum of speed, an Italian trio coasted past me. As they did so, Giovanni Perricelli slapped me encouragingly on the back.

Behind me I heard Edmund shout again, 'And when you finish, I'm going to give you this flag.'

I snarled under my breath, 'I don't want your fucking flag.' I stared ahead and thought...*up the road? I've still got nearly twenty miles to go. I'll have to find somewhere else to drop out. Some place where no one will stop me.*

I trudged on past the drinks zone. Not there. Too many people knew me. Then, with impeccably bad timing, I heard another recognisable voice. I glanced up. Across to my left beyond the high wire fence I saw David Fox again, this time running and shouting like a mad man along the ridge of the grass embankment.

Over and over again, he shouted, 'C'mon, Chris, keep going. That's it, you're doing great...'

I knew Foxy was fit and ready for the Melbourne marathon the following week and he would therefore have no trouble in keeping that type of running up all day. My best hope, I thought, was to slink off course somewhere at the far end. It would be packed with people, and they would surely be distracted by the men hurtling around the circuit.

Minutes later I was striding towards the gantry and past the recorders. It was noisy, dominated by cries of, 'Go Australia, go, Deakesy.' More walkers blitzed past me, including Nickolay Matyukhin, one of the Russians who I had beaten the previous season in Italy. The crowds cheered wildly. Demoralised, I walked on. As the searing pain scrambled my mind, the cheering subsided to a muffled drone. I needed a quiet escape route, a hole to crawl into.

In a subconscious state I accepted the offered sponge from a girl whose smile was transparently sympathetic. I could respond with no more than a weak smile. A few strides later I stopped. A race official stepped forward, stared me in the eye and said, 'Finito?' I was devoid of all energy. Like a referee counting out a floored boxer, the official waved his hands palms down. He asked again, this time in English, 'Are you finished?'

Before I could respond, a chorus of voices from a short distance away demanded that I keep going. I looked beyond the race official, through a gap in the marquees to where a band of people on a section of Olympic Park Hill were gesturing wildly to me to carry on. Amongst those shouting, clusters of people appeared to be trying to grab my attention by waving union jack flags. Overwhelmed, I was still consumed with the futility of starting again.

Away from my own race performance: It was just past eleven when the race official climbed the step ladder to place a third disk against number 1692. The temperature had risen to a sweltering thirty degrees centigrade; the hottest day of the games. Like Valentin Kononen, several other walkers had been shown the red disqualification baton by the chief judge and disconsolately required to unpin their race numbers. Others had succumbed to heat and exhaustion. Arturo Di Mezza was an early casualty after vomiting for the last time at around the thirty kilometre mark. The surprise and disappointment of the Italian's retirement was surpassed when Valeriy Spitsyn stepped off the circuit shaking his head dejectedly. In all, eight competitors dropped out.

Approaching the forty kilometre mark the lead group was down to four. Nathan Deakes was keeping the locals happy by producing the race of his life and going shoulder to shoulder with Korzeniowski. Two Mexicans made up the quartet until Herman Sanchez's determined look turned to one of tortured anguish when he saw the red baton waved at him. For a short time the lead group numbered three.

Back in the stadium the race progress was being monitored in the glass fronted control room that overlooked the track. In between that morning's athletic events, the walk had also been shown periodically on the two giant LCD screens. The last qualifying group of women sprint relay runners had just crossed the finish line. Meanwhile, a ripple of applause greeted the arrival of the second qualifying group in the women's javelin. They were being escorted in single file out into the packed arena.

In the control room, Executive producer, Greg Bowman got a nod from his assistant producer. Reassuringly on one monitor he could see that the last of the traffic cones, leading from the tunnel out onto the track, were all but in place. Korzeniowski could be seen out in front on the monitor approaching the stadium. He had a clear lead as he turned up onto the track towards the final one hundred metre straight. Thunderous applause and cheering accompanied his sprint to the finish. Moments later he was flinging his weary arms in the air. The clock stopped at 3:42.22. He sunk to his knees and soaked up the adulation.

The Pole was on a victory lap draped in his national flag when Aigars Fadejevs punched the air in delight on his approach to the finish line and a silver medal. The young Latvian had mounted a late charge through the field. A minute later Joel Sanchez stopped the clock in 3:44.36. Both Valentin Massana and Nickolay Matyukhin reeled in Nathan Deakes before the finish.

The PA system informed the crowd that Deakes was achieving a lifetime best performance. Greg Bowman and his team joined in with the rapturous reception afforded to the Australian. 'Brilliant,' he said. 'That was brilliant.' He leaned back in his chair. 'Okay, how long before the last of these guys come in?' He raised his voice. 'Can someone find out please? We've got relays to get through. And it looks like it will be tight.'

A voice came across on the communications loop. 'Greg. Duane here. The word from the road circuit is that most walkers should finish within half an hour.'

'Most,' Bowman queried.

'Well, there are a couple of guys...an Irishman and a Brit. They're quite a bit off the pace. I think the Irish guy will make it. The British walker looks like he's suffering big time. He's stopped quite a few times and is a couple of laps down. We have doubts he'll finish.'

'Okay mate. We'll keep an eye on it.'

Thirty-five minutes later Jamie Costin, walking in the green vest of Ireland, crossed the finish line in 38th position – more than a kilometre behind the Hungarian ahead of him. The 4 x 400 metre runners were primed and ready to go. The aim was that all rounds would be completed on time by the end of the scheduled morning session.

Bowman looked at the monitor. He was concerned that the predicament of the British walker had the potential to be disruptive. The team in the control room recognised that. There were mutterings among them. A voice piped up. 'We could let him finish *outside* the stadium.'

Bowman was unimpressed by the suggestion. He liked precision, and yet was left with uncertainties to ponder. Decisions had to be made, and quick.

'Boss. The first group of relay runners are out.'

Out on the road loop, drink stations were being dismantled, kilometre markers were being taken down. The crowds had long dwindled to the handful of spectators slow to leave.

With every passing minute my scuffed strides seemed to get louder. Only the occasional whimpered groan interfered with my erratic breathing. My salty skin was turning a devilish pink. Unable to muster the strength to take the last sponge, my lips felt primed to crack. The road ahead, now virtually deserted, had long descended into a meandering blur. Numbed by the physical pain; the thought of trudging down *that road,* twice more, threatened to suck me into an ever darkening abyss. I was jolted back to the present.

'Well done mate,' a race steward shouted. 'Keep going.'

I acknowledged the friendly encouragement with a feeble nod of thanks. Minutes later I was passing the remnants of the drinks zone. Lisa was ready with a bottle and a sponge. There was a demonic look in her eye. The urgency with which she demanded that I take both could not be ignored.

At the turn there was the bleak sight of staff disentangling the steel barriers. The flag was gone, as were my loyal supporters. A South American judge offered a discreet clap and willed me on. The quest to finish the walk from hell seemed ever pointless. My spirits were lifted by the encouragement from familiar voices, first by Barbara Shillabeer ignoring the pain in her aching knee, then by Edmund heard further on in the distance – the flag now draped around him like a caped crusader. Foxy reappeared jogging and shouting along the length of the grass embankment. And, waiting at the far end amongst the last of a few diehard picnickers on Olympic Park Hill, a solitary union jack flag bearer who, when I passed by, were all whipped up for one last rousing rallying call.

The bell for the final lap rang out. Mesmerised by its sound, I was barely able to comprehend that I was actually striding out down toward the Great Dividing Range for the twenty third and last time; less than two miles to the finish line. I had to keep going now. But who cared? I felt embarrassed and conspicuous. If it wasn't for me, these friendly enthusiastic people could pack up and move on.

I was heartened by the actions of stewards, volunteers and even police officers. Momentarily they stopped their clear up duties, stepped forward and applauded my efforts around the near deserted loop. My mind was flooded with memories of past Olympic walks. I had so wanted this to be the best. To race fast and hard and not just survive. That dream had long vanished. Instead I had just endured my slowest ever fifty kilometre walk. Desperate thoughts of walking back alone into an empty stadium had to be ignored.

I felt an unremitting sense of relief when finally directed away from the two kilometre loop. Grimacing with pain I strode along the cordoned off route back to the stadium. The giant metal girders soon loomed large to my left. In my peripheral vision I saw Foxy and Edmund dodging and weaving past pedestrians as they ran in close attendance shouting encouragement:

'That's it, Chris. Fan-bloody-tastic!'

'Keep going, Chris. Well done. It's going to be worth it. Brilliant...'

I strode along the road until guided left toward the mouth of the stadium entrance. I caught a glimpse of my friends being stopped abruptly by security.

'Sorry guys,' I heard the guard say. 'The public aren't allowed beyond this point.'

I felt their despair as I headed towards the gaping dark tunnel ahead of me.

In the long winding subway, wall lights partially lifted the gloom. After nearly five hours I finally felt some respite from the burning sun. It was eerily quiet until I reached a line of stewards' whose applause echoed along the concreted passageway. Accepting their congratulations as sympathetic, I could only muster a weak responsive smile as I passed by. Pushing on, my chin dropped again to my chest, each stride marked by an amplified scuff. The end, as ignominious as it felt, was imminently within sight. The destructive feeling had little time to fester when I rounded a bend and saw natural light filtering in. Lifting my head a first window sighting of the arena lay ahead. My heart missed a beat. I was mystified. To my surprise, people were still in the stadium.

Outside, and unknown to me, was the last group of relay runners each ready and waiting standing in one corner of the stadium. Their run should have been the final action of the early session. Since entering the tunnel, my approach had been shown on the huge LCD screens. In anticipation of my emergence into full view, words boomed out from the public address system:

'Ladies and gentlemen, in spite of injury, in the tunnel and approaching the track at the end of his fifty kilometre walk, you will see the British walker, Chris Maddocks. This is his fifth Olympic Games.'

Applause and cheering started to swell. The announcer recited the words of Baron Pierre de Coubertin, the founding father of the modern Olympic movement: 'The most important thing in the Olympic Games is not the winning, but taking part.' He paused as the cheering grew. 'The essential thing in life is not conquering, but fighting well.' With that, the thumping drum beat of the Proclaimers' song, *I'm Gonna Be (500 miles)*, pumped out over the stadium. The crowd clapped and stomped in time with the song's intro' rhythm, the sound of which I first heard as I walked on and began my exit from the tunnel.

Immediately hit by blinding sunlight, an eruption of noise cascaded over me. One hundred-thousand spectators were rising to their feet, creating a wall of sound.

Walking out onto the track and veering right, the enormity of it all electrified me. My legs threatened to buckle. The finish line at the far end had yet

236

to be reached. Tears welled up in my eyes, my anguished progress down the track was accompanied by the crowd singing along with the chorus *But I would walk 500 miles, and I would walk 500 more...*I could hardly comprehend what was happening.

Determined that my last competitive strides should be good, I walked tall and proud toward the finish line. The pained expression I had carried for 31 miles softened as a feeling of wonderment swept over me. The end imminent, I looked to the heavens and lifted my weary arms skywards. My final steps were greeted with a crescendo of crowd noise. I covered my face with my hands. Someone handed me a bottle of water and I poured some of the cool contents over my head. I turned and thanked the crowd by lifting my hands high again to all corners of the stadium. The gesture was greeted with a rousing finale of cheering.

Shaking my head in utter disbelief, I walked off the track. As I did so, a song by Nancy Sinatra belted out over the tannoy...*these boots were made for walkin', and that's just what they'll do. One of these days these boots are gonna walk all over you...*

Patiently waiting trackside for the first post-race analysis was a BBC crew. I embarked on thirty minutes of one emotionally charged interview after another.

There was little that the team medics could do for me so soon after the race. My torn, strained, stretched muscles would simply take time to heal. After being eased off the treatment table and aided by a team doctor, my walk through the empty corridors within the bowels of the stadium was pitifully slow. Everything hurt – the proverbial steam roller had done its damage. I was too weary, too bemused to comprehend either the upbeat words of the doctor or make any sense of the immediate reaction to my hellish walk. Perhaps it was fitting then that the first person we should bump into outside the stadium was Mark McCallister. The Chaplain was all smiles as he extended his hand to congratulate me. He told us that he had made an early dash back to the stadium in order to see other athletes on the British team who he was also committed to supporting. The fact that he was able to describe in such passionate detail what it was like when I arrived back in the stadium, and how proud he felt, went someway to helping me appreciate what had just happened and how it had seemingly affected those that witnessed it.

Far from refreshing, the effects of a shower back at the village apartment revived me in a manner befitting someone suffering from an unwise, unprotected extra hour spent in the mid-day sun. Concealed beneath sunglasses and a light cotton shirt, I was sure that my white rimmed eyes and vest-shaped *tan* was not a good look. I stepped out into the sunshine and started my lone walk through a bustling Olympic village and an anticipated reunion with my friends from

Plymouth. En route, the outstretched congratulatory hand of David Hemery, President of UK athletics, was as unexpected as it was welcomed. Tall and lean, Hemery had a star presence that I admired. When the former Olympic hurdles champion said he had been in the stadium assisting the British sprint squads and had witnessed my race finish, and added how proud he was, I was lost for words.

Words failed me again when I walked into the hospitality lodge and was greeted by smiling faces and a spontaneous round of applause led by Edmund and Barbara, their Australian hosts, David Fox and from staff members who had seen the walk on television.

A couple of hours passed, by which time refreshments had been consumed and all minutiae of the race walk had been discussed. Prematurely extracting himself from the group, Edmund had taken up pole position in front of the large TV screen and had been catching up on the day's Olympic highlights when he excitedly alerted everyone to look at the screen. As was usual, the end of the BBC programme was accompanied by a short rendition of Heather Small's song, *Proud.* Heads turned and necks were craned as I was seen striding down the stadium track, with the final freeze-frame shot showing my anguished look at the finish line, arms aloft.

I looked on open-mouthed, accepting the pats on the back with as much good grace as my sore body would allow.

Meeting up with David Fox the following morning for a day of sight-seeing and relaxation had originally seemed like a good idea, particularly as it was to start outside the magnificent Sydney Opera House. Given that I could barely move because of stiffness, I was surprised that I had arrived first. Seated and relieved to take the weight off my feet, I soaked up the glorious sunshine and the breathtaking views of Darling Harbour and the Harbour Bridge, taking time to think about my earlier phone call with my mother.

She had said how proud she was, that I was in all the papers and the phone had not stopped ringing. She warned me not to worry about what they had written in the *Sun.* In what she assured me was a good article, apparently I was described as a snail in the headlines, and compared to Eric the Eel, the hapless yet inspirational black swimmer from Equatorial Guinea. I sighed at the thought. The arrival of my friend lightened my mood again.

'I've got a couple of Australian newspapers in my rucksack. Want to see them?' he asked.

I smiled at Foxy's obvious enthusiasm. 'Okay,' I replied.

Foxy plucked out one newspaper. He flicked through to the sports pages, until he found the large picture of Robert Korzeniowski on his knees at the finish line. 'There...read that.'

I browsed through the half-page piece headlined *Pole wins gold.* I smiled at the sub-heading *Brit receives hero's welcome,* before reading on. 'Yeah, good, thanks for showing me that.'

'You think *that's* good.' Foxy excitedly offered the other newspaper. 'Look at the sports section, front page.'

I rested the *Australian* newspaper on my lap. I stared at the huge dynamic picture of me looking skywards whilst crossing the finish line my arms spread-wide and aloft. 'Bloody hell,' I mumbled. Headlined in bold print it read *50km journey past pain barrier...*

'Go on read it. It's fantastic.' Foxy pointed at the paper and a small picture of Greg Bowman. 'That guy there says what happened yesterday was one of the highlights of the games; right up there with Cathy Freeman. It's great. Go on read it.'

A few minutes later I carefully folded the newspaper and handed it back. 'I need a drink.'

Seventeen days after a spectacular opening ceremony, the Olympic flame was finally extinguished. The Games of the 27th Olympiad were over. At Sydney airport the following day, autograph hunters were out in force, attracted by a mass exodus of athletes whose skill, endurance and years of perseverance had contributed to what most authorities considered the best Olympic Games ever.

For Great Britain, the haul of medals, including eleven golds, had journalists waxing lyrical about the team enjoying its most successful Games for over eighty years. In such exalted company, I ordinarily would not have expected any attention from other travellers as I killed time wandering around the duty-free shops.

Posing for photographs and answering questions from smiling sports fans about how I felt, and what was it like when I finished my race, were answered with the reticence that I believed it deserved. Some of the strongest, fittest, most accomplished athletes in the world were in their midst, and short of using a walking stick to get around, I still felt like an old man looking for somewhere to lie down. 'Yeah, I feel good thanks,' I'd replied with a sheepish nod. 'Thanks for your support,' I'd said with some embarrassment and genuine appreciation.

Three hours after our arrival at the airport, Britain's team of 300 were called for departure. When I was pulled to one side by Simon Clegg, the BOA's Chef De Mission, I listened like an uneasy schoolboy might when addressed by the head teacher only then to be reassured, *don't look so worried, you haven't done anything wrong.* Reminded that the long haul flight to London would fly via Singapore, a spell in the pilot's cockpit during a take-off or landing phase was offered. I accepted a take-off slot with bemused gratitude. The other symbolically prestigious places were allocated to rowers, Steve Redgrave and Matthew Pinsent, cyclist, Jason Queally, modern pentathlete, Stephanie Cook, boxer, Audley Harrison, and fellow athletic team member, Denise Lewis – all Olympic gold medallists and, as a special perk courtesy of British Airways, all upgraded to first-class.

Several hours later, I was sitting comfortably amongst the majority of the team when I got the nod to move along and join the others in the first-class section in preparation for my final call to the cockpit. Seated next to super-heavyweight Audley Harrison, the extra minutes allowed just enough time for my own autograph book to do the rounds before our 747 Jumbo Jet started its taxi procedures and take off from Singapore.

By the time I returned to my seat in economy class, most of my team colleagues were sleepy and blissfully unaware of my fanciful thoughts of looping the loop up there on cloud nine.

PART SEVEN

Part Seven: Beyond Sydney

I cannot pretend that there was any great fanfare when I arrived back in Plymouth. In many ways it was like any other return from a major championship. People wanted to know what it was like and how I felt about my race. Where it was different, was the number and diversity of folk who not only recognised me but wanted to stop me in the street and just share what they had seen and to offer a few complimentary words. It was an incredibly humbling experience. The level of media requests for post-race interviews was certainly greater than any I had previously encountered. I was happy to oblige, so sure was I that this kind of attention would undoubtedly be short-lived.

It was suggested that what I needed was an agent to help me financially capitalize on this new found notoriety. I made a few enquiries and consequentially was put in touch with a former international athlete who provided this service to a number of successful sports persons, retired or otherwise. His positive response to my approach filled me with optimism, an optimism that would, over the following months begin to wane with each flimsy excuse and postponed London meeting, until such time our telephone conversations simply petered out. With that, the apparent window of opportunity closed. Around the same time, I was reminded that things could have been different had I stayed in touch with my self-proclaimed manager, Mike Judd.

It is true we had lost touch for most of the intervening years between us leaving Exeter University and him tracking me down to the veterinary surgery in Plymouth. He had read some of the newspaper coverage that I was enjoying since my return from Sydney. When he rang, there was no cordial introduction, merely the sound of him chastising me for my total lack of recognition towards him in the press, and that I would stoop to any level to see my own name in lights, namely, loafing around at the back of the field at the Olympics. Our friendship was duly rekindled.

One of the more persistent journalists that contacted me was Duncan Mackay. His insistence that I might attend the British Athletics Writer's Awards evening towards the end of November was met with unintended indifference. When first told about it on the telephone, I was non-committal about accepting the invitation. Initially I made my own flimsy excuses about not attending, until on the third call I eluded to the cost of me getting to London. I was virtually penniless by then, but could not bring myself to say so. Only when he said my intercity rail ticket could be reimbursed did I finally say *yes*. As I had never previously been invited, I had no idea what the evening entailed. I thought I sensed some gratitude when I said that my girlfriend lived in London, and therefore there would be no additional expenses claim. The date was set.

241

Commuters stood at least ten deep on the platform at Victoria station. Inside the long line of carriages, the tightly packed passengers were becoming increasingly agitated by the delay. The doors were taken an age to open. Finally, they jolted open allowing the disgruntled masses to spill out. Once most had disembarked, there was a near frenzied surge to board the tube.

'This is the northbound Victoria line train,' the train driver announced. 'Please move right down inside the carriage to allow more folks to get on.' He paused. 'Move right down inside please. It's Friday evenin'. The weekend has just started, and we'd all like to get home. Please move inside the carriages so everyone can board the train. I know it's a bit squashy, but you never know, you might meet a new friend, maybe someone to spend the weekend with.' I liked his optimism. 'Mind the closing doors please,' he said. The doors almost closed, before reopening. The driver's optimism appeared short-lived. 'Ladies and gents, the beeping noise coming from the doors means they're about to close. It does not mean throw yourself or your bags into the doors. Thank you.' After two more attempts, the carriage doors slid shut.

The train shuddered away. I grabbed at the overhead handrail and steadied myself. The emaciated Mohican standing next to me did the same. The Mohican badly needed a wash and some strong deodorant, so I turned my head away though fresh air was in short supply. I felt hot and overdressed. The long grey pure wool retro coat was too much over my best navy blue suit. The white shirt and black bow tie looked smart but felt increasingly clammy around my neck.

The train driver's voice was heard again. 'Sorry to say this ladies and gents. It's happened again. More delays on your Victoria line and all sorts of trouble on the Jubilee. Gawd only knows what's going on there. It's gonna take more than our new mayor, Ken Livingstone to sort that tube out. By the way, Green Park is our next stop. Thank you.'

I looked through a small gap under the Mohican's arm. Richard Pannell's daughter Katie was seated sandwiched between a fat West Indian lady and a middle-aged man clutching several bulky polythene bags on his lap. I made eye contact with Katie. She looked stunning in her new black sparkly dress that she had bought specially for the occasion. She caught my heavy sigh. I regretted not paying the extra and opting for a taxi ride across London from the home she shared with her friend in Docklands.

'This is Green Park ladies and gents. Welcome to Grreeen Park. Change here for the Piccadilly line and, the Jubilee line if you're really desperate. Hope you've got loads of time if you have to go for that one. This is Grreeen Park.'

The tube jolted to a stop. I shuffled to join Katie on the platform. We followed the throng heading for the escalators. Once out in the supposedly fresh air, we were pointed in the direction of the Park Lane Hotel – a five minute walk away and only a stone's throw from Buckingham Palace. Katie insisted on walking, in spite of wearing high heels.

Minutes later the hotel was in sight. Some of the guests were arriving by limousine. I hailed a taxi. I insisted that our arrival should at least look good. The fare cost three pound to go the hundred yards. A waste, Katie said.

Stepping out of the cab we looked up at the impressive façade of the hotel. The steps up to the entrance through imposing granite pillars gave immediate notice of its five-star grandeur. Katie could hardly contain her delight. With an air of mock demure, she took my arm.

Inside, a smartly attired doorman pointed across the red carpeted foyer towards the appropriate check-in desk. Ahead, a few other late arriving guests were leaning over a table checking their dinner reservation. While Katie and I waited, we were encouraged to look at the wine list. My eyes flitted over the options. My heart skipped several beats. Taking a deep breath, I whispered, 'Hmm...got any preference, Katie?'

She stared at the wine list. She casually smiled at the receptionist and said, 'Excuse us a moment. She yanked my arm, and gestured for me to move away from the table and out of earshot. 'Maddocks,' she hissed, 'what are you doing?'

'Choosing a wine.'

'Oh really,' she whispered. 'And which one did you have in mind? A red? Perhaps a nice dry white? You know, I saw a lovely French Cabernet Sauvignon - only fifty-five quid. Or did you eyeball the cheapest bottle on the list. Mmm, what was it again?'

'Twenty-eight pound,' I said meekly.

'Ah good, you did see it.' She looked me sternly in the eye. 'If you're trying to impress me, forget it. We'll get a drink from the bar.' She looked around, 'There must be one here somewhere.'

A voice from across the foyer interrupted us. 'Chris!' A man strolled briskly toward us, his hand outstretched. 'Duncan Mackay. Pleased that you could make it.' He shook my hand, I said *Hi*. 'You had us a bit worried,' he said. 'Most of the other guests have already gone through to the ballroom suite and taken their seat.'

Mackay grinned. 'Well, I know that we've spoke a few times on the telephone, but I don't think we've ever actually met.'

I nodded. 'No, I don't think so. Erm, this is my...girlfriend, Katie.'

'Pleased to meet you, Katie,' he said shaking her hand. 'Okay. The two of you are on table thirty-five. You'll see it over to your left as you walk into the ballroom suite.' He pointed toward the expansive staircase. 'It's up there on the first floor, straight ahead. There are about ten people to each table. We've organised it so as there's a mix of athletes and their guests, along with journalists and various corporate people on each table. If you'd like to go on up, first course will be served soon. There should be wine on the table; the corporate bods normally take care of that. Well, I've got a few things to do.' He smiled and started to walk away. 'I'll see you later. Enjoy your evening.'

'Thanks,' I said. I looked at Katie.

She smiled. 'Well, he was friendly.'

We walked on toward the staircase. She said, 'I'm thirsty. I wouldn't mind a glass of water. And, since when have I been your girlfriend, Maddocks? I don't have to hold your hand or anything silly like that, do I?'

'No.'

'Good.' She took my hand anyway.

It felt like I had just clasped hands with my sister. Given our age difference, I could have been holding hands with a daughter. Katie knew I had little time since accepting the invitation to drum up a new girlfriend and that I appreciated her pretending to be my partner for the evening, even if it was done under sufferance.

The seventy year old ballroom suite looked positively sumptuous that night; 1920's art deco style at its most glorious. The ballroom's rich history was much discussed during the five course dinner. In the early years, under the bright lights and subtle shades of pink, hundreds of partying revellers would have once enjoyed the risqué dancing of Flappers up on the stage. More recently, I learned that the luxurious suite had been used when filming period scenes from classic British television dramas like Brideshead Revisited and Jeeves and Wooster. There were no monocled aristocrats this time amongst the 400 diners who were directing their heartfelt applause towards the five teenage girls up on the stage.

Dazzled by a bombardment of flash bulbs the young women clutched their engraved trophies and smiled with blushing pride for the cameras. During the previous month, the sprint relay squad had won world championship gold in Cuba. They were the surprise recipients of the young athlete of the year prize; the first time in the organising committee's history that the award had been presented to a team rather than an individual. The clapping eventually subsided. They stepped down off the stage.

Katie leant forward and whispered to me. 'Is that the last one?'

I was still clapping. 'I think so,' I answered.

Meanwhile up on stage from behind a lectern the MC shuffled his papers, adjusted his microphone and readied himself to speak again.

Paul Dickenson was an established television commentator. Formerly a successful international hammer thrower, his bulk was now squeezed snugly into a dinner jacket. He was amongst many friends, old and new. Apart from the current athletics Olympic team, there were also previous winners and former British Olympic greats. Earlier in the evening he had introduced a special short compilation film of highlights from the athletic year.

On a huge rear projection screen with a soundtrack of Heather Small singing *Proud*, footage appeared of early season cross-country running, road races, and the most memorable Olympic moments seen on BBC television. I was still loosening my trouser belt after an over indulgence when an extended clip of me finishing my race in Sydney was beamed up on the screen. I had to bite my lip, so humbled was I by the resultant cheer that accompanied the moment. Heather's lyrics, *what have you done today to make you feel proud...* were even more poignant given the unexpected enthusiastic recognition from my more illustrious peers. I think even Katie discreetly wiped away a tear.

Few people were surprised when Jonathan Edwards received the award for male athlete of the year. Mark Lewis-Francis was an outstanding favourite for the junior male award. Winning the 100 metre sprint in Cuba was a great achievement. He had been given a generous round of applause when Dickenson announced his name. Tongue-tied, the black teenager had managed a few customary thank-you acknowledgements before strutting off stage.

Denise Lewis looked both beautiful and sexy in her gold dress. Her whoop of delight and beaming smile when accepting her award for top female matched the radiance displayed so prominently on advertising posters since her win in Sydney.

Paul Dickenson cast an eye across the ballroom. The five junior girls were returning to their seats. He cleared his throat with a light cough. He had one other *special* award to announce. To present the award he invited up onto the stage Jean Pickering, and her son Sean. Both were warmly applauded as the spotlight followed them to the front of the ballroom. Jean was the widow of the great television sports commentator, Ron Pickering, who died in 1991. Their son, Sean, was an international hammer thrower and a successful businessman. Dickenson waited for the noise to subside. He began by speaking about *a man who had been around for a long time. Twenty-three years on the international athletic scene. In spite of that longevity had seldom received the recognition that he deserved. Until, in the twilight of his career, he walked into the limelight.*

Smiling eyes suddenly turned towards our table. I started to sink into my chair. The realisation that it was *me* to whom Dickenson was referring was almost too much. I barely heard the remainder of the tribute, until, 'and in appreciation of his services to British athletics, the Ron Pickering Memorial Award goes to...' I felt the heat of the spotlight descend upon me. I did not clearly hear my name amid the back slapping and cheering. Dumbstruck, I remained rooted to my chair.

I heard Katie's voice. 'Go on Chris. It's you!' I looked at her. She had tears in her eyes. In a state of shock, I rose to my feet, and from the back of the ballroom I began to weave my way past the tables, shaking outstretched hands as I went. Two months had passed since my legs had felt so weak.

Moments later I was holding a boxed engraved cut-glass decanter, and standing in front of the lectern, my heart pounding. I scanned the ballroom. It looked bigger from the stage. Smiling faces looked back up at me. I caught glimpses of familiar features, some that until that moment I had not realised were present at the function. At the far end, I saw Katie. She had one hand cupped over her mouth. I paused, and composed myself.

'Wow! This is amazing. I hadn't expected this. I was just happy to be here; and get a free dinner.' The laughter relaxed me. I glanced across to Dickenson and enquired, 'It is free isn't it?' The extra laughs bought me some time to think. I breathed deeply. 'Oh blimey, my friends who know me would tell you that I'm not usually lost for words...'

Twelve minutes later I was stepping down off the stage to rapturous applause. Denise Lewis stepped forward to give me a congratulatory hug. A whirlwind of flash photography and handshakes slowed my progress back to my table.

Soon afterwards I was told that as an award recipient I now had a lifetime invitation to the annual ceremony; interesting, because nothing arrived in the post the following year, or any subsequent year.

Actually, I have in fact been back – just the once. In 2002 one of my post-graduate friends on the journalism course persuaded me to contact the organisers and arrange tickets for two. Having a bloke by my side probably did not look nearly as good as Katie did on my arm. Nevertheless, it was gratifying to see James revelling in the opportunity to mix with the stars that night. For me, the circumstances may have been different, but I did get to go up on stage again and speak to Paul Dickenson. I would have preferred to have kept my head down at the back of the ballroom and sent someone else like my mate up to collect the draw prize. But, once the spotlight descended there was no hiding. Paul grabbed the opportunity to interview me and ask what I was doing these days. I was an aspiring journalist then, and said so.

POSTSCRIPT

Obviously, it was not part of my grand plan to become a postman, it just happened. Shortly after it did in 2004, I was talking to my old school mate, Richard Jarman. We were at the gym, and during a breather from lifting weights and aerobic work on the treadmill, he expressed some concern over my gloomy demeanour.

'What you need is a girlfriend,' he said.

Now I hasten to add, it had not been quite as long as it might at first appear. Suffice to say though, that Richard was aware that in the midst of my various leaps from one job to another, I had gone through a simultaneous fallow period in the romantic stakes, and for reasons such as these, I was feeling particularly low.

'Is there anyone in here that you fancy,' he asked.

The next bench lift would wait until I scanned the room. It was surprisingly busy that evening and as a consequence, there were choices. I spotted a woman running on the treadmill. 'I quite like that one,' I said. I had seen the petite blonde once or twice before, but had no idea who she was.

'Speak to her then,' Richard said.

So, I did. Now I appreciate this sounds like I had picked out a favourite sweet in a shop, but in my defence we did talk for a while before I asked her out. It transpired that she and a friend were novice runners and had secured a place to run the 2005 London marathon. I said that I knew a bit about training and if they wished I could help them with their schedules.

Little did I know it, but I had met my soul mate. Fiona and I were married in 2009. Our wedding at a quintessential English village was picture perfect. Many of my athlete friends attended, including Edmund who read so eloquently in church for us. All the Pannell family were there. Even Murray Lambden's late arrival from the Isle of Man was just in time to allow him to capture special impromptu photographs of my beautiful wife-to-be on the arm of her dad, with bridesmaid Millie in tow.

I have a lot to be thankful for. Indeed, I felt a sense of pride in May 2011 when an American TV executive made contact and said NBC would like me as part of their commentary team during the three walk events at the London Olympics. I was flattered that the impact made during my competitive career was far from forgotten; an additional prize perhaps for all those years trying to reach the top. Our gorgeous baby daughter was born in June 2011...now that *is* the greatest prize of all.

Acknowledgements

Recollections of people, places, and periods of my life have prompted the full gamut of emotions. Endless hours rummaging through scrapbooks, looking at old letters and photographs, thumbing through my diaries. As a life-long collector, some would say 'hoarder', I was able to access these invaluable sources for precise detail at will. Of course, I also relied on my memory when recalling scenes, knowing that an honest representation was a moral prerequisite, no matter how it might be perceived.

Throughout the process of writing this autobiography, I was forever mindful of who might be included and who was excluded; the latter category invariably caused me more anxiety than the former. So, to all those family and friends in my formative years and beyond, including the wonderful group of reprobates at the gym in Plymouth, and the long list of unnamed athletes and associates all of whom contributed to my sports career and life experiences, I say a heartfelt *sorry* if you feel aggrieved at any omission. Short of writing War and Peace part 2, space simply would not allow me to refer to everyone who crossed my path and made a difference.

I would however like to offer special thanks here to a number of good people, and they include: All the medics who helped keep me going, particularly, Ian Stewart, Dr Brian Gurry, and Mike Elliot who were so generous with their time. John Constandinou whose words of wisdom helped me more than most to get my story published. Topsy Turner, Glaswegian, former International boxer and current owner of the gym I now frequent, whose infectious and occasionally abusive enthusiasm cajoled me persistently to produce a book for him to read – if only so as he could make sense of my nostalgic ramblings. Sid Clarke, whose warped sense of humour was much needed as was his coaching advice during the latter half of the 1980's. Greg Bowman, Executive Producer at three Olympic Games whose authoritative explanations post-race allowed me to describe decisive moments made from behind the scenes in Sydney.

Support during my racing career came in many guises. Tony Perkins, baggage-boy extraordinaire on many a long trip abroad. Closer to home, Wally Emery masterminded many races in the South West, an unsung hero if ever there was one. Encouraging voices from the roadside, particularly when the going got tough, were heard from the likes of Colin Young and Paul Warburton. Indeed, the wonderful thing about being involved in sport is how it unites people with a common interest – for a sports nut like me that can never be underestimated. The world of athletics is full of good people; the race walking fraternity, from club level to World and Olympic level is like one big extended family, a family I have been privileged to feel a part of. Friendships made along the way will last forever. The likes of Murray Lambden, George Nibre, and Geoff Wightman I only see

248

occasionally, but feel richer for having shared memorable times. Thank you to each and every one.

Finally, and I mean it this time. Fiona, to you, I perhaps owe the greatest thanks...

PHOTOGRAPHY

Photographs courtesy of the author except:

Alf Tupper: © D.C.Thomson

Me at 14 years old: © Lee Flaws/Tiverton Gazette

Pictured with my sea cadet team-mates: © Lee Flaws/Tiverton Gazette

Modelling my first ever GB tracksuit: © swmg

Mum showing gritty determination: © Lee Flaws/Tiverton Gazette

Athletics Weekly cover: © Graham Maynard

The National 35km cup: © Guy Newman/The Herald, Plymouth

I'm praying that the Princess Royal: © Grup/Jaume Muntaner

Surprisingly this photograph: © Alistair Morrison

Chiropractor Kevin Kelly promises: © Lynn Johnson/The Herald, Plymouth

Just a few of my scrapbooks: © Mark Shearman – Athletics Images

Startrack coaching in Plymouth: © swmg

Assisting Edmund in the surgery: © Mark Shearman – Athletics Images

Journalist Phil Stoneham's idea: © Al Stewart/swmg

Racing 50kms in Sydney: © Mark Shearman – Athletics Images

That flag, given to me by Edmund: © John Allen/The Herald, Plymouth

Cover photograph: © Newspix/Phil Hillyard